Witch
Hunt

Witch
Hunt

Essays on the
U.S. AUTO INDUSTRY
and the
BLITHERING IDIOTS
Who Almost Killed It

Peter M. De Lorenzo

Edited by
Janice J. Putman

octane press

octane press

Edition 1.0, March 2011

ISBN-10: 0-9821733-7-7
ISBN-13: 978-0-9821733-7-4

Book and cover design by Tom Heffron

www.octanepress.com

Printed in the United States of America

For the True Believers

*The ones who, in the face of a business that
grows more rigid, regulated, and risk-averse by the day,
remain unwavering in their passion, commitment,
and dedication to the essence of the machine and
what makes it a living, breathing, mechanical
conduit of our hopes and dreams.*

Contents

Preface

ON THE MORNING OF JUNE 1, 1999, I sent out a series of guerrilla emails to assorted members of the media with a link to issue number one of Autoextremist.com. Growing up in a car family, I was able to experience Detroit's heyday like few others. That, combined with more than two decades in auto advertising, left me with a depth and breadth of knowledge about the business—as well as an incendiary point of view about it all. I knew that I had a lot to say and no one else was saying what needed to be said quite the way I could say it.

From the very first issue of Autoextremist.com I described in painful detail how the Detroit automakers had lost their way and how they were clueless about their true place in the automotive world. I zeroed in on the countless missteps and the mind-numbing culture of bureaucratic mediocrity that was the cancer eating Detroit car companies from within.

To say the automobile business has changed dramatically since that June morning is a supreme understatement. Detroit's car companies went from being totally clueless to starting to claw their way back into the game to veering toward almost total collapse.

Zero to oblivion in just over a decade, basically.

Through it all, Autoextremist.com prevailed, telling the real story behind the story and exposing the poseurs and the hopelessly clueless—the people who were directly and indirectly responsible for the disintegration of this country's automobile industry and, in turn, the American industrial fabric—as well as the brilliant visionaries who still lead the True Believers at work at these companies today with guts, gritty determination, a conviction in the mission, and a will to win that will fuel the passion for this business for a new generation.

Today, Autoextremist.com is considered to be one of *the* most influential publications of its kind in the business. But that position has not come without constant criticism, specifically for the look and feel of the website itself. There are no splashy pop-ups, no cool videos designed to hold the minimal attention of the ADD Generation, no contests, no comment boxes so that the general decline of the American educational system can be put on display in all of its cringe-inducing glory, and no legions of underpaid kids uploading vacuous "content" twenty-four hours a day.

That last point—the fact that we only update the website weekly—was the deal-breaker for a lot of the card-carrying members of the short-attention-span hordes out there, and we were dismissed by most of them as being so positively out of touch with the up-to-the-minute M.O. of the Internet that we were not just ancient, we were inconsequential.

Did it have an effect on me? Hardly. When I started Autoextremist.com I had no intention of pandering to my audience. Hell, I didn't even know if there was going to *be* an audience to pander to in the first place. But gradually, others began to gravitate toward the site, and we began to influence the influencers—including upper-level industry executives, financial analysts, members of the media, and the motorsports community. The reason most often given for the growing popularity and influence of the website?

The Writing.

It has always been about *the writing* at Autoextremist.com, and that's not likely to change anytime soon.

So then, here it is: The Writing. The "best of the best" of my essays covering the implosion and resurrection of the U.S. auto industry during the last three years.

It is at times an excruciatingly painful and sad story, at other times pathetic and laughable, and still other times exhilarating and life affirming. You would swear it was fiction in parts if you had not watched it unfold for yourself, but at the end of the day it's all true. And the lessons from this era will resonate for decades to come.

Peter M. De Lorenzo

FOUNDER AND EDITOR-IN-CHIEF, AUTOEXTREMIST.COM
BIRMINGHAM, MICHIGAN
SEPTEMBER 24, 2010

Introduction

THIS COUNTRY IS AT A CROSSROADS. We are now faced with a burgeoning national crisis that is challenging virtually every aspect of the American way of life as we know it, including the ability to own a home, the opportunity to have a job, and even one of the fundamental freedoms that we have long enjoyed in this vast nation: the freedom of mobility.

That the domestic automobile industry has been a bellwether of this country's looming national crisis is no secret, at least not to the learned people who understand the key role that our auto industry plays in this nation's economic health as a whole. Detroit first faced the reality of the global economy and what it really means long before the rest of the country had to give it even a second thought.

As the economies of China, India, and Russia have emerged, the demand for the world's resources has pushed prices through the stratosphere. The costs of everything that go into the manufacturing of an automobile—steel, aluminum, rubber, glass, plastic, precious metals, oil, etc.—have gone up dramatically in the last several years, putting tremendous pressure on the auto companies and their suppliers.

Combine that with the auto companies having to deal with healthcare, pension funding, and labor costs in a global economy that has no time for such "trivial" concerns, and it's no wonder that Detroit has long been the canary in the coal mine for U.S. economic experts.

And now, with rocketing gasoline prices pushing Detroit to the brink of disaster, and the crushing housing situation actually getting worse, this nation is facing a perfect storm of circumstances, the likes of which it hasn't had to face since the onset of World War II.

Back then the automobile industry responded to a national need unlike any other part of the manufacturing sector. From April 1942 until the beginning of 1945, no cars were produced in the United States. Detroit's entire output was given over to producing war machines and the materials this country needed. Think about *that* for a moment.

Yes, it was a different time and a different era, but I would argue that the biggest difference back then was that this country was at war, *but not with itself* like it is today. Back then a common goal unified this country like no other time before, or since.

Today, we've become a nation of warring factions hell-bent on destroying each other, even if it means destroying this country from within in the process.

Our government leaders have placed their own special interests above the overall health and needs of the country at every opportunity, even turning their backs on key manufacturing sectors—the domestic automobile industry being just one example—no matter what the long-term consequences might be, as long as it was the expedient thing to do, both personally and politically.

Our public discourse has dissolved into a disgusting cacophony of unbridled near-hatred wrapped in juvenile put-downs and three-second sound bites designed to vanquish and humiliate, rather than help us illuminate and understand the critical issues facing this country, and it shows no signs of abating anytime soon.

Our national obsession with psychoanalysis that grew out of the "I'm okay, you're okay" '70s has unleashed a firestorm that has almost crippled our modern society in a paralyzing fog of correctness. A direct result is that our educational system has been dumbed down and geared to the lowest common denominator to such an extent that we're now faced with legions of kids growing up in a pass/fail world of no harm, no foul, and no consequences whatsoever for their actions. Young strivers and achievers are not only growing fewer in number, they're being shoved aside and mocked for their inner discipline and desire to succeed, and it won't be long before this nation is swarmed over by dunderheads who pride themselves on their relentless mediocrity and who aspire only to drag this country down with them.

This country needs an enema. Either that or it needs to press the reset button and start over.

We need to go back and understand why this country was formed and why it's important that we not only survive as a nation, but thrive with the principles of our founding fathers alive and intact.

We are now living in a world that places little emphasis on what America once was, but rather waits to see which America will go forward from this moment in history. And it's no surprise that some would love to see America come to an end.

Are we going to hold those beautiful words of the Declaration of Independence close? Or are we going to dissolve into a sniveling, mewling embarrassment of a nation that once had it all but threw it away in a cloud of indifference, incompetence, and rampant mediocrity?

Are we going to rekindle the ideals and the unwavering moral purpose of those whom Tom Brokaw so eloquently dubbed "The Greatest Generation," those whose sacrifices allow us to live freely in this country today? Or are we going to just sit back, shrug our shoulders, and let whatever happens happen, sending a giant message of "whatever" out to the world?

Are we going to be a nation of blue-sky dreamers who say, "Why not?" Or are we going to be a country of sodden, lazy consumers who can only mutter, "Why bother?"

It really is up to us as a nation at this juncture, isn't it?

But it's going to require the kinds of words, concepts, and, most important, the *actions* that have been anathema around here for quite some time.

Words like *sacrifice, discipline, focus,* and *commitment.*

Concepts like believing in—and caring for—each other, while having our leaders put this country's long-term interests in front of self interests and special interests.

And actions like mustering this nation's brilliant technical resources and mind power, and unifying it with our manufacturing expertise to forge a new urgency of purpose with an unwavering focus on getting this country back in shape and on its game.

I, for one, strongly believe that it's not too late for this country to get on track and start functioning as a unified nation once again. And faced with the most daunting set of circumstances in seventy years—a crumbling housing industry, an automobile industry in grave crisis, and a global reality that threatens to tear this nation asunder—I really don't think we have much of a choice.

We didn't get this far as a nation by allowing things to be dictated to us. At key moments in our history we have *always* risen to the occasion, responding to dire threats and looming crises with a sense of unity and an overriding purpose that has transcended and overcome all challenges.

And we are now at one of those key moments again.

We're once again being reminded of the price of our independence.

Let's hope we're all ready to do our part.

Part One

The Winds of Change

Chapter 1

Dawn of the Reduced Expectations Era

*Ominous winds of change were blowing across Detroit and the entire domestic automobile industry and, by January 2008, the sense of foreboding that hung in the air was fueled by the daily icy winter shellacking. These weren't, however, just wintry blasts to remind us we lived in the Midwest. No, these were the winds of furious and fundamental change about to grab the industry by the throat and not let go. We opened the month with the 427th issue of Autoextremist.com, **eight and one half** years after we started back on June 1, 1999. And on that ninth day of January 2008, the frigid winds of reality were sweeping over this town with an inevitability that was both swift and unforgiving.*

FOR THE FIRST TIME IN 102 YEARS, the Ford Motor Company finds itself the No. 3 automaker here in the North American market, supplanted by Toyota. Toyota became the No. 2 automaker in the U.S. last week by outselling Ford by 61,962 vehicles in 2007 (2.62 million vehicles to 2.56 million). Toyota's U.S. market share is currently at 16.8 percent to Ford's 16.4 percent.

In Ford's case, the company is finally dealing with the fundamental reality that you can't keep churning out cars and trucks at a rate over and above the demand for them. This has been the hardest lesson for the Detroit-based automakers, but it is one that had to be learned—or else. Ford is forgetting the old volume and statistical bragging game that dominated this town for so long and instead is doubling down on reality by focusing on designing and building cars and trucks that people actually want to buy, abandoning the strategy of manufacturing for manufacturing's sake.

Ford insists they won't waver from their new Alan Mulally–instilled mantra, and even though there will be more bad news emanating from Dearborn as they get their proverbial shit together, I believe them. Ford simply has no choice, and being relegated to No. 3 in the U.S. is—and should be—the least of their concerns at the moment.

This is just the beginning of the news about Toyota vs. Detroit in 2008, however, because it's inevitable that Toyota will also surpass General Motors globally in sales to become the world's largest automaker sometime this year.

Speaking of GM, they're embarking on the centennial celebration of the company this year. Unlike Ford's centennial celebration of a few years ago, which went big on that company's heritage, GM's is all about the future and what's "Next" for the company, complete with an hyper-intensive Internet-fueled communication effort that will feature everything just short of massive group hugs around the globe by the time it's all over. All well and good, I suppose, as GM is obsessed with convincing the world that they are indeed hip enough to understand, but I question an effort that ignores history. Especially a history as rich as GM's.

Ford got their celebration right, with a creative blend of old and new, while GM seems overly desperate to forget about what got them to this point. You know what they say about people who choose to ignore history, and in GM's case I have a foreboding sense of déjà vu about this so-called Next centennial effort.

Starting with the fact that last week CEO Rick Wagoner, in the midst of talking about GM's centennial, waffled about the timing of the Chevrolet Volt, GM's potential world-beater of a plug-in hybrid electric car that is slated for 2010 as a 2011 model. GM is mounting an all-hands-on-deck effort for the Volt led by chief product guru Bob Lutz, with the best and the brightest the company has to offer present and accounted for on the project. But Wagoner's statement, in which he implied that the 2010 target date was a hoped-for goal but that they couldn't guarantee it, sent up an unexpected red flag that made me wince.

Why? In the bad old days of GM, the hype was always stronger than the products, and GM got crucified—and deservedly so—for conducting their business that way. But now, with such excellent products as the Cadillac CTS, Buick Enclave, Chevrolet Malibu, Chevrolet Corvette, Saturn Aura, and Tahoe 2 Mode Hybrid here and others on the way, I thought GM was finally out of the premature hype game once and for all. But the fact that they've featured the Volt in actual advertising (which I deem to be a crucial mistake) and basically are revolving their entire Green strategy around the car—while starting to be vague on the timing—well, that adds up to a heaping, steaming bowl of Not Good in my estimation.

If this is truly the "Next" GM, then they better get their house in order, starting with the managing of their product message in a manner that's consistent with what they're actually able to deliver to market. This is a show-me/prove-it-to-me business now with no room for error and zero room for hype that can't be backed up. The skeptics out there in the world are just itching to come down hard on GM if this Volt project doesn't measure up or if it falls short of its mark. And believe me, I will be the first one to double-barrel GM if they blow this one.

As for Wagoner's speech to the Consumer Electronics Show yesterday in Las Vegas, in which he touted GM's future product philosophy as being one filled with electronic wonders and devices that will get between the driver and the act of driving—for the drivers' benefit and for safety's sake, of course—I am beyond underwhelmed. Robo cars and gee-whiz electronics for electronics' sake do not suggest a visionary future to me. It does suggest, however, that GM is starting to focus on the wrong things again.

Besides the fact that electronic "nannies" have an obvious down-side—on one hand they can make average drivers somewhat better, but on the other they can be oppressive irritants that actually remove the driver from the equation—if GM's future product platform revolves around creating a rolling electronic think pad masquerading as an automobile, then they're in danger of embarking on a journey that will ultimately destroy all the new product gains they've made in the last few years.

Great cars and trucks result from a focused consistency in product philosophy and an unwavering commitment to excellence in design, engineering, performance, overall operating efficiency and quality—all of the things that GM seems to have finally figured out of late after wandering around lost in the desert for the previous 25 years.

But if GM actually believes that they can hang their hat on electronics alone, no matter how advanced and futuristic or wonderful they might be—in place of fundamental product integrity—I'm not buying it in the least.

GM is walking a very fine line here. It's one thing to embrace the future with a sense of wonderment and discovery; it's quite another to become overly dependent on systems that forcibly remove a driver from the act of driving whenever it's deemed convenient.

At this point "GMnext" sounds like a giant not so much to me until proven otherwise.

Let's get back to the fact that this is issue No. 427 of Auto-extremist.com. The number *427* has always been magical here in the Motor City. In the '60s, a 427-cubic-inch V-8 was the go-fast ingredient that powered everything from low-profile "sleeper" family sedans to blistering-fast Corvettes and Cobras—and a field full of NASCAR stockers to boot. Even today, a 427-cubic-inch V-8 lives and breathes in the brilliant Corvette Z06, standing as the last link to a bygone era.

And bygone era it is, as the automakers that compete in the North American market slowly but surely gear up for the new fuel-economy regulations that will transform this nation's fleet for good. As if to emphatically underscore this transformation, GM announced last week that it had canceled plans to build a new double-overhead-cam gasoline V-8 for its luxury cars that was scheduled for production in its Tonawanda, New York, engine facility beginning in 2009. Word is that this new engine was truly spectacular, delivering an outstanding combination of power, torque, smoothness, and overall operating efficiency that rivaled anything out there in the automotive world. Now, it's only the first visible casualty in what will become a long line of fundamental changes as the automakers wrestle with the reality of these new fuel-economy standards.

V-8s in luxury sedans and sports cars will fade away except in the most exotic of applications, replaced by direct-injection V-6 and super-clean diesel engines. For example, the new direct-injected V-6 in the 2008 Cadillac CTS (which develops 304 horsepower) will become the biggest engine available in a Cadillac by 2010. Gasoline V-8s in general will gradually be replaced by diesels, especially in full-size trucks and SUVs (ironically the Tonawanda plant will get to build GM's all-new 4.5-liter diesel V-8 engine that will see production in 2010). And V-6 engines will give way to four-cylinders whenever possible. These changes will filter throughout every segment and manufacturer vehicle lineup across the industry, with engines getting smaller and the choices we're used to becoming far more limited in scope.

Speaking of history, this point in time reminds me so much of the early '70s it's uncanny. Back then, it was the switch to unleaded fuel, catalytic converters, and the recalculation of horsepower ratings that sent the auto industry into a tailspin. That was followed by gasoline shortages (both real and imagined) and new fuel-economy standards, turning the business upside down. The nadir of it all for me was when Chevrolet actually called a Camaro with 165 "net" horsepower a Z-28.

The future for the automobile business looked grim back then, a bleak landscape for regular motorists and enthusiasts alike. But as we well know now, the automakers learned to do wonderfully creative things with their engines and drivetrains, using computers to transform the way that our cars and trucks were designed, engineered, and built. And we ended up embarking on a new Golden Age of motoring that would culminate in the spectacular automobiles we have available to us today—the finest the world has ever seen.

While we bask in the glory of these outstanding machines at almost every price point right now, in the coming few years we will be reminded at virtually every turn that as we transition from the Horsepower Era to the Reduced Expectations Era, our vehicles will gradually have the excitement factor dialed out of them.

Will we see the same magnitude of technical breakthroughs that will allow the industry to eventually transcend these new standards and build desirable vehicles again? At least desirable in the sense of genuine driving enjoyment, without having the electronic crusade removing the driver from the equation altogether? I believe we will. But the transition is going to be exceedingly painful before we get there, because the reality of the situation is such that things will have to get worse before they're able to get better again.

The same can also be said for this nation's domestic automobile industry in 2008. Things are going to get even worse before they can get better again.

It's just inevitable.

Chapter 2

With friends like these . . .

In the throes of an election year, we watched the political candidates from both parties—after vilifying Detroit for being the cause of nearly every societal and economic ill currently facing the nation—fall all over themselves as they traipsed across the state sounding concerned about our well-being and the well-being of one of America's founding industries. Not many were buying it. After all, these were the same politicians who—just a couple of months before—cited Detroit and everything about the automobile industry as being emblematic of what was wrong with America.

IT WOULD BE INTERESTING and enlightening to see John McCain, Hillary Rodham Clinton, and Barack Obama showing up at various insider fundraisers and Detroit auto plants of late, trying to convey how important the domestic automobile industry is to this country's manufacturing base—and its future—if it weren't for the fact that their so-called concern was disingenuous, if not flat-out phony.

After all, aren't these the same politicians who derisively chastised Detroit at every turn earlier in the campaign? Aren't these the same presidential candidates who just a few months ago vilified the Detroit automakers as being weak and out of touch with the realities of the global economy? Yup, same ones. But now the Michigan vote is back on the front burner, and thus these three politicos are stumbling all over each other to show how much they "get" Detroit and understand its importance to America's manufacturing base.

Hell, for a mildly amusing diversion we even had a phalanx of candidates and their entourages parachute in to the Detroit Auto

Show in January so they could ramble on vaguely about Michigan's "problems," as if we all suffered from a medical condition that needed to be addressed. That they confirmed that they knew little about this state and that they didn't have the first clue as to what they're talking about when it comes to the domestic automobile business (except for maybe Romney, who's an ex-homey) was not a surprise. Nor was it surprising that their measurable impact on the proceedings was less than zero.

Not that we're surprised or shocked by any of this. No, even out here in "Michigan—The Flyover State" we understand that there is a dramatic difference between conducting a campaign for president as opposed to actually *being* the president. We understand the difference between empty campaign promises and real substance in a political speech, too, so forgive us for taking everything said by these candidates with a giant grain of salt.

Despite their recent glad-handing forays into plants in Michigan, Ohio, Wisconsin, etc., these three politicians and their advisors have demonstrated repeatedly that their grasp of the issues facing Detroit and the entire domestic auto industry—and ultimately America's ability to remain a viable manufacturing entity in the global economy, for that matter—is fleeting, at best. Not only do they seem to have trouble understanding the ramifications of a crippled domestic auto industry (beyond the platitudes in their speeches, of course), they seem to subscribe to the popular theory that Detroit can get back on track with a snap of the finger and an instant jolt of technology, and then things will magically be all better overnight.

Oh, if it were that easy.

I've said repeatedly in this column over the last few years and in my book, *The United States of Toyota*, that Detroit, Inc. was the canary in the coal mine for the rest of the country when it came to the fundamental issues facing all of us as a nation.

The healthcare crisis and the difficult pension-funding problems hovering over this nation like a hangover that just won't go away? The domestic automobile industry was wrestling with these issues long before the rest of the country decided that there even *was* a problem.

The threat to America's standing in the world because of the gradual erosion of our manufacturing base? Detroit has been in the throes of that vexing issue for *years*.

Only one of the candidates truly understood Detroit's canary-in-the-coal-mine role, but he's no longer involved in the process. Perhaps if the three serious contenders who remain are interested in ripping off other candidates' speeches, they should go back and look up some of Mitt Romney's speeches, because they just might actually learn something for a change—and some of these issues might actually start to sink in.

The attention given to this state by these three political candidates is mildly amusing—seeing as it smacks of a fishing expedition for friends in low places that they ultimately couldn't care less about—and it does shed some light on the domestic automobile industry's problems once again, but I'm afraid the platitudes are just that, and after the campaign is over we'll be right back where we started.

And when the dust settles a year from now, these facts will remain: Between one in twelve and one in fourteen jobs in this nation are still either directly or indirectly related to the domestic automobile business. And to those citizens far removed from this part of the country or this business who would insist that "it won't affect me" if we lose part or all of the domestic automobile industry, I would say you're being naïve.

And to those others who suggest something to the effect that "Detroit should just go Green and things will be all better overnight," I would say that you're in need of a serious reality check as to how much of an investment in time and money is actually involved in delivering these future technologies to the American consumer public on a massive scale, no matter what the Henrik Fiskers of the world say.

Make no mistake—the bottom line in this discussion hasn't changed since I began writing about it three years ago. This country's fundamental ability to manufacture things in the global arena is absolutely crucial to the long-term health of the entire nation, and it continues to be under severe threat from so-called allies and adversaries alike.

We cannot exist as Starbucks Nation alone—as much as some would like to believe we can—and we can't keep paying attention to this country's problems only when it's convenient fodder for the campaign trail on the fly, either.

It would be nice if the three remaining serious contenders for president displayed even a modicum of understanding of the issues facing the domestic automobile industry—and this nation—for more than the time it takes for one of their touch-and-go campaign visits here.

But then again, that might be too much to ask.

After all, with friends like these in Washington, why should we worry, right?

Chapter 3

Detroit's King of Delusion

People who don't live in this region of the country—and in Michigan in particular—have no idea what it's like to have grown up in an environment that has been corrupted by years of the union "entitlement" mentality. A corrosive, pervasive, dishearteningly unrealistic mindset, it has created an overwhelmingly negative cloud that has hung over this state, the city of Detroit, and the entire auto industry for decades. It courses through the veins of the Detroit city government, causing paralysis that has brought the city to its knees. It has thwarted forward progress for businesses large and small, and it continues to be a fundamental detriment to progress in the American automobile industry. This isn't the last time you will read about unions and specifically the United Auto Workers union in this book.

WHAT YEAR IS IT AGAIN? 1968? 1978? How about 1988? No, actually, as most of us know, it's 2008. But remarkably, there is one entity headquartered in this town that refuses to acknowledge reality, history, the writing on the wall, or anything even remotely resembling rational thought, for that matter. The United Auto Workers union, that staunch bastion of head-in-the-sand, wrong-headed thinking—at least when what masquerades as their woefully skewed version of "thinking" rears its ugly head—launched a strike against American Axle & Manufacturing Holdings Inc. late Monday after negotiations broke down on a new labor deal.

What's involved? 3,650 American Axle workers in Michigan and New York walked off the job and hit the picket lines, jeopardizing all truck production at GM, American Axle's largest customer by far.

What part of this action seemed even remotely like a good idea? The domestic automobile industry—a.k.a. "Detroit"—has been in freefall for the better part of twenty-five years. This inexorable downward spiral has been punctuated by alarming annual losses in market share to the Asian and German manufacturers, as what was once formerly known as the "Big Three" saw their fortunes plummet. Detroit watched in horror as an entire generation of buyers, tired of mediocre products with average to dismal quality, abandoned the domestic manufacturers for imported brands in droves—never to return.

Pummeled by a $1,500-per-vehicle cost disadvantage brought on by absurdly expensive, union-driven healthcare costs—the most expensive and comprehensive programs of their kind in the nation—and crushing pension-funding expenses, Detroit reeled as it tried to regain footing in the market, only to find that its way back was blocked by an uncooperative UAW and compounded by the fact that government-sanctioned currency manipulation was giving their Asian competitors a $1,500 minimum *advantage* on every car and truck sold in this market—this on top of the built-in cost disadvantages the Detroit automakers started out with.

But Detroit, determined to fight back, started to blow up their obsolete processes and—paced by GM—rediscovered the fundamental law of this business that they had wandered away from so cavalierly in the past. And that is that The Product is and always will be King.

Hope emerged as GM rediscovered its product *mojo* and signs of life started to appear in the other Detroit manufacturers as well after years of being lost in the desert. And the UAW even got it together— or so it seemed anyway—agreeing to a series of what appeared to be landmark labor agreements last fall that would allow Detroit to at least approach being on a level playing field with their Asian and German rivals in terms of cost.

But I never bought into the words "groundbreaking" and "historic"—the terms bandied about last fall by the media in reference to the UAW—because I knew that deep down this labor organization was and is fundamentally flawed. That the UAW's M.O. is not one of enlightened cooperation, but one of irrational, unflinching, relentless entitlement. That the words "We'll get what we deserve" resonate far more through its depleted ranks than "We'll have to do what's best in order to see these companies remain competitive."

The UAW only acquiesced to those agreements last fall because they had no other choice. Detroit was shrinking at a horrific pace and its market share couldn't support anything but a dramatic consolidation, which meant that jobs would have to be cut and wages and benefits would have to be seriously reduced—or else. And at that point, the halcyon days of the UAW were indeed over.

While too many in the media back then were quick to canonize Ron Gettelfinger, the UAW president, and prematurely hail him as being some sort of "visionary" labor leader after those negotiations, I didn't. Because I never thought the moniker "statesmanlike" should be used in reference to this intransigent, misguided, narrow-minded, and maliciously inflexible individual who at any moment could and would choose to derail crucial agreements with the auto manufacturers or their suppliers, just because he could.

And as if right on cue, he demonstrated his true colors last fall when in the midst of those so-called historic agreements he authorized utterly futile and worthless work stoppages against the Detroit automakers in a pathetic, grandstanding gesture.

And now, here we go again.

In the face of massive layoffs in the automobile business as the Detroit manufacturers fight for their very survival, and with the state of Michigan mired in a monumental recession—one directly attributable to the dire straits the automakers find themselves in—the likes of which has never been seen before, and with foreclosures and unemployment at record levels, and with the mood grim as desperation sets in for countless citizens in this region, this miserable excuse for a leader does the most *un*-statesmanlike thing he could possibly do by calling for a strike against American Axle that absolutely no one can afford, least of all the workers involved.

It's no wonder that Steve Miller, the blunt, no-nonsense, straight-talking Delphi CEO, reserves particular ire for Gettelfinger in his new autobiography, *The Turnaround Kid: What I Learned Rescuing America's Most Troubled Companies*, published by HarperCollins. Miller sums up the UAW front man this way: "Gettelfinger was a big disappointment. An industry in crisis needs leaders who can rise above the tactics of intimidation that may have worked decades earlier."

Uh, no kidding.

Ron Gettelfinger is quite simply Detroit's King of Delusion, a Neanderthal figure operating in a hermetically sealed time warp that prevents even a shred of reality or rational thinking to enter into his—or the UAW's—atmosphere. As a matter of fact, he and his counterpart at the Canadian Auto Workers union—the equally thick-headed and wildly irrelevant Buzz Hargrove—are industry anachronisms who have become blatantly and painfully obsolete.

Even if this strike action were to end today, there's no hiding the fact that Ron Gettelfinger is a small-minded irritant, a man who relishes being an obstinate obstacle to progress, and a petty grandstander at every turn, just because he can.

And his so-called act grew tiresome years ago.

Chapter 4

The Highly Compensated Bunglers from Cerberus wreak havoc on Chrysler

I relentlessly pounded Cerberus for months for a raft of egregious behaviors and sins, big and huge. Cerberus, the super-slick, cold-hearted mercenaries who couched their takeover of Chrysler in glowing "We're doing what's right for America" terms, is (and was) like the (three-headed) dog in the neighborhood who chases cars from sunup to sundown, never catching one. Then, one day, the dog catches a car and hasn't even the foggiest notion what to do with it. Cerberus is that dog, and Chrysler was its car. And as I predicted, Cerberus would eventually go down in flames after finding out in no uncertain terms that carpetbagging hedge-fund opportunists were no match for an industry as thoroughly complicated as the automobile business.

SOME PEOPLE THINK that I've been far too hard on the folks out in Auburn Hills. After all, Cerberus CEO Stephen Feinberg has likened his company's efforts to "save" Chrysler as being part and parcel of fighting for truth, justice, and the American Way. Feinberg's quest was even referred to as his "patriotic" duty by his apologist-in-chief, Chrysler CEO "Minimum Bob" Nardelli, the ex–Home Depot guy who, by the way, has truly distinguished himself as being hands down the wrong guy at the wrong time in charge of the wrong company.

Memo to our Autoextremist.com readers: It's not as if I have to go out of my way to find things to write about when it comes to Chrysler. As a matter of fact, I have studiously *avoided* writing about the highly compensated bunglers out in Auburn Hills, because if I didn't, I could have easily written about them every week.

And now, here we go again, because those wacky, wonderful folks who give new meaning to the term *utter futility* are back front and center with yet another lame-brained scheme to engage America's car-buying consumers.

Let's review a few things first, shall we? Remember, Cerberus Capital Management is the company that professes to be visionary stewards of the fabric of America instead of the churn-and-burn specialists that they actually are. Lest anyone get the wrong impression here, they're not the Little Sisters of Charity by any means. They're in it for the money—and that's fine, man, as The Dude would say—we're into profit just as much as the next guy, I just don't like it when Cerberus pretends to be something they're not, which they seem to do on a daily basis.

Make no mistake, when Cerberus jumped head first into the idea of taking Chrysler off of Daimler's hands (after the Germans had finished running it well and truly into the ground), they had gold-dipped sugar plums dancing in their heads—because *there was gold in them thar Auburn Hills!*

They'd rarely been wrong before, and besides, how tough could the car business be? After all, the so-called Cerberus culture still hinges on the residual Masters of the Universe mentality left over from the '80s version of Wall Street, and they figured no one could outsmart them, especially a dying vestige of a rust-belt industry slumped against the ropes.

Oh how wrong they were.

Despite spouting glowing phrases like "We're in this for the long haul" and "We're going to do justice to this iconic American brand," Cerberus found out in about ten minutes that they had gotten themselves into a mess that they were ill equipped to handle. On top of a lurid set of negatives—a dismal product mix, disillusioned dealers, virtually nonexistent cash flow, and the fact that the majority of the company's manufacturing (at least in the plants that are still open) is going directly into the rental car fleets—Cerberus was sailing Detroit's version of the *Titanic* into the iceberg-filled waters of the worst U.S. economy in years.

To make matters even worse, Cerberus went out and actually *recruited* Bob Nardelli to run the whole show, which made the efficacy of this enterprise suspect from the get-go. Then, they went out and hired a disgruntled Jim Press away from Toyota. Press, who had been moved up and out of the day-to-day fray at the Japanese automaker, and who was just itching for something of substance to do after being disrespected by his Japanese handlers, yielded to the siren call of a giant back-end payoff (estimated at $52 million) should the Cerberus turnaround of Chrysler succeed. That it required flipping his personal switch and disavowing twenty-three years of blatant anti-Detroit bashing while misleading the industry media on a regular basis—exposing his built-in duplicities for one and all to see—was something he hoped we'd all forget to notice. We didn't.

Was this a corporate marriage made in heaven? Hardly. The fact that Press and Nardelli don't speak is common knowledge. Though repeatedly denied, these two have about as much in common as Barack and Hillary. Press views Nardelli as an interloping mercenary lightweight who is grossly unfit to hold sway on key product decisions (and he's dead right on this count, of course). Nardelli is convinced that he's the smartest guy in the room—any room—which tends to get in the way of listening, unless you fancy the dulcet tones of your own voice, or the sound of one hand clapping.

Oh, I almost forgot, added to this unwieldy clash of egos was one Deborah Meyer, an ex-Toyota marketing maven who was hired before Jim Press. The problem? Jim Press doesn't care for Ms. Meyer. The other problem? Nardelli has little use for Meyer, either, trusting his personal marketing guru, the relentlessly overhyped Peter Arnell, instead.

So what does Ms. Meyer do to stake her claim in this mess? She comes up with the idea of recruiting up to 5,000 people to become members of something called the Customer Advisory Board, which will be an online forum where Chrysler employees will listen to direct input from interested parties—and then go forth to allegedly build better Chrysler products. This is all part of Meyer's "We listen" ad campaign, which is trying to convince the American car-buying public that by listening to its customers, Chrysler will make its future cars and trucks great.

Now, I don't know about you, but this is akin to letting the inmates run the asylum, only this won't be some modern-day, feel-good remake of *One Flew Over the Cuckoo's Nest*. Rather, it will be the automotive industry equivalent of *The Voice of the Customer Gone Wild*.

Creating forums to listen to the voice of the customer? How about if they just set up listening kiosks at America's shopping malls to soak up the kaleidoscope of cumulative wisdom generated by your average gaggle of Teen Queens about the vicissitudes of the car business?

Meyer was quoted as saying, "We want to harness insights and customer dreams into things we can use concretely with our different groups, such as engineering, design, marketing."

Well, I guess if you can't come up with the goods on your own, why not, right? *Right.* Grasping at straws doesn't even begin to convey the lunacy of this move.

While Chrysler soaks up the white noise from their touchy-feely customer forums and contemplates the wonder of it all, other car companies (at least the good ones, anyway) will go about the serious business of designing, engineering, and executing the best cars and trucks they can possibly bring to the street.

While Chrysler listens to its "Customer Advisory Board" and pauses to make sure everyone gets a collective group hug for their efforts, other car companies will put the pedal down—hard—and disappear down the road.

So, when it comes to the Gang Who Couldn't Shoot Straight out in Auburn Hills, I guess I won't run out of things to write about anytime soon.

After all, you just can't make this shit up.

Chapter 5

GM's 20 percent Solution

Several years ago when I argued that GM would have to get smaller here in the United States in order to become better suited to its newly downscale position in the global automotive world, the minions—big and small—down at the RenCen took great umbrage with even the mere whiff of such a suggestion. Chief among those who dismissed the notion out of hand was none other than GM CEO Rick Wagoner, who, when queried about the idea by another journalist, scoffed dismissively at such a notion. Getting smaller to get more fit and ultimately get better is anathema to an accountant's mindset, apparently, and "The Rick" as I referred to him, wanted nothing to do with it. But, as I delighted in pointing out, when you spend all of your time reacting in business, instead of focusing on being proactive, bad things and bad days inevitably happen. And for GM—and the entire domestic-based automobile business—the bad days were well and truly here. As for my vision for what GM needed to do in order to survive? It eventually would come true as GM jettisoned Saturn, Saab, Pontiac, and Hummer in order to appease their government overlords and live to fight another day. The new GM would focus on Chevrolet, Cadillac, Buick, and GMC.

YESTERDAY, RICK WAGONER outlined a series of drastic moves in conjunction with GM's annual shareholder's meeting that are directly attributable to the recent spike in the pump price of gasoline and the collapse of the large SUV and "casual use" light-truck market. Specifically, the shuttering of three truck plants: Oshawa Truck Assembly in Canada (which builds the Chevy Silverado and GMC

Sierra); Moraine, Ohio (which builds the Chevy TrailBlazer, GMC Envoy, and Saab 9-7x); and Janesville, Wisconsin (which builds medium-duty trucks and the Tahoe, Suburban, and Yukon). And also the elimination of Chevrolet Kodiak medium-duty truck production in Toluca, Mexico, by the end of this year.

GM also stunned the assembled media multitudes yesterday by announcing that "GM is undertaking a strategic review of the Hummer brand to determine its fit within the GM portfolio. At this point, the company is considering all options, from a complete revamp of the product lineup to a partial or complete sale of the brand."

No, no one knew that the pump price of gas would jump 50 percent in a matter of just a couple of months, so Wagoner & Co. can't be blamed for that, but the signs of the end of the full-size SUV and "casual use" light-truck market were everywhere long before now. I first wrote about the "SUV Bubble" three years ago, and though vehemently chastised and accused by some for exercising my own wishful thinking on a market that showed no signs of distress whatsoever, I knew in my gut that the American car-buying consumer had reached the end of the line with these vehicles and that the fad of driving lumbering SUVs and city-slicker pickups for personal daily transportation had just about run its course.

Why this was a surprise to anyone in the executive suites of the Detroit automakers is shocking to me. Yes, Detroit built massive amounts of profitability into building these behemoths, but while gorging at the trough of those seemingly endless profits, isn't it just a little bit odd that no one bothered to pick their head up and ask the fundamental question "What if?" As in what if the American consumer finally woke up and realized that these SUVs and light trucks they were using to run up to the Home Depot and the local market made zero sense? What if the global demand for the world's resources forced the price of oil to record highs? And what if the subsequent consumer reaction was swift and final?

The shocking lack of foresight displayed by GM and The Other Two has now been replaced, of course, by a frenzied storm of activity to get with the "smaller and more efficient" program. That these automakers were clearly caught flatfooted in all of this is embarrassing and inexcusable, especially when some of the companies sell competitive products in other markets where the price of gasoline is double what we're paying, on average, today.

Before you label this as just another case of hindsight being 20/20, let me be clear: The reason I'm slamming this point home today is that what's going on now is consummate proof that the classic Detroit mindset of sticking with something for way too long and running it into the ground—whether it made sense or not—has finally caught up with them with a finality that has not only been swift, but brutal.

What does it mean? It means that right now, the Detroit car business model that has been in place for the last thirty-five years has been blown to smithereens. Everything that passed for standard operating procedure before is simply no longer applicable. The spike in gasoline prices has the American car-buying public scared straight. And this isn't just a brief little flirtation with global reality this time, because even the most obtuse Americans seem to get it now.

Not long ago the debate raging was about the new EPA mileage requirements and how they would affect Detroit and the rest of the automobile industry. There was deep conjecture and distress about how the American driving public would not be ready for the European fleet model of smaller cars and drastically more efficient smaller trucks and crossovers. Those worries seem kind of quaint now, don't they?

On the flip side, and to be fair to Wagoner, GM also announced some good things yesterday. They're bringing an all-new global compact car program to America to be branded a Chevrolet sometime in 2010 (the Cruze, with a direct-injected, 1.4-liter turbo, no less). That this will be a direct competitor to the next-gen Ford Focus is no shock. They're also bringing a new Aveo here (okay, maybe that's not so good).

Oh, yes, and the GM board of directors—that tedious monument to steady-as-she-goes, rubber-stamp thinking, that Band of Do Nothing Brothers that has sat back and presided over the company's

75 percent decline in value since 2000—has approved the funding for the production "go" of the all-new and all-electric (with ICE support) Chevy Volt. *Halle-frickin'-luja.*

That the approval of the Volt comes *three years* after Bob Lutz first suggested it internally says a lot about the company, and it says a lot about the fact that left to their own devices, bean counters will never take the visionary path or venture to put their stake in the ground and believe in something that could actually be a game-changer.

The bottom line in all of this is that global events are now conspiring to *force* GM to be a company that controls only 20 percent of the U.S. market after its leadership not only refused to admit that it was even a realistic notion, but adamantly scoffed that their business would even come to that.

Wagoner summed up his company's announcements with this: "These moves are all in response to the rapid rise in oil prices and the resulting changes in the U.S., changes that we believe are more structural than cyclical. While some of the actions, especially the capacity reductions, are very difficult, they are necessary to adjust to changing market and economic conditions and to keep GM's U.S. turnaround on track and moving forward."

GM's turnaround in the U.S. "on track and moving forward?" Please. First order of business for Wagoner & Co.? Stop publicly talking about "the GM turnaround" in the North American market or anywhere else, for that matter, because the GM "turnaround" is in turnaround, yet again.

Would a more visionary management structure have seen these cataclysmic events brewing on the horizon and taken steps sooner to prepare the company for today's globally dictated reality?

Yes and yes.

GM will of course derive much of its future profitability in Asia, so GM's current management team will likely dine on those profits for quite some time to come, but that doesn't absolve Rick Wagoner & Co. for not seeing the negative possibilities or exploring the ramifications and the "what ifs."

As for GM in North America, that 20 percent solution is no longer a pipe dream, but its day-to-day operational reality.

It would have been nice if they had envisioned and planned for it, rather than just reacted to it, but that's asking entirely too much, apparently.

Chapter 6

What would Jack do?
Don't ask

In the worst economy this country had seen in decades, and with the highest gasoline prices in history bringing the Detroit automakers to their knees, "Minimum Bob" Nardelli—the ex–Jack Welch/GE acolyte appointed by Cerberus to resurrect Chrysler—officially pirouetted off the gangplank and into the deep end of irrelevance in the summer of 2008 with his latest misguided attempt at setting priorities for the beleaguered car company. Tom Walsh from the Detroit Free Press *reported that Chrysler was embarking on an "intensive new leadership program" for its top three hundred executives in keeping with Nardelli's blind adherence to the Jack Welchian mindset that's rampant at Cerberus, a financial company filled to the brim with GE alums. Needless to say, it didn't go well. Eventually, Nardelli would be broomed from the auto biz along with his Cerberus cronies, but they would welcome him back with open arms and award him yet another assignment so he could set about "fixing" another American corporation, his serial incompetence remarkably intact.*

HMMM, LET'S SEE. Gas is heading for $5 per gallon and the biggest news Chrysler has is a new Dodge Ram Pickup due late this summer? Not exactly what I would call encouraging, to put it mildly. Not to mention the fact that Chrysler's quality ratings are in the toilet. And Nardelli determines that this is the best possible time to run his top executives through a *leadership* program?

How out of touch can this guy possibly be?

Beyond category out-of-touch, apparently. *This* is the guy who has been overwhelmed and overmatched ever since he hit the ground strolling in Auburn Hills. *This* is the guy, after all, who bristled with the cocky arrogance of his Cerberus handlers, even as he did his best "Aw, shucks, we're just here to help" routine with the media and anyone else who would listen. And *this* is the guy who has managed to preside over the final dismantling of what at various times was a pretty damn good car company.

Cerberus has hit the wall with Chrysler. Clearly unprepared for having things *not* go its way, the company has run up against the one irrefutable High-Octane Truth about the car business, which is: No matter how successful you are in other arenas or endeavors, and no matter how much money you've made along the way in whatever it is you are allegedly good at, the car business is unlike any other business in the world, and nothing—*nothing*—you've done up until this point can prepare you for the sheer complexity and daunting challenges of it.

When Cerberus decided to take a flyer on Chrysler, it assembled a "dream team" of managers who would get the thing up and running and headed to profitability in no time—at least that was The Plan. That they were unaware that assembling a dream team of managers is something altogether different from having them actually *function* as a team is surprising, given their alleged brilliance, but that's neither here nor there at this point. Suffice to say the bitter reality for Cerberus is that it is hopelessly at a loss as to what to do with the company.

That they picked the wrong guy, at the wrong time, for the wrong assignment to lead the charge was a key mistake, but it was only the second of many. Because when the basic idea behind the enterprise is flawed to begin with—that a bunch of money managers with no car business experience can resurrect a floundering car company in an industry decimated by the inertia of unprecedented change—there was literally no hope for this endeavor from the get-go.

Let's be clear here: The absolute *last* thing Chrysler management needs right now is some touchy-feely management program on "leadership." You do that when you're fat, happy, and looking at six straight quarters of profitability and increased market share.

That doesn't apply in this case. Not even close, as a matter of fact. When you're on the ropes and gasping for breath like Chrysler is, there isn't a management training program on the face of the Earth that will do you a lick of good.

That's something that the GE-addled brains at Cerberus just can't fathom, apparently.

Let me put it another way: This is not the time to ask "What would Jack do?" Jack doesn't have the first clue about the car business, and he wouldn't even know where to begin.

Memo to "Minimum Bob" and Cerberus:

You need product.

And you need customers.

And then, repeat after me: *The Rest of it Doesn't Matter.*

Chapter 7

Politicians? We don't need no stinkin' politicians

If the citizens of Michigan and the employees of its automotive industry ever decided to measure our self worth by the attention received from the two men running for president in 2008, then we'd all be feeling the love, even though that affection was about as meaningful or as substantive as a giant ball of cotton candy. Judging by the frequency of the two presidential candidates' trips to Detroit back in those days, I half expected to see them manning the barista station at the local Starbucks, asking me if I wanted an extra shot. It was getting that ridiculous. Oh, yes, we here in Michigan understood that we were key to the general election that November. We got it. But then both *candidates managed to distinguish themselves by their utter lack of understanding of the issues facing this state, and ultimately the nation, when it came to the erosion of our manufacturing sector, and by their almost laughable perspective on what will "fix" the Detroit car companies.*

PRESIDENT BARACK OBAMA has been backpedaling on his view of America's car companies ever since he blasted them in a speech before the Economic Club of Detroit last February. Back then Detroit was totally responsible for its plight, and Barack was going to fix things first by chastising them for their blatant incompetence and then by jamming technological "help" (of a virtually meaningless amount) down Detroit's throat so that the local automakers could get with the

29

program. Oh, and add new higher fuel-economy requirements to help speed the change too.

It was a ballsy speech at the time and, I naïvely thought, a measure of Obama's convictions, which was admirable. But that was until he showed up a couple of months later decrying the sad state of Detroit and its car companies and lamenting what has happened to the men and women displaced by the plummeting fortunes of the automakers—and saying he would help us all rise up and get back on our feet again.

Now, I get the fact that things said on the campaign trail mean little (like zero) once a candidate is actually in the White House, but still, Obama's flip-flopping has bordered on the transparently pathetic. And here he was in Detroit just this past Monday night (at Joe Louis Arena) spouting his views—listen carefully, folks, because clever speechwriting does not constitute a cohesive policy in my book—saying we're going to be alright because he will pull Detroit up by its bootstraps through new green technology and enlightened trade policies—all while he's saving the planet, ending wars, and fixing whatever else ails this country.

Wow. All that and Al Gore's endorsement, too.

But then again, John McCain is no better. Once again he's muttering about his lame-brained "gas tax–free" summer to "help the American people," which is so resoundingly stupid I can barely muster the words to describe it, other than the fact that it marks a new low in pandering for votes in this country. What next, John? Every citizen who votes for you gets a free gas card worth a hundred gallons if you're elected? It's *that* absurd.

McCain is also a founding member (along with Obama) of the "finger snap" brigade when it comes to talking about fixing Detroit's problems. As in, each candidate has policy advisors who clearly know jack about the depth and breadth of the U.S. manufacturing crisis that Detroit has signaled—given its canary-in-the-coal-mine role in the manufacturing sector—and, completely ignoring that, generate a series of finger-snap initiatives that look great in side-by-side comparisons in the media and sound great in stump speeches, but in effect do little to seriously address the underlying problems on the table. But then it's on to the next issue, problem not solved but "addressed" enough for the media and the average voter. Talk about the quintessential definition of lip service.

I would caution both McCain and Obama's handlers and their advisors on the following going forward:

1. THE CRISIS IN DETROIT GOES FAR BEYOND THIS STATE AND THIS REGION. This nation's automakers are still either directly or indirectly responsible for between one in twelve and one in fourteen jobs in this country. There is no amount of finessing or masking of this industry's importance to the health and well-being of this country's economy, and there's no amount of fixing, reinventing, "greening," or replacing this key industry overnight with a finger snap. If the domestic automobile business is allowed to fade into oblivion, it won't be a regional crisis like the steel industry's collapse in Pennsylvania; it will be a national crisis that will devastate vast swaths of the American fabric.

2. WASHINGTON'S REFUSAL—AND THAT MEANS YOU, McCAIN AND OBAMA—TO BOLSTER ONE OF ITS COUNTRY'S STRATEGIC INDUSTRIES WITH THE KIND OF SUPPORT THAT COMPETING GOVERNMENTS GIVE TO THEIR OWN INDUSTRIES IS GLOBALLY JUVENILE AND BLATANTLY IRRESPONSIBLE. For the record, it's tiresome to see companies—and not just car companies—waltz into this country and be given free rein to wreak havoc on whole sectors of the economy with impunity. No, this isn't a protectionist screed—it's a reality forced upon this country by a new global viciousness that would like nothing better than to see the U.S. suffer catastrophic travails. The time for cheap talk and paper policies to save one of this country's most crucial industries is over. This nation is either going to have to be saved with a coherent strategy based on long-term solutions and globally realistic trade policies, or it will have to face the ugly consequences. And I mean ugly.

3. STOP TREATING AMERICA'S SO-CALLED ENERGY POLICY AS A STRATEGIC AFTERTHOUGHT. I've read your statements and I've heard your speeches, but I've seen and heard nothing concrete about *what you're actually going to do about it*. Why is that? Why is it easier to blame Detroit (or whoever the whipping boy du jour is) for *all* of this country's problems than it is to stand back and be realistic about our energy needs going forward, and knowing that Detroit will have to play not just a bit part, but a crucial role? And no, this problem isn't going to be solved by a bunch of venture capitalists in Silicon Valley promoting their magic cars, either. Unless you plan on earmarking trillions of dollars for a comprehensive national mass-transit program in this country (which would take at least twenty years to become a reality, at best), then you better work with the automakers and the energy companies and craft a policy that makes the most sense for the entire nation.

4. IT'S ABOUT THE GREEN THING. We get it, and every citizen of this country gets it now. Green responsibility will be part of American life going forward. But please, *please* dispense with the bullshit that attaining some sort of environmental happy place is just a presidential term away. The most capable technical minds in the world are working overtime on the transportation systems of the future—meaning what we'll be driving five, ten, and twenty years from now—and yes, a lot of them are right here in the Motor City. You remember us, right? The place both you and your advisors have conveniently written off at least a hundred times in the last eighteen months—except for our votes, of course. After all, you may be vacuous, transparent, hopelessly naïve, and incredibly unrealistic, but you're not stupid.

Suffice to say it's a good thing that more than a fair number of people around here remain skeptical of the election rhetoric and politically empty gestures generated by Mr. Obama and Mr. McCain in this campaign. Yes, we will be presented with the most drastically contrasting choice in candidates since the Nixon-Kennedy election—blah, blah, blah—but the reality is that these two men will say or do whatever they think they need to say or do in the coming months to get elected. And that might be political reality, but it still stinks.

No, we don't need no stinkin' politicians.

What we *do* need, however, are serious, committed people willing to do the due diligence necessary to make the focused, informed, and *rational* decisions that will help shore up one of this country's essential industries and guide our energy policy for years to come.

Chapter 8

Obama and McCain
must step up to history

No, I never thought the previous column would instantly put an end to the wild flailing about by the presidential candidates (and their ever-attentive staffers) in their quest to solve The Energy Thing, which seemed to go hand-in-hand with dealing with The Detroit Thing. And then there was The Economy Thing, which seemed to meld into Every Thing at that point in the campaign, given the perilous state of this nation's economy and the tumultuous effect high gas prices were having on every facet of American life. But I didn't think John McCain would weigh in the next week with his solution to our energy problems—and of course Detroit's predicament—which was a predictable mishmash of conjecture and confusion amounting to not so much. It wasn't hard to see why McCain lost the election, as every time he opened his mouth it got worse.

JOHN MCCAIN (or should I say the staffers assigned to addressing the problem) came up with the following for our contemplation this week in a speech given at Fresno State University: a proposed $300 million prize for whoever can develop a better automobile battery, and $5,000 tax credits for consumers who buy new zero-emission vehicles—a so-called Clean Car Challenge to encourage U.S. automakers to develop zero-emission vehicles. It will be somewhere in the neighborhood of 2012 before we see a sizable number of these vehicles on our roads, at the earliest, but who's counting? This "challenge" would be added to McCain's support for overturning the federal ban on offshore oil drilling and the consideration of more nuclear power facilities (with the affected states' approval, of course).

"In the quest for alternatives to oil, our government has thrown around enough money subsidizing special interests and excusing failure. From now on, we will encourage heroic efforts in engineering, and we will reward the greatest success," McCain said in his speech.

McCain also insisted that this new battery should deliver power at 30 percent of current costs and have "the size, capacity, cost, and power to leapfrog the commercially available plug-in hybrids or electric cars."

Whoa, that's quite a feat. But McCain didn't stop there, because he also suggested that foreign automakers such as Honda and Toyota would be eligible for the prize, since the Japanese companies have large manufacturing plants in the United States.

Let's stop right there and back up a moment.

I would think that if there was a class called America's Energy Policy 101 somewhere in Washington, D.C., that part of the basic fundamentals of that policy would be to protect this nation's energy security first and foremost with concerted actions independent from other nations. Yes, we all understand it's a global world out there and that idealistic alliances and partnerships are part and parcel of the new world order, but McCain has it wrong here.

First of all, $300 million is chump change in the world of advanced technology and serious research and development. It's the technical equivalent of a cup of coffee when you're dealing with battery development and battery-powered vehicles, and it just won't cut it. It's this "finger snap" attitude again that drives me crazy—that these problems would be oh so easily solvable if Detroit would just get off its ass. And, if it won't do it, why, our government leaders will just turn to Toyota to solve our problems.

What part of this even remotely constitutes sound judgment?

No, at this point in our nation's history, what this country really needs is the technical equivalent of a '60s "moon shot" to help deal with our future energy and transportation needs.

When President John F. Kennedy delivered his speech about going to the moon, in person, before a joint session of Congress on May 25, 1961, his words were at once chilling and exhilarating. This was a challenge that was not only hard to imagine, it was all but insurmountable, but we were going for it, he said—and we would succeed—but it would come through the kind of sacrifice and determination that this nation hadn't mustered since World War II.

Here are some excerpts from that speech:

> *Now it is time to take longer strides—time for a great new American enterprise—time for this nation to take a clearly leading role in space achievement, which in many ways may hold the key to our future on Earth. ...*
>
> *I believe we should go to the moon. But I think every citizen of this country as well as the Members of the Congress should consider the matter carefully in making their judgment, to which we have given attention over many weeks and months, because it is a heavy burden, and there is no sense in agreeing or desiring that the United States take an affirmative position in outer space, unless we are prepared to do the work and bear the burdens to make it successful. If we are not, we should decide today and this year.*
>
> *This decision demands a major national commitment of scientific and technical manpower, materiel, and facilities, and the possibility of their diversion from other important activities where they are already thinly spread. It means a degree of dedication, organization, and discipline which have not always characterized our research and development efforts. It means we cannot afford undue work stoppages, inflated costs of material or talent, wasteful interagency rivalries, or a high turnover of key personnel.*
>
> *New objectives and new money cannot solve these problems. They could in fact, aggravate them further—unless every scientist, every engineer, every serviceman, every*

technician, contractor, and civil servant gives his personal
pledge that this nation will move forward, with the full speed
of freedom, in the exciting adventure of space.

The decision to go to the moon was a momentous one. As NASA describes it, "Only the construction of the Panama Canal in modern peacetime and the Manhattan Project in war were comparable in scope. NASA's overall human spaceflight efforts were guided by Kennedy's speech; Projects Mercury (at least in its latter stages), Gemini, and Apollo were designed to execute Kennedy's goal. His goal was achieved on July 20, 1969, when Apollo 11 commander Neil Armstrong stepped off the Lunar Module's ladder and onto the Moon's surface."

That's big-time stuff, folks. But solving this country's energy future is every bit as big as the Manhattan Project or the construction of the Panama Canal, because it involves the very future of this nation. And that's why it distresses me to see these two men who are running for president (and their handlers) seemingly not grasping what's before them at this very moment in history.

Let me go back to President Kennedy's speech: "I believe we possess all the resources and talents necessary. But the facts of the matter are that we have never made the national decisions or marshaled the national resources required for such leadership. We have never specified long-range goals on an urgent time schedule, or managed our resources and our time so as to insure their fulfillment."

Truer words were never spoken, and they apply doubly today. This country is brimming with the talent, vision, and resources necessary to accelerate battery development and explore alternative propulsion, or whatever the technical need is that's on the table for our future transportation needs. But the fact of the matter is that as a nation we have never made the commitment necessary to address our energy issues, or marshaled the resources necessary to even make a dent in the problems we're now facing.

Our leaders in Washington have shirked their responsibility and squandered every opportunity to set long-range goals and create a sense of urgency with the American people when it comes to our energy future, and now we're paying the price for it.

Mr. Obama and Mr. McCain both insist that they know what's best for us going forward when it comes to energy security, but I'm not convinced of that. They talk around the issue, throw out knee-jerk platitudes, and generally sink into campaign rhetoric at the drop of a hat. And none of that is doing this country one damn bit of good at this point.

Both of our presidential candidates should go back and read President Kennedy's speech from that day in May 1961, and then maybe—just maybe—they will begin to grasp what's needed at this juncture in history.

McCain wanting to "encourage heroic efforts in engineering" doesn't even begin to scratch the surface of what's needed right now. Perhaps a sizable portion of NASA's endeavors should be immediately switched over to the kind of research and development that would actually help this country in the near term—the next fifteen years— when it comes to our energy challenges. At least that would be one place to start.

This nation's energy crisis demands a sense of urgency, a sense of national purpose, and the marshaling of our technical resources on the level of which we haven't seen since the race to the moon began. It will take the brilliance of our finest talent and an unwavering commitment on a national basis to achieve our goals.

And it will take one of our two presidential candidates to step up and actually demonstrate the kind of leadership needed to see this country through one of the most pivotal moments in its history.

Part Two

The Doomsday Scenario

Chapter 9

GM's defining moment

After writing about General Motors' foibles and occasional triumphs—and its too many models/too many divisions/too many dealers conundrum—for nine years and counting, it was remarkable that $5 per gallon gasoline had done what the executive brain trust at GM could never do during the modern era: force the company to face the reality that it must drastically and fundamentally change its organizational structure. Why it took the cataclysmic event of a radical adjustment in what this country paid for a gallon of gas to trigger GM management's decision to finally address the Achilles heel that had crippled the company in this new global automotive world was beyond me, given that GM's multiple-division structure—a legacy from when it controlled 48 percent of the U.S. market way back in the '60s—had become woefully obsolete at least fifteen years ago. But there was more to the story. And this is the column where I called for Rick Wagoner to step down. Wagoner eventually would be unceremoniously dismissed by the Obama task force, a clear scapegoat and "the body" the administration needed to demonstrate to the American people that they were on this whole "fixing Detroit" thing.

GM IS ON THE BRINK OF DISASTER today because its executive leadership—along with its embarrassing rubber-stamp board of directors—steadfastly refused to acknowledge the fact that the company could not function properly as a viable corporate enterprise while still configured to produce and sell *double* the market share that it actually has in the U.S.

And while GM managers sat back and watched that market share inexorably slip away over the last fifteen years as Asian and European competitors took huge chunks of its business away, they continuously postponed taking the steps necessary—when they weren't avoiding them altogether—to reconfigure the company for the future. And now, they're out of time.

What happened? How could a company with the kind of tremendously deep talent and brain power at its disposal that GM has be caught so out of position and be so out of touch with what's going on to the point that it has now been left mumbling "woulda, coulda, shoulda" to itself while facing the consequences of their inactions and lack of foresight?

After years of writing about this industry and analyzing GM, I can safely say the answer comes down to a very simple realization, and that is that *no one* at GM—from CEO Rick Wagoner on down—ever actually believed that what was happening in the U.S. market was really going to continue, that somehow, some way GM would rise up again and return to its rightful place as the biggest car company in the world. In other words, a level of hubris is alive and well within General Motors that is absolutely breathtaking to contemplate.

I know because I have observed it up close. I have seen it in the way the company still treats its suppliers, for starters. But that's not where the real trouble was and still is at GM. It's the vast middle management layer—that gray morass of mediocrity that I have referred to with such contempt over the years—that has absolutely destroyed GM from within.

I have watched in horror as these bureaucratic middle managers functioned as if the world revolved around their little fiefdoms inside the company, and listened in stunned disbelief to their shockingly narrow-minded perspectives on the automotive world and their place in it. Their willful naïveté took on a life of its own, and their cancerous go-along-to-get-along mentality paralyzed the company at every turn, no matter how attuned or enlightened the leadership regime in place was at any given time.

But GM's vast gray middle has always been a problem, even in its heyday, which means that ultimately the buck has to stop at the top—with the series of leaders over the years who allowed GM to wallow in its mediocrity and who ultimately are responsible for GM's predicament today.

Yes, you can blame Washington for allowing the import manufacturers to run rampant in the U.S. market with none of the penalties, duties, or restrictions that their governments slapped on *our* domestic manufacturers when they tried to compete in their home markets, but that doesn't account for the fifteen-year period (the late '70s to the mid-'90s) when Detroit built piss-poor vehicles that turned a sizable chunk of American consumers away from buying domestic-built cars and trucks, and for good too.

And you can blame the cost-prohibitive contracts that the Detroit manufacturers entered into with their unions, based on the impossible notion that the good times would go on forever and that there would always be money to cover the bills in the end.

And you can say that the global economy brutally altered GM's (and Detroit's) fortunes at an accelerated rate that no one could have predicted, yet those same manufacturers were savvy enough in some cases to take advantage of those new markets, while blowing their position in *this* market to smithereens, which defies explanation.

And you can argue that no chief executive of a car company— foreign or domestic—had any idea that the price of gasoline would go through the roof in a three-month period, destroying much of their business overnight, yet these same manufacturers all did business in Europe where gas has been traditionally two and even three times as expensive as in the U.S., so none of that thinking ever crept into their future-planning sessions here? I find it hard to believe, and frankly inexcusable at this point.

But there *were* definitive signs warning us of what was headed our way long before this spring. The aftermath of Hurricane Katrina and the ensuing gas price spike—along with the emerging economies around the world—should have given the powers that be at these car companies at least a clue that America's gasoline "holiday" was about to be permanently brought to a close.

And the full-size SUV market was showing signs of deterioration long before $5 gas prices permanently disabled it. American consumers—a faddish lot, by every measure—had started to lose interest in the hulking trucks three years ago (I referred to it as the growing "SUV bubble" at that time).

But none of that hand-wringing really matters now because today General Motors, once this country's shining beacon of industrial might and a symbol of success around the world, is less than a year away from outright disaster and the distinct possibility that it will go bankrupt, or will have to consider an alliance with another manufacturer to survive. (I can't even imagine where GM would be right now if it wasn't for its Bob Lutz–led product offensive—Chevrolet Malibu, Buick Enclave, Cadillac CTS, etc.—which has kept the company afloat in these desperate times.)

With the dire straits that GM finds itself in today, CEO Rick Wagoner is now being forced to act on a course of action that he has openly scoffed at up until now, which is to consider a wholesale reappraisal of divisional operations in favor of a company-wide retrenching around the two GM divisions that still matter—Chevrolet and Cadillac.

Once upon a time, when it controlled half the market, GM needed all of its divisions to adequately cover the entire spectrum of market segments in the U.S. Now, with less than 20 percent of the U.S. market, GM can ill afford to keep its eight divisional balls in the air. And as a result, GM management is *finally* admitting that Alfred Sloan's divisional "ladder" model has reached the end of the line.

So what's next for this once-proud company? At this critical juncture in GM's history it will need lots of things to go its way if it is to survive as an independent entity. That includes its new product offensive, which can't miss in any segment. When you're fat and happy and on a roll, you can afford a product stumble once in a while, but when you're in GM's situation, a product misstep could be the difference between survival and bankruptcy. I see absolutely no margin for error here.

And GM's dealers will finally have to accept the fact that what once was will never be again, and that whole parts of GM will simply go dormant until further notice. GM Divisions may continue to exist on paper, but unless you're connected to a Cadillac or Chevrolet franchise, the future is bleak. A couple of Buick models (Enclave and the next-gen LaCrosse) and some Pontiacs (the four-cylinder G5, G6, and Vibe) will survive, and GMC trucks will soldier on, but cars and trucks that don't sell or don't have the potential for success won't be supported by any marketing efforts in the current environment.

Where does this leave Saturn and Saab? On the edge. And GM is already shopping Hummer to potential buyers.

But more important, where does all of this leave Rick Wagoner?

Though Wagoner did orchestrate GM's expansion into emerging markets (discounting the Fiat fiasco), and he did make a brilliant move to bring Bob Lutz on board—which frankly saved the company, in retrospect—he is, after all, the CEO who insisted on a huge, expanded push into the full-size SUV market just three years ago.

He is the CEO who flat-out dismissed the concept of GM "getting smaller to get better" so it could be more aligned with its shrinking footprint in the U.S. market as something that didn't even merit consideration. But now he and his team are scrambling while being forced to contemplate just that—and to a radical degree, too—by reacting to an idea that could have, and *should* have been acted upon several years ago.

He is the CEO who has presided over the most calamitous period in company history, with GM now worth just 25 percent of what it was when he took the reins as its chief executive, and with GM stock at the lowest point since the early 1950s.

Rick Wagoner is the one constant in any discussion of GM's recent history and its current crisis, and yet he remains at the helm of the company with hardly a worry or query from GM's logic-challenged board of directors. (How this board has managed to escape scrutiny for its blatant incompetence is beyond all comprehension and something that must be addressed if GM is going to go forward in a positive direction from this crucial point in its history.)

And if GM is going to go forward, now is the perfect moment for Rick Wagoner to step aside. He's had some hits, yes, but the many misses will forever cloud his tenure as CEO of what once was the world's largest and most successful industrial company.

On the precipice of GM's centennial year, the time is right for Rick Wagoner's term to come to an end.

In his place, GM needs Fritz Henderson—its current COO and the executive already pre-positioned to succeed Wagoner—to take the reins of the company. No, Henderson isn't the greatest thing since sliced bread, but he is the right guy at this pivotal, defining moment in GM history. Henderson is a visionary (never Wagoner's strong suit) and he will be more than willing to make the tough decisions necessary, and to set about reconfiguring GM for its survival.

Then maybe, just maybe, GM might have a shot to be around for another hundred years.

Chapter 10

The Trifecta of
Not Good

For the last several years, the war cry emanating from Detroit's top executives has been that the "perception gap" between consumer impressions of domestic cars and trucks and the reality—in terms of quality, safety, design, performance, handling, durability, efficiency, value, etc.—was giant and patently unfair, because the vehicles Detroit was turning out were vastly improved over the bad memories festering in buyers' minds. And for the most part, they were right. The contemporary products coming from Detroit were seriously competitive and in some cases actually equal to their German and Asian rivals, but the lingering perception gap in the minds of American consumers was so negatively skewed against even the idea of considering an American car or truck, that Detroit marketers could make little if any headway when it came to convincing shoppers to give their domestic entries a serious look. The same questions dominated the discussions of Detroit marketers in meeting after meeting: How do we convince them that we're worth a look if they won't even give us a glance to begin with? How can we possibly fortify our brand identity when we're not even on these consumers' radar screens? How do we close that perception gap when these people are clinging to bad memories of a decade (or more) ago? How can we get through to those who won't give us the time of day that we're not the same car company that we once were? How, indeed? Today, there's still an intense, ongoing battle for the hearts and minds of the American car-buying consumer.

IF YOU HAD ANYTHING TO DO with marketing at the Detroit car companies in the last decade, you didn't have time to think about much of anything else. Needless to say, "closing the gap" was what kept everyone up nights here in the Motor City.

And now, just as Detroit is showing marked improvement (well, at least GM and Ford, at any rate) and bringing to market solid, competitive entries in several different segments, the spike in gasoline prices has rocked the Detroit automakers to their core and left them reeling, because their SUV profit centers have been ripped to shreds in just three months.

An old friend of mine from Northern California (the anti-car, anti-Detroit capital of the universe) called me Monday morning and asked a litany of questions that could have been culled from the evening network news broadcasts. For instance, "Why did Detroit keep making those lumbering SUVs when they could see the writing on the wall?" "When are they going to get these high-mileage hybrids and electric cars on the road?" "What is taking so damn long?"

Just in case you've been away on vacation for a few years the answers to those questions are: 1. Because it was easier for the Detroit automakers to wallow in short-term, short-sighted SUV profits than it was to muster the *cojones* to stand up and say "We need to make dramatic moves for our future or we won't have one." 2. They'll be making a lot of PR noise over the next eighteen months, but the reality is that you won't see alternative propulsion vehicles on the road from a domestic manufacturer in any quantities until 2011. 3. Developing advanced-technology vehicles takes more than a finger snap to get the job done. Those last few years of clinging to the fading fortunes of the SUV market have proved costly for Detroit—and devastatingly so—because it is now lagging behind its two top Asian rivals by nothing less than a five-year swing.

For people far removed from the auto biz, especially in places populated by porkmeister lawmakers (Washington, D.C.), radical, one-dimensional environmentalists (California), and unbridled greed merchants (Wall Street), there was never any "perception gap" shrinkage to begin with. They never noticed that Detroit had made a huge leap in capability and credibility, and now that it's all over the media that Detroit has been caught flatfooted *yet again*, you can almost hear entire segments of the consumer public jettisoning Detroit from their thinking—permanently.

In other words, any chance of that perception gap being narrowed anytime soon was blown to smithereens by $5 per gallon gasoline prices.

Unfortunately for Detroit, the battle that went on over the last few years to close the perception gap has been rendered meaningless by going to the SUV profit well one too many times. In what can only be described as the last gasp from The Land of Short-Term Thinking, Detroit sealed its current turmoil in a hail of indecision, non-decisions, and monumentally bone-headed decisions. Or, as we like to say around here, the Trifecta of Not Good.

Now, instead of getting consumers to focus on the good news from Detroit—which is the fact that the domestic manufacturers are building products that can and *do* compete in every meaningful aspect with vehicles from the imported manufacturers, with many more on the way—the national consciousness has been focused on the fact that Detroit is out of touch with the times, and out of touch with the needs and wants of the American consumer.

It may not be fair, and it may not take into account what's coming product-wise over the next twenty-four to thirty-six months, but for Detroit, this negative perception is now the new reality.

Chapter 11

Ford's Radical Transformation

Now that the story was starting to get out about Ford's dramatic future product plans, I went on record as saying that Ford, under the leadership of CEO Alan Mulally, would be the best-positioned American automaker for this still-new century. It was a strong statement, but I felt it to be an accurate one. No automobile manufacturer had undergone a more fundamental internal transformation than Ford. And by fundamental I mean everything, *beginning with a philosophical shift in the way the company approached its business under Mulally, whose laser-like focus had altered the company to such an extent that it was barely recognizable in less than two years. Ford was clearly emerging as the American car company to be reckoned with. Today Ford is the* most successful American automaker and a *global* force *to be reckoned with.*

ALAN MULALLY HAS PURGED the paralyzing bureaucratic fiefdoms that thrived for years at Ford; he has eliminated the classic Detroit policy of designing, engineering, and producing vehicles in a vacuum—something that has absolutely crippled the domestic automakers for years—and he has trained his entire team's focus on the one thing that can in fact save the company, which is, of course, The Product.

I know what you're thinking, that all of this stuff is so obvious that it really shouldn't even be noteworthy at this point, but believe me, what will come out in tomorrow's announcement from Ford can't even begin to tell the story of what has gone on behind the scenes. The announcement will only address the obvious future direction of Ford's product transformation, but the rest of the story is still being written, because it's an ongoing process that gets refined, pushed, and tweaked every single week by Mulally and his team.

The short story behind the announcement is this: Alan Mulally has completely abandoned what worked for the previous thirty years (and what has been made painfully obsolete over the last three months in this new "real price" energy world we live in) and has taken Ford in a new direction that basically eliminates the distinction between what Ford is in Europe and around the world, and what Ford is in the United States market, in terms of the cars offered.

In the old days of Detroit, Ford (and GM) made cars for different markets around the world, and what worked in Europe was never even considered for the U.S. except in a few individual instances, because the driving was different "over there" and the price of fuel was dramatically higher, which thus forced the need for a completely separate range of products than what we were used to.

In Ford's case, American driving enthusiasts whined for years about the terrific Fords available in Europe that were never available here, and when Ford did venture to bring one of their stellar European products over here, they would never stick with it long enough to make a difference in the larger scheme of things because the company was designed to make money on producing large cars and even larger trucks.

All of that has now changed in one tumultuous quarter.

Mulally could have made a series of incremental steps, which is part and parcel of the Rick Wagoner school of "managing the downward spiral," but he knew if he hesitated or made only gradual moves, then Ford wouldn't be around long enough for it to matter. So instead Mulally emboldened his team with marching orders that did away with the word "transition" and focused their *raison d'être* on *transformation*, and the results will be truly breathtaking to see, to the point that, in just twenty-four months, Ford's product lineup will bear little resemblance to today's lineup.

The only way I can describe just how radical Ford's future-product push is in terms that the casual observer of the auto biz can understand is that Mulally and his team have actually *skipped* a model cycle with these new cars headed for the U.S. market; instead of a series of baby-step changes over the next three years, Ford will bring its 2012–2014 products forward to the 2010–2011 timeframe in a blaze of models and configurations that will set the U.S. market—and its competitors—on its ear.

We're talking a full range of smaller, more efficient sedans, sport coupes, crossovers, people movers, and even urban delivery vehicles that will change people's perceptions of what the Ford Motor Company is almost overnight.

Will Ford still make trucks and some larger vehicles? Absolutely. There will be a core group of American pickup buyers needing the vehicles for work applications, so that business will remain steady for the foreseeable future. It will be a much smaller market than what it once was, but it will still be viable for years to come nonetheless.

But the everyday "face" of Ford on America's streets and byways will be radically transformed by these dramatically designed and executed new passenger cars, and it will be a refreshing sight to behold.

It's actually fitting that an ex-Boeing engineer has led Ford's fundamental transformation, given the fact that Henry Ford's exploits into the aviation business were so noteworthy.

And it's fitting, too, that the one American automobile company that basically pioneered this industry—and that is celebrating the 100th anniversary of its vaunted Model T this year—is the company that will lead the domestic automobile business into the future.

Things are about to come full circle for the American auto industry, and for the legacy—and the future—of the Ford Motor Company, the timing couldn't be better.

Chapter 12

Down for the count: Crunch time for Detroit and the nation

After all of the hand-wringing about product, all of the second-guessing and Monday-morning quarterbacking about what the Detroit automakers did or didn't do to arrive at the predicament they find themselves in, it had come down to this: The Detroit Three did not have enough money over the short term—the next two to three years—to 1. Weather the financial storm caused by the collapse of the SUV and personal-use light-truck market brought on by high gasoline prices; 2. Bring new, more efficient vehicles to showrooms (while converting former pickup and SUV plants to build them); and 3. Accelerate the development of advanced-technology electric and plug-in electric vehicles in order to get them to showrooms in a timely fashion. Let's contemplate those words again: Not enough money, *as in the necessary cash to survive* as an industry *during this, the biggest production transformation/conversion since World War II. It turned out that* The End *was nigh for two of the Detroit Three.*

I HAVE MADE LIGHT IN RECENT MONTHS that the two presidential candidates are in this state so frequently now that I half expect one morning to see one of them delivering my newspaper (Barack Obama was here in Michigan Monday, John McCain was here yesterday). But there's nothing funny in the least about what's going on in Michigan or in the domestic automobile industry.

This industry, one that still either directly or indirectly accounts for between one in twelve and one in fourteen jobs in this country, is teetering off the edge of a cliff, dangling by a thin thread of "If we can just hang on until 2010, things will be better." But it's clear now that things *won't* be better for the industry two or three years down the road if it can't survive long enough to stay in business in the interim. And it's also becoming very clear that the domestic automobile industry won't be able to survive without some sort of government-sanctioned short-term loan package.

Obama was in Michigan on Monday touting $4 billion in guaranteed loans and tax credits for Detroit (McCain hasn't weighed in on the subject as of yet), but that is a mere drop in the bucket compared to what the domestic automobile industry actually needs. Estimates are flying around behind the scenes and in the media as to what this all might really cost. How does $8 to $10 billion for revamping the plants just to get these new electric vehicles built sound? Or how about another $25 to $30 billion on top of that over the next three years just to keep these auto companies afloat and out of bankruptcy? Tom Walsh, who writes for the *Detroit Free Press*, researched that $40 billion figure, and it's mind-numbing.

That the politicos in Washington are finally becoming alarmed as to what a wholesale implosion of the domestic automobile industry would do to the country is why the subject of guaranteed short-term government loans is suddenly part of the presidential debate. Whether you believe that the Detroit automakers deserve help or not, there's no question that the consequences of inaction would be dire for the economy and the country.

So here we are. After all of the posturing and the hand-wringing that I referred to at the beginning of this column, the reality is that one of America's key manufacturing industries is down for the count. It does little good at this juncture to rehash how we arrived at this point, because what matters now is what we, as a country, are going to do about it.

Do we collectively shrug our shoulders and say "they"—as in Detroit—deserved it and go out and buy more Toyotas, Hyundais, or whatever the next automotive flavor of the month from the Pan-Asian region is?

Do we, as a country, continue to underwrite the long and painful downward spiral of our nation as we watch industry after industry relegated to second-tier status because of our lethargic "whatever" attitude and our abject refusal to understand the end-of-life-as-we-know-it implications of the continued erosion of our manufacturing base in the new global economy?

Do we continue to operate as a loose confederation of "Balkanized" states, at odds with each other across the country at every turn, while turning our backs on our fellow citizens as long as it doesn't directly affect our day-to-day lives? After all, it's much easier to refer to what's going on in this industry as a "Detroit crisis" or a "Michigan problem" or one of those issues for the forlorn "flyover states" instead of what it really is: an *American* problem, and one that will deeply affect all of us if allowed to continue.

Or do we, as a nation, learn about and come to terms with the issues involved and work to understand the Big Picture implications, and then resolve to do something about it through our representatives in Washington?

I've said it before in *The United States of Toyota* and repeatedly in this column, and I don't mind saying it again today: We, as a country, cannot exist as Starbucks Nation alone. We cannot come to the table in this new global economy only as a nation of slothful consumers, a people who have completely lost the ability to create or manufacture things—and even worse, the will to muster the energy to care—because once we lose that, then the day we lose touch with the basic fabric of our nation won't be far behind.

And make no mistake about it, once that happens, other nations will be glad to start dictating our quality of life to us in no uncertain terms.

Sound appealing? I didn't think so.

The state of Michigan is on the front burner in the presidential campaign of 2008—that we already knew. But now the fate of this country's domestic automobile industry is in serious jeopardy, and the catastrophic implications to our national economy if Detroit goes down are almost too staggering to contemplate.

And how each of these presidential candidates responds to this crisis will be telling, for Detroit, this region, *and* the nation.

Chapter 13

For once the short-term thinking isn't coming from Detroit

Now that gas prices had softened a bit, faint sounds of warning were starting to creep into the media's coverage of the auto business. The gist of the bleating? That Detroit may have overreacted by tearing up its future-product plans to skew their upcoming product lineups toward vehicles that deliver dramatic leaps in fuel efficiency. To say that notion was flat-out absurd was an understatement. Anyone who thought that the pullback in gasoline prices was anything but a temporary lull was kidding themselves. The global pressure put on the price of oil by Russia's, China's, and India's burgeoning economies will continue to wreak havoc on the U.S. price at the pump as those countries consume more and more of the world's resources. And besides that stark reality, did we really need to be reminded that one of the main reasons for Russia's incursion into Georgia that month had everything to do with gaining control of a massive oil pipeline to the West? And did we really need to be reminded, too, that the next gas price spike would be more severe than the most recent one? I certainly hoped not.

CONSUMERS MAKING RIDICULOUS "sell low, buy high" auto-purchase decisions in the Oil Panic of 2008 made no sense whatsoever. So to think that there are some people out there who now believe that the latest pullback in gas prices means that happy times are here again shouldn't really surprise anyone.

The ironic part of this is that for once the Detroit Two are ahead of this story. GM and Ford, in particular, have made some tough calls in the last five months to dramatically alter their product portfolios in the coming years. Part of that was driven, of course, by the looming stiff increases in the EPA mileage requirements, but the reality for these automakers and their planning teams was the reasoned belief that the era of "cheap" oil was well and truly over, and to think any other way was to be foolhardy and irresponsible.

That some analysts are now hand-wringing about whether or not Detroit overreacted to the price of oil is yet more proof (as if we really needed any) that the Detroit Two cannot win this PR battle, no matter what they do or what they say. Not with consumers who hate Detroit, not with the "finger snap" environmentalists who think that the solution to all of our troubles is but a couple $100 billion away, and not with the vipers in the media looking for their next Detroit "implosion" story, either.

Consumers who want Detroit to die bring their own reasons for their thinking to the table (some of it based on bad ownership experiences, too much of it based on the "it won't affect me" and "who cares" syndromes), the knee-jerk environmentalists can't be reasoned with, and those in the media who relish reporting on Detroit's imminent demise are doing what they do best because that particular form of train-wreck journalism has become a staple of the American media scene—and it is what it is. There is no amount of corporate PR in the world that will convince these factions that there is new, clear thinking at work in Detroit

But I reserve particular ire for the self-proclaimed "expert" analysts who are now starting to question Detroit's commitment to revamping their product lines for fuel efficiency, terming it "overreacting." It's just ludicrous thinking. These are the same analysts, remember, who previously harped on Detroit's slow move to change, and they as much as anyone should understand the concept of lead time and what it means in this business. That they're weighing in now with their instant analysis about product commitments that had to be made for the 2010–2011 timeframe because gas has dropped 30 cents a gallon says more about their underlying motivation than anything I could possibly say at this point.

GM and Ford product planners made the right call. Yes, they will offer a diverse lineup of vehicles accounting for all the various needs that our nation's fleet has to accommodate (even SUVs too), but the new mainstream passenger cars on the way will be fuel-efficient and right for the globally intense world we live in today.

As they should be.

As stunning as it may seem, for once the short-term thinking in this country isn't coming from Detroit.

Who could have possibly envisioned *that*?

Chapter 14

Detroit has lost the image war, and now it's time to move on

It was all over but the shouting, hand-wringing, and whining, but the facts were clearer than ever: In the fall of 2008 America didn't care about Detroit, and Americans couldn't be convinced to abandon their ingrained—and mostly inaccurate—perceptions that Detroit builds "inferior" vehicles. It was getting uglier by the minute.

FOR SEVERAL YEARS NOW, I have been writing about the gap that exists between the quality and integrity of the cars and trucks that Detroit builds and the negative perception of these vehicles that a growing number of Americans share. And it has been made clear to me by the overwhelmingly negative tone of the emails we receive, and from the comments I get in person from people on the road—and from the blatant anti-Detroit stance that exists in the majority of the media—that the battle to win the hearts and minds of Americans is over for Detroit, and there's no amount of advertising and PR spin money that will change the negative tide mounting against it.

The reality of the situation is that people just don't care. I've heard it countless times in countless ways: "It won't affect me if Detroit goes down, why should I care?" "Detroit deserves what they're getting." "It's just another tired industry that will be replaced by something else, so what?"

And for the denizens of Detroit 2.0 to actually think that there's enough time and money to counteract this negativity is a false hope.

Because this isn't the same America that mustered the will and the fierce pride to counteract global evil in the Second World War. This isn't the same America whose "blue sky" thinking and unbridled creativity responded to a challenge and propelled the rocket age to new heights. And this isn't the same America that once shared a common purpose and perspective on what this country stands for.

Instead, this country has become a jaded and fractionalized nation of consumer sponges driven by the lackadaisical mantras of *Whatever* and *What's in it for me?* A nation whose people couldn't be bothered with such esoteric concepts as this country's eroding manufacturing base and the nation's burgeoning inability to lead on the world stage.

So where does Detroit go from here?

I believe that turning away from this debilitating quest to change the American consumer mindset by massaging the message and endlessly cooking the formula of communicating Detroit's fundamental goodness will actually prove to be oddly freeing for the Detroit manufacturers (at least the ones still standing by 2011). Because then they can focus all of their attention on the only thing that can ultimately save them, which is building products that consumers find compelling in every respect.

(This is much tougher than it sounds, as GM in particular has found out of late. The Cadillac CTS and Chevrolet Malibu are fine cars, but GM still has to cajole consumers into buying them. Yes, these excellent new products are making headway for GM in the market, but the road is painfully slow and deliberate. GM has found out the hard way that this perception gap—which was twenty-five years in the making—cannot be changed overnight)

That GM and Ford are finding the road to success in global markets easier than in their own backyards is even more reason to shift their priorities. The North American market will be in freefall for these two manufacturers until they hit bottom, and then they can slowly build it back up from there. And the only way that is going to happen is by building products that bristle with advanced technology, impressive efficiency, and bold design. Products that, in the end, simply cannot be found anywhere else, which admittedly is a *very* tall order.

For Detroit to continue down this path of beating the proverbial dead horse—in this case courting an American consumer public that frankly doesn't give a shit—with countless messages about what they're doing better and what's going right is a monumental waste of time and money.

The image war is over for Detroit, and it's time to move on.

At this juncture Detroit has only one move left, and that is to get through to the American consumer by building outstanding products that have no ifs, ands, or buts attached to them. Machines that not only stand out, but stand above the rest. Anything less than that kind of superlative execution will hasten the demise of these companies altogether, or at least marginalize them into becoming regional players in their home country.

Chapter 15

"GMnext"?
How about GMWhat have
you done for us lately?

The first one hundred years went by in a blur; at least they did at GM's centennial celebration that September morning at its headquarters in the Renaissance Center, hard by the Detroit River. GM intentionally raced through its first century in the opening minute of the hour-long program, as the whole point of its forward-looking "GMnext" initiative was to talk about where the company was going, not where it had been. The company then capped a rousing, around-the-world "live" tour of its far-reaching global operations with the unveiling of the production-ready Chevrolet Volt—the company's all-new electric car—with GM CEO Rick Wagoner making the point that "The Volt symbolizes General Motors' commitment to the future." Little did anyone know that the Volt would eventually come to symbolize much more than that. "GMnext" would turn out to be a one-way ticket to bankruptcy.

AH YES, THE VOLT. No, it's not just the "reinvention of the car," as GM likes to say (although it very well could be)—it's the company's lead-image spear for the next two years, the one vehicle that has the potential to not only change the game itself, but one that just might have the ability to change two decades of accrued negative perceptions that have pulverized GM's image.

Let me repeat one key word here, the Volt has the *potential* to do a lot of great things for GM and the auto business as a whole. But will it? And better yet, *can it?*

GM is convinced. As a matter of fact, they're so bullish about the Volt that they've bet the very existence of the company on its success, and they've hung their collective asses so far out in the breeze on this one that anything less than absolute vindication on all of its promised performance targets would be such a massive black eye for the company that GM would never recover.

But now what? One reality of "GM*next*" is that it will require the biggest balancing act in modern automotive history, because GM now has the monumental task of convincing the American consumer public that the Volt will:

1. ESTABLISH GM AS THE INDUSTRY'S TECHNOLOGICAL-ECOLOGICAL LEADER.

2. USHER IN THE DAWN OF THE "ELECTRIFICATION" OF THE AUTOMOBILE.

GM hopes to do all of this while maintaining the public's interest in a vehicle that won't be in showrooms until the end of 2010.

And while GM is doing that, it still must continue to sell its improved portfolio of cars, trucks, and crossovers, the ones that are still straining to gain grudging respect in this market.

Combine this challenge with the precarious nature of the nation's financial future—what with the implosion of Wall Street roiling the economy—and you have a quest that's unprecedented in the annals of automotive history.

As I've stated in previous columns of late, the idea of Detroit convincing the American consumer buying public that their cars and trucks are worthy has become a fool's errand, because America and Americans frankly couldn't care less. The domestic auto industry is wrestling with the reality that it simply cannot change a generation of buyers' overwhelmingly negative perceptions about its products, even though most of that negativity isn't applicable to the vehicles being produced today.

The Volt, however, has the *potential* to change all that.

The Volt has captured the imagination of a large portion of the media and a large squadron of savvy consumers looking for The Next Big Green Thing. And GM has, in turn, managed to capture marketing lightning in a bottle with it.

But how long can it last? And how long can GM keep the public and the media's fascination with the car "on point" in the coming twenty-six months?

Though not an apples-to-apples comparison, how GM has handled the upcoming Camaro is a case, in my estimation, of how *not* to do it. The Camaro won't be available in showrooms until next March, yet after its slam-bang intro at the Detroit auto show in January of 2006, it has starred in the movie *Transformers* and has become so ubiquitous at car shows across the country that the newness is all but worn off.

Is this the fate of the Volt? The fact that it's slated to appear in the second chapter of *Transformers* (along with a bunch of other GM production vehicles and concepts) being filmed right now for next summer does not exactly bode well. Let that be a caution to GM marketers going forward.

There's no question that if the Volt delivers on its promise of forty reliable, trouble-free miles on a single electric charge—even if it does cost $40,000 and GM won't build a lot of them—it *will* change how the game is played, and GM *will* establish itself as the unquestioned environmentally forward-thinking automobile company.

But at the end of the day there's another, more ominous reality hanging over GM and the euphoric potential of the Volt.

And that is that after a century of dominance and a storied existence as one of America's corporate icons, "GM*next*" isn't about the next one hundred years at all.

Rather, "GM*next*" is about whether or not GM can survive its precarious financial standing—the one that is haunting every move the company makes—long enough to see the Volt come to fruition in the first place.

Chapter 16

A doomsday scenario unfolds for Detroit

First it was the mortgage loan meltdown, followed by the gasoline price spike the previous spring. Then the collapse of the "casual use" light-truck and SUV market—almost the entire source of Detroit's profitability—came immediately afterward. Then it was the perilous slowdown of the economy, resulting in the precipitous drop in car and truck sales. Add in the turmoil on Wall Street and the teetering banking crisis, and you had the ugly icing on an already bitter cake. Then, in the midst of the nation's banking crisis, the credit crisis—or lack of it—threatened to derail Detroit's best-laid plans for its very survival.

It is one thing for the Detroit car companies to muster the expertise, the technical resources, and the strategic imperative to reposition themselves for a resurgence in 2010, because their backs are to the wall and it's a relentless, 24/7 siege to keep on track and keep focused on where they *want* to be, as opposed to where they are now.

It's quite another to have the very lifeblood of their business—available credit—yanked out right from under them, leaving them with painfully few options going forward.

The $25 billion in government loans at a favorable interest rate is one component of Detroit's lifeline that will be spent on new technologies and the development of more fuel-efficient vehicles for 2010. That's a given. One that comes with strings but one that was sorely needed in order for Detroit to fuel its future product programs.

But if consumers can't get credit to buy vehicles right now, or if it becomes extremely difficult to get credit even if a consumer's credit rating is outstanding, then we're talking about the collapse of the entire domestic automobile industry as we know it. Not just another negative step in a long line of negative steps for Detroit, but an imminent and outright collapse.

A lineup of glittering new products—no matter how technologically advanced or wildly efficient they are—counts for exactly nothing if consumers can't afford them. And this isn't just Detroit's problem, either. All car manufacturers will be in the same boat unless this credit situation is solved—and soon.

But the Detroit automakers are already under severe pressure because their cash position is beyond precarious to begin with. When you're burning through $1 to $2 billion a *month*, it starts to add up, which is why the Detroit automakers are hanging by a thread. The best guesstimates for GM and Ford is that the endgame is only eighteen short months away, *if* the "burn" rate continues at the breakneck pace it's going now and there's no dramatic turnaround in their fortunes. Chrysler? They will partner with another company in that timeframe, no matter what happens.

Losing access to credit is a Doomsday scenario that no one in Detroit—or the rest of the country for that matter—is prepared for. How could anyone be prepared for such a cataclysmic upheaval in the way America runs?

It's easy for some to say that maybe this is the best thing that could happen, that the country needed a major correction in its credit addiction so that we could get back on track, but as good as that may sound theoretically, it spells disaster in a kaleidoscope of ways—for every sector of the economy—and particularly for the domestic automobile business.

The U.S. auto industry is teetering on the brink and has been for months. It has been one thing after another followed by another for Detroit, and each new turn of the screw redefines bad as we know it.

And just how much worse can it get?

Not much, because Detroit's giant bowl of Not Good is already filled to the brim.

With the domestic automakers planning on launching a brace of pivotal new vehicles for the 2010 model year, there is at least a shred of hope that two of the automakers can survive. New products, new technologies, and compelling new fuel-efficient vehicles are on the way. But talking about all the great stuff coming in 2010 and surviving until then are two entirely different things.

Unless and until cooler heads prevail in Washington—which apparently is asking a lot—and the political grandstanding can be set aside for a day, then Detroit simply doesn't have until 2010.

If people can't get loans to buy cars or trucks, then it's Game Over for Detroit.

Chapter 17

In the Land of Not Good, hysteria sets in

The swirling maelstrom of conjecture, rumor, and fabrication that enveloped the Motor City (a.k.a. The Land of Not Good) in October of 2008 concerning GM and Chrysler had spun completely out of control. So much had been said by so many people who knew so little about what was going on, that it was truly breathtaking to contemplate. As a matter of fact, I had never seen anything like it in all my years in this business. With that in mind, I thought it would be a good idea to take a deep breath and talk about what we knew first, before we ventured into how any future scenarios might have played out.

FIRST OF ALL, as I've been warning for quite some time, the Cerberus "miracle" planned for the resurrection of Chrysler was a flat-out disaster waiting to happen. And unfortunately for the people at Chrysler, my prediction is unfolding as you read this. That Cerberus was completely out of their league and unencumbered with the first shred of knowledge or expertise required to turn around a flailing, ailing, and deflating American automotive icon is a known fact.

And on top of that, the unbridled hubris that they brought to the table, which deluded them into thinking that they actually could venture into one of the most challenging businesses in the world—at exactly the most crucial juncture in American automotive history—and emerge with a nice big payday in a couple of years, is beyond comprehension.

That Cerberus assembled a "dream team" (at least in their estimation) consisting of Bob Nardelli—a man who was such an abject failure at Home Depot that the company has taken years to recover—and Jim Press, the architect of the modern miracle that is Toyota in the United States today, and assumed that they could just throw a switch and it would all be good, makes me question the sanity of the powers that be at Cerberus.

That the Cerberus brain trust was *that* out of touch and *that* detached from the reality of the situation is simply scary. There's really no other word for it. Needless to say, the fact that things didn't go swimmingly for the Cerberus "dream team" was no surprise in the least. Assembling a team of alleged all-stars on paper doesn't automatically translate into a winning performance, and Cerberus proved that timeless adage once again, but with dramatically painful consequences unique to its self-inflicted predicament.

To make matters worse, Chrysler's public pronouncements have consisted of a particularly insidious form of overpromise, underdeliver bluster from the very beginning. Nardelli's obnoxiously tinged arrogance combined with Press's incessant habit of lecturing the media about how super things were—as opposed to how truly horrific things actually were—wore thin months ago. And it seemed that the grimmer the sales numbers were for the domestic auto industry—with month after month of catastrophic results led by Chrysler's shockingly dismal performance—the more the rhetoric by Nardelli and Press was ratcheted up. And the more Chrysler's credibility plummeted.

As a matter of fact, as recently as two weeks ago, Chrysler was at it again, this time led by COO Tom LaSorda—a nice guy who has unfortunately been turned into the "Baghdad Bob" of the domestic auto industry by this Cerberus-orchestrated nightmare—extolling the virtues of Chrysler's future electric-vehicle program, a program that has little chance of happening in a future scenario of a Cerberus-planned exit strategy from the auto business.

The fact that this embarrassing smoke-and-mirrors "it won't be long now" public disinformation campaign has continued along unfettered—without even the whiff of reality emanating from Chrysler—has been absolutely reprehensible, in my estimation.

With all of this in mind, then, let's talk about the so-called merger.

A disastrous scenario by any measure.

Let me get this straight right off the bat: The reality of a merger between GM and Chrysler would be an unmitigated disaster of incalculable proportion, one that would decimate both companies. You can spare me with the "economies of scale" argument (the darling rationale of "expert" analysts by the droves), too, because as logical as those arguments may be, the fact of the matter is that putting two companies together that are already slumped against the ropes and gasping for air is sheer lunacy.

When you have one company that has too many models, too many divisions, and too many dealers, how could you possibly think that combining that company with *another* company that has too many models, too many divisions, and too many dealers would be a good idea?

I just about choked in my cornflakes, reading some pundits extoll the size of the newly merged company, as if that would somehow justify all of the negatives associated with these two companies coming together.

It doesn't. Not even close, as a matter of fact.

Besides, the "size" of the merged company wouldn't resemble any of the estimates, not if any rational thought came into play.

No, the real meat of the GM-Chrysler talks revolved around Cerberus wanting out—and wanting out *right now*—of Chrysler. And if everyone would step back and let that thought percolate for a minute, then there might, and let me say that word again—*might*—have been some logic to a GM-Chrysler deal. But that deal wouldn't have been a merger. Instead it would have been a takeover, with GM relieving Cerberus of control of Chrysler.

The important thing to remember in all of this is that Cerberus is privately admitting for the first time—despite its tediously embarrassing pronouncements to the contrary—that they are done with the car business.

The Cerberus obsession with Chrysler was akin to the dog in the neighborhood that likes to chase cars all day. But then, after finally catching a car, the dog doesn't have the first clue as to what to do next. Cerberus caught its car in the guise of Chrysler, and armed with zero cumulative knowledge about the business, it demonstrated its relentless cluelessness and utter futility at every turn.

If there had been any agreement at all between GM and Chrysler, it would have revolved around GM taking control over Chrysler's assets in exchange for the rest of its stake in GMAC. That way, Cerberus would walk away with 100 percent of GMAC and GM would be left to sort out what to do with Chrysler's existing operations.

GM's interest in Chrysler: Why? And would it have been workable?

Why would GM have been interested in doing this if its situation is already beyond precarious? There are three reasons from GM's point of view, actually (beyond the usual mention of cost savings): 1. To gain control of the Jeep brand, so it could be merged with Hummer (that is until Hummer is sold); 2. To gain control of Chrysler's minivan franchise and its engineering and development expertise in that segment; and 3. To prevent a major global competitor from gaining a major foothold in the U.S. market by taking over Chrysler and its dealer network. (Analysts have also mentioned Chrysler's $11.7 billion in cash on hand as a lure for GM, but even if that cash is verified, I remain highly skeptical that it's enough, given the horrendous task at hand in figuring out what to do with the parts of Chrysler that GM doesn't want.)

It should be obvious that under any takeover scenario Chrysler would be gutted of people and nameplates. After all, the last thing GM needs is more truck and SUV capacity—or more cars to sell for that matter—so the likelihood of GM hanging on to the vast middle management bureaucracy of Chrysler, or its mediocre product portfolio, is slim and none. In short, GM would cherry-pick only what it wanted from Chrysler, which means that the impact in terms of human capital would be absolutely devastating. How bad would it be?

I estimate 80 percent of the current Chrysler workforce would have to be eliminated for any of it to work.

Even if GM had gained control over Chrysler and only took interest in Jeeps and minivans, *would* it have worked? From where I sit, no, because GM has been operating with a divisional structure that grew obsolete 25 years ago, while refusing to acknowledge the reality of its too many models/too many divisions/too many dealers conundrum. So, with GM already teetering on the edge of corporate disaster, why would they have wanted to add to the confusion?

With Cerberus done with Chrysler, the fate of the auto company based in Auburn Hills has been set. Within six months, Chrysler will be taken over or "parted out." Either way, Chrysler will cease to exist as we know it by next spring, if not sooner.

As for GM, the fact that the company's management is exploring all options at this juncture is telling. Yes, the national and global financial crisis and the paralysis in the credit markets have been brutal to Detroit in particular, but GM's "talks" with other automakers smacks of desperation, there is no doubt about it. Especially with the news that GM approached Ford on the idea of a more formal, large-scale partnership (beyond the small technical partnership they already share in a few engineering areas) even *before* the Chrysler discussions, according to Bill Vlasic, reporting for the *New York Times*. Those talks went nowhere, as Ford wants to go on its own path.

As hard as it may be to believe, GM may be next up behind Chrysler to face elimination, consolidation, or ruination. The first one hundred years for GM blew by in a blur. The next twelve months, on the other hand, are shaping up to be an excruciatingly painful siege that could determine the very existence of the company.

Simply incredible.

Needless to say, we have a developing situation here in the Motor City. I just hope we can survive the hysteria long enough to sort it all out.

Part Three

Pitchforks and Torches

Chapter 18

After the smoke clears, it's time for America, Inc.

By now it should have been obvious to even the most casual observers that the domestic automobile industry was on the verge of total collapse. Already reeling from the gas spike earlier in the year and the subsequent decimation of the light-truck and SUV markets, the national financial crisis had conspired to cut the amount of survival time for two of the three domestic automobile makers from years to just months, leaving General Motors and the Cerberus-owned Chrysler LLC teetering on the brink of bankruptcy.

IT HAS ALSO FINALLY BECOME OBVIOUS to even the most jaded anti-Detroit zealots in Washington and around the country that a collapse of the domestic automobile industry would be a cataclysmic event with devastating and far-reaching consequences that would threaten to shake this country's economic future to its core.

The urgency of this looming economic disaster—which initially was just a sideshow compared to the national and international financial crisis—is now on the front burner for this country's decision makers, and is one of the prime topics in the presidential race, too.

It is clear that GM is in direct talks with the White House about receiving an early injection of money—from either the $25 billion already promised to the Detroit Three or the $700 billion financial institution bailout package—in order to ease the financial blow to employees and dealers as a result of its acquisition of Chrysler from Cerberus. And that agreement may in fact have already been made.

The alternative? There is no good alternative. If GM were able to acquire Chrysler (although the financial wherewithal for GM to do it completely on its own just isn't there) straight up, the immediate cessation of most of Chrysler's operations and the brutal dismissal of 80 percent of its employees—not to mention the utter devastation to thousands of dealers across the nation—would plunge this country toward economic disaster on top of an already deepening recession.

Free-market theorizing aside, we have long since passed the point of no return in this matter. If this country allows one of its key manufacturing pillars to slip into insolvency, it would set off a dark chain of events that would reach into every sector of the economy and would not only devastate the states where Detroit has its manufacturing and parts facilities, but would affect every state of the union.

There are still some out there who don't believe this "Detroit thing" will have anything to do with their lives or livelihoods, of course. It's hard for some people to understand that because Detroit and Michigan ("The Flyover State") are viewed as relics from an ancient country no one remembers anymore, even though one in fourteen jobs in the U.S. are *still* either directly or indirectly dependent on the domestic automobile industry. I really don't know how else I could possibly present those figures in order to get through to people out there that they should care deeply about what's going on in Detroit and Washington right now, because it's real and it *will* affect you, no matter where you are or how flush your circumstances are.

Even though I am absolutely convinced that the idea of GM acquiring Chrysler is fraught with opportunities for abject failure on a grand scale, the White House will make the decision that a managed dissolution of Chrysler over time under GM's stewardship would be preferable to an immediate corporate blowup.

But let's move beyond that for a moment. Let's operate under the assumption that with government assistance GM *does* take over Chrysler. Now what? Critics are quick to point out that Detroit can't continue to do business as usual and that accountability and some measure of performance deliverables have to be built into the "strings" of any loan package. And I say fine to all of that, except I must point out the reality that it hasn't been business as usual here and that Detroit has been racing to revamp its product offerings for going on five years now (lead time is not a concept that people outside this business find easy to understand).

But I am really much more concerned about the negative and wildly naïve attitude that has been allowed to fester in and around Washington and across the country of late, the attitude that suggests that our manufacturing base and this country's ability to make things somehow doesn't matter in this brave new consumer nation that the U.S. has become in the twenty-first century.

It's the same attitude that suggests—if not outright promotes—the idea that we can exist in some alternative consumerist universe of our own creation, a Starbucks Nation of "whatever" consumers who don't really care where whatever it is we're coveting comes from as long as it's here now and c-h-e-a-p.

This is the same attitude that has left this country ill-prepared for the burgeoning realities of this global world we're living in. And this "whatever" posture that has become far too commonplace in our nation, and the idea that this will all work out somehow—because it always has—is not only beyond scary, it's just flat-out wrong.

I've said this before and I will say it again: This nation is at a crossroads. Our idyllic, textbook, free-market notions and our "Aw, shucks, we just want you to play nice with us like we play nice with you" Jimmy Stewart–like attitude that we continue to try to foist off on jaded nation-state competitors that just don't care are simply obsolete in this new global economy.

Other nations have taken advantage of Uncle Sam's quaint view of the world for years, to the point where they must privately refer to us as "Uncle Sap."

We've allowed other nations to come into this country virtually unimpeded, and have showered them with lavish, long-term tax breaks and incentives for good measure. Yes, jobs were created, but now we're waking up to the fact that American-owned manufacturing strongholds are fewer in number because our manufacturing base has been slowly but surely eroded from within.

Just a few examples? We allowed Japanese automobile manufacturers to dump vehicles in this market—vehicles that carried none of our American workers' healthcare or pension overhead burdens of any kind—for *years* while the Japanese government did everything in their power to keep American-made vehicles from being sold over there. We also watched as Japan, Inc. willfully and consistently manipulated the yen in their automakers' favor—to the point that Toyota was making millions of dollars every quarter just on currency manipulation alone—while our own government shrugged their shoulders and mustered little or no protest, saying "Gee, we wish you guys wouldn't do that," or some such nonsense.

Where did all of this leave the Detroit automakers? The manufacturing powerhouse that forged this nation's middle class and once powered the "Arsenal of Democracy" in World War II? The companies that allowed millions of people to make a decent living, send kids to college, and allow communities big and small across this nation to thrive for the better part of one hundred years?

Broke down and busted on the side of the road, that's where.

Make no mistake, Detroit was more than culpable for their predicament, that has already been well documented by me and others ad nauseam. But trying to compete with Japanese vehicles that started out with a $3,000 cost advantage before they even hit the dealership lots while paying for healthcare and pension funding that grew exponentially with each passing model year was a debilitating, no-win game for Detroit. And now that game is well and truly over.

After the smoke clears, the dust settles, and the hand-wringing and political posturing stops over this Detroit bailout, this country will be faced with some difficult choices going forward.

Do we want to continue to compete in this brutally competitive global economy with hat in hand and shuffling feet, hoping countries treat us nice and with respect? Or do we wake up, smell the coffee, and realize that these countries are only in it for the money—*our* money—

and they will do everything in their power to get their hands on it, even if it means turning us into a nation of consumer zombies with little left to stand on other than our revolving plastic.

If we want to shore up this nation and we want to get this country back on track, then we're going to not only have to make some difficult sacrifices, we're going to have start playing tough in this new global marketplace. And that means that the gloves will have to come off in Washington. This country needs to start thinking in terms of "America, Inc.," and that means, first and foremost, rebuilding our manufacturing base and supporting our American companies—no matter what sector they're competing in—because to not do so in this global economy borders on the criminal.

The reality about all of this is that countries from all over the globe *love* to do business here, and they love to do so for a reason. And that reason is because we don't ask them to sacrifice much to come over and set up shop here. As a matter of fact, we make it real easy for them. Twenty-five years of tax break incentives? Sure, why the hell not?! Free land? Come on down!

The bottom line is that this type of total economic acquiescence on the part of our government—at the national *and* local levels—will have to change, and dramatically so.

Don't agree with a "bailout" or loan for Detroit? Then what if every foreign auto manufacturer—*whether they have plants here or not*—had to pay anywhere from $250 to $1,500 per vehicle sold (on a sliding scale) to do business here? (Because no matter how much they say that they've created jobs in the states they operate in, and that they shouldn't be penalized for doing so, at the end of the day their profits return to their home countries. And to pretend otherwise is to have your head in the sand.) And then what if that money went directly into a fund to help support American workers' pensions or an education fund for their families?

The idea that in this global economy our free-market policies will be accepted and embraced and that everyone will play nice with us because we want to play nice with them is simply absurd and woefully out of touch. America must change its ways if we are to survive as a global leader, economic and otherwise.

The bottom line in this discussion is that we have a multitude of problems in this country that will take time, sacrifice, hard work, and collective effort to solve. And we're only going to be able to do that if we're unified as a nation, and we compete in the global marketplace as "America, Inc."

Chapter 19

Dear President-Elect Obama

Well, the inevitable happened. Buoyed by great speechwriting and the magic elixir of youthful exuberance—with a healthy dose of the "change" mantra thrown in for good measure—Barack Obama became the forty-fourth president of the United States after John McCain shot his campaign in the head by choosing a ill-qualified political hack from Alaska to be a heartbeat away from the presidency. The nation had spoken, and now it was time for a little levity and perspective. Two years later, Obama would get his ass handed to him by a pissed-off electorate. And that whole "change" thing? Not. So. Much.

WELL, YOU DID IT. Words like "historical," "unprecedented," and "fundamental shift" are being bandied about this morning, and they're all true. You have already accomplished what a lot of people thought you could never do: Get voters to abandon their fog of complacency and actually come to the polls and vote—the single most important act a citizen of this great country can do—and to galvanize this nation like no politician has in decades. The people voted for a new beginning. They voted for that elusive but promising term, *change*. And they voted—more so, perhaps, than any other reason—for hope. A tall order indeed.

So I congratulate you, sir. But alas, your moment of triumph is destined to be incredibly short-lived, because I'm afraid this country has no time for a victory lap. The problems and issues we're facing are threatening to collectively overwhelm us, and we need visionary leadership from you and our representatives in Washington. And we need it right now.

We need you all to set aside the kind of polarizing, shrill, and divisive debate that we've come to expect out of Washington in recent years, because it's like we're watching a bad TV show that we can't turn off.

We need you to purge the aura of vindictiveness that seems to permeate what passes for "leadership" in Washington these days, because it's so off-putting that we're losing hope—there's that word again—losing hope in our leadership, hope in our system, and hope in our future.

It's like we the citizens don't matter anymore, because we've been swept aside in favor of lobbyists, special interests, and financial "wizards" who have let us down at every turn, and who have left whole parts of this country reeling and hurting and desperate.

And worse yet, all of this has left us feeling that we've become part of a country that none of us recognize anymore. No, this isn't some nostalgia-laced longing for us to go back in time to some post-card America that can't be re-created; instead it's a fervent wish and desire to get this country back on an even keel.

Is that too much to ask?

We need to get back to being a country filled with hardworking people who care about striving and achieving and who care about each other, rather than a country paralyzed by legions of self-absorbed citizens who have mastered the two most distressing phrases in America today: "What's in it for me?" and "Whatever."

It's not the country we grew up with, Mr. Obama. It's not the country that survived financial ruin in the early '30s, world wars, cold wars, and every threat imaginable. It's not the country that nurtured blue-sky dreamers and entrepreneurs at every turn, the country that rewarded ingenuity, hard work, and success, the country that did great things across a broad spectrum of disciplines, avocations, and pursuits.

Instead we've become a nation of bitter, vicious factions, an embarrassingly bad circus of pointing fingers and relentless huffing and puffing—consumed by narrow-minded thinkers and narrow-minded thinking—while there's real work to be done and real challenges to face.

Speaking of which, right now we're facing a financial crisis that is threatening to plunge this country into a full-on depression. And that crisis was brought on by a system based on financial instruments that could be manipulated by a few for tremendous gain by those same few. But allowing that much financial decision-making to be entrusted to a few—and just assuming they'd do the right thing for the country as a whole—proved to be disastrous, and unfortunately when that house of illusion collapsed it took us all down with it. There is plenty of blame to go around and much of it has been assigned already, so I'm not going to belabor that point today.

But of all the things on your plate—our financial institutions' implosion, the continuing military actions in Iraq and Afghanistan, the looming threat of a newly belligerent Russia, the myriad strategic threats, the endless global issues, and the pitiful shape of our educational system—there is one imminent crisis that threatens to derail your presidency before it even gets out of the gate, and that is the certain collapse of the domestic automobile industry and the looming consequences to our nation if swift action isn't taken.

This is about real work, sir. The kind of work that built this country from scratch and powered this nation to a level of greatness never seen before. The kind of work that has defined our nation's soul for as long as we can remember. The kind of work that helped the middle class thrive and flourish.

And that kind of real work has been undermined at every turn, unfortunately. The American manufacturing sector has been eroding for years. Wildly naïve government policies in the face of a global marketplace with little inclination to adhere to our view of how business should be conducted is one reason for this, and lobbyists who are bought and paid for by foreign governments and industries are another.

Our national obsession for getting things on the cheap—the Wal-Mart syndrome—isn't helping, either. We have become a nation of bargain hunters, consumer zombies addicted to deals that feed into our instant gratification and "right now" mindset. Unfortunately, that mindset is helping destroy our country from within by contributing to the decline of our manufacturing sector. And this is having a devastating effect on our long-term strategic future, too.

Let me get back to the issues facing the domestic automobile industry, one of the pillars of our manufacturing base in this country. The threat to the Detroit Three has far-reaching implications for all of us. One in fourteen jobs is either directly or indirectly connected to the domestic automobile industry. Repeat that figure to yourself because it's daunting. We're not just talking about the threat to one of America's core industries here, and it's not just Michigan or the other scarred "flyover states" that will be devastated by this either, because there are automotive suppliers and dealerships big and small all across the country that will be immediately affected if Detroit is allowed to go bankrupt. And for a nation teetering on a deep recession, I don't need to tell you that a bankrupt Detroit could send this nation over the edge.

Spare me the free-market proselytizing and the collegiate-level economic theorizing that is popular with so many whenever this is mentioned, because there's no time for that anymore. The debate about whether or not Detroit needs financial help? That ship has sailed. We've gone way past the point of no return at this juncture because Detroit is just months away from catastrophe. Now it's only a question of how much money and how soon it can get here. I'm sure you and your advisors are well aware of the urgency at this point.

Mr. Obama, you come to be the forty-fourth president of the United States at the most pivotal time in our nation's history. Not since the calamity of the Great Depression or the harrowing threat to our democracy in World War II has this nation been on the brink of unfathomable disaster.

The posturing, stump speeches, and pat speeches that went over so well on the campaign trail count for exactly zero right now. We all know the difference between campaign rhetoric and substantive analysis, discussion, and decision-making, so at this point we're not really interested in hearing one more word.

Instead we want rolled-up sleeves, clear thinking, and a clean sheet of paper. We want the Best and the Brightest that this country can muster, and we want those individuals to attack our problems with a zeal that we haven't seen in Washington in at least forty years.

We need action, Mr. Obama, because for too long we've seen inaction, excuses, and a general shirking of responsibility and accountability at every turn in Washington.

But most of all, sir, we need hope.

Hope that our representatives will have the strength, the courage, and the vision to step up and deliver the kind of leadership that this nation so desperately needs.

Hope that our nation is not on the precipice of a cataclysmic decline but instead is on the verge of a great new era of innovation, creativity, and global leadership.

And finally, hope that you can make a difference. Hope that you can get this country back on track. And hope that there's somehow and some way that you can bring us all together again.

We're counting on you, Mr. Obama.

Chapter 20

Tick, tick, tick. . .

So it had come down to this for General Motors: one hundred years of living, breathing American industrial and social history was on the precipice of total disaster, with the once-glittering corporate icon facing certain collapse if some sort of government financial aid package was not put together over the next sixty days. Think about that for a moment. The company that basically powered this nation through a century of progress and helped it muster the strength to fight world wars—while contributing immeasurably to the fabric of America and the development of our vast middle class—was on the verge of filing bankruptcy.

UNBEKNOWNST TO THE LEGIONS of people out there in "fractured" America, the ones who fill the Internet with bile and who project such a level of viciousness and unbridled glee at the thought of the collapse of our domestic automobile industry as if it were—amazingly enough—some warped opportunity for celebration, there are countless towns, big and small, scattered all across this nation that have grown up with GM as their main employer and the main source of income for thousands of American families.

I am absolutely convinced that the people who hate "Detroit" and want it to implode have not even the faintest of clues as to what it really means if it were allowed to happen. To those instant experts out there who are reveling at the thought of a major part of our country's industrial fabric collapsing, I say be careful what you wish for—because if GM is allowed to fail, it will take the entire domestic auto industry down with it—meaning thousands of suppliers and dealers in towns making up a cross-section of America will go under too.

For the record, there are around 14,000 domestic-oriented deal-ers in the U.S. employing approximately 740,000 people with a payroll of around $35 billion—that's billion with a "B." But that's just the dealer side of the equation. When you add in the suppliers and all of the associated businesses that either directly or indirectly depend on Detroit for their livelihoods, we're talking almost three million people who would be out of work in a matter of just a few months, adding up to a $150 billion loss in personal income.

Let's take California, for instance. Judging by our reader mail, there seems to be a large contingent of people out there who adamantly believe that "Detroit deserves to die" etc., etc., and that whatever happens "won't affect me." But GM and the domestic auto industry's collapse will most definitely affect Californians as well. NUMMI, a joint operation between GM and Toyota and the only San Francisco Bay Area car factory (the Toyota Corolla, Toyota Tacoma, and Pontiac Vibe are built there), is already reducing shifts and may even shut down its Tacoma pickup truck line due to the burgeoning economic slowdown. One of our readers who understands the ramifications of a domestic industry collapse passed this interesting local news report along about NUMMI, which read, "There are tens of thousands of additional jobs on the line besides the 5,000 at NUMMI. There are over 1,000 suppliers in California that provide parts. They in turn employ 50,000 people."

That's just one factory. Now multiply that by the staggering totals involved if GM—which has twenty-two stamping plants and twenty-six powertrain plants in North America on top of its assembly facilities—and the rest of the domestic automobile industry is allowed to fail. The tentacles of this kind of cataclysmic disaster would spread throughout the nation like a virus that could not be contained.

I really don't know why it's so easy for people out there to dismiss the collapse of the domestic automobile industry as being some minor event that won't affect them in the least, because each person who is part of that figure of three million represents a real family and real human story. It's the mom-and-pop diners, stores, and peripheral neighborhood businesses that depend on the workers who toil at these factories and plants for their livelihoods too. There are towns all across America that would simply dry up and blow away if the local GM or supplier plant shut down. That's not an exaggeration, that's a simple fact.

I have been vilified of late by numerous critics for shifting my commentary to a more political tone over this election year, but I don't offer any apologies. This country is not only in the throes of a financial crisis, it's in the throes of a fundamental identity crisis as well. We as a nation have been lulled into thinking that things will work out and that any unpleasantness headed our way will be mere speed bumps on our journey to becoming a state of perpetual consumer bliss.

Well, it just doesn't work that way, folks.

We live in a global economy that isn't big on history or what we as a nation once did or stood for. We have to compete, or else we will arrive at a point when our national future will transition from being one of destiny to one dictated to us by an unsavory set of circumstances and interests not in line in the least with our hopes, our dreams, or our thinking.

In order to compete in this global economy we have to get smarter in our schools and with our educational policies. A high school graduation rate of 50 to 60 percent should be anathema in our inner cities instead of too often the rule. Remedial classes for kids entering college (who are not able to handle freshman classes) should become a thing of the past. And our teachers need to be compensated realistically and properly so more of our brightest people will sign up to help shape our kids' futures.

Even though we as a nation don't seem to have the stomach for hard work and sacrifice any longer—hell, I'm not sure those words and their meanings are even in the lexicon of vast swaths of our population—we must get tougher in the midst of this global economy, and we have to steel ourselves for the kind of battles we'll face. And that means shoring up our manufacturing and supporting our homegrown industries that are so intertwined with communities all across this still great nation. It also means that President-elect Obama will not only be president of the United States, he will have to be CEO of America, Inc., too.

And America Inc. not only needs to be rebuilt, it needs to be fortified with new determination because there are far too many talented and creative people in this nation who can do extraordinary things and we need to make the idea—the idea that we can innovate, create, build, *and* manufacture things that are the envy of the world—cool again, and take pride in doing so as well.

In short, this nation needs a wake-up call.

Anyone who thinks this country will not be thrown into a full-blown depression if the domestic automobile industry is allowed to fail is simply kidding themselves. We are facing a perfect storm of events that could spell disaster if we as a nation don't act and act fast. And it would take *years* for this country to recover, too.

As I've said repeatedly, the time for all of the idyllic "let the free market run its course" hand-wringing is over. It's far too late for that. This country's leadership needs to get these loans to GM and the rest of the domestic automobile industry in the next sixty days, or life as we've come to know it in this country—and I mean *every* part of this country, not just here in the Motor City—will be severely and unequivocally altered.

That *tick, tick, tick* you hear?

It's time running out on the future of America.

Let's hope that what needs to get done will in fact get done, before it's too late.

Chapter 21

New Detroit vs. Old Detroit in Washington

That week in November I had done several live and taped radio interviews across the country and with the BBC in London. A spirited interview with Diane Tucker appearing in The Huffington Post *entitled, "Journalist to GOP: You're 100 Percent Wrong About U.S. Automakers," and I had several national and international TV appearances slated over the next few days, too. The subject? The looming implosion of Detroit, of course. People wanted to know the who, what, when, where, and why of this whole thing, and they wanted to know about the cost, both in terms of taxpayer money needed and the real cost to the economy if the Detroit automakers didn't receive those bridge loans. The din out there in the media at the time was so anti-Detroit and anti-"bailout" that I welcomed the opportunity to present the other side of the debate, even if it appeared with each passing day that Detroit was running out of time and unable to break through the negative media clutter that enveloped the industry at every turn. And after that death march of a hearing before the Senate Banking Committee, I was even more pessimistic.*

WHEN ALAN MULALLY, Rick Wagoner, Bob Nardelli, and Ron Gettelfinger sat down in front of the microphones, I knew it wasn't going to be good, especially when Peter Morici—the relentlessly self-promoting economics professor from the University of Maryland—sat down next to them. Which senator was responsible for inviting him is anyone's guess, but it was clear that this was a setup from the get go.

We then had to watch as each of these U.S. senators spewed their particular brand of inaccuracies and flat-out misconceptions about the automobile industry in their opening statements. A very few were actually worth listening to—and I mean like two—while most of the others were so blatantly self-serving and out of touch with reality that it was painful to watch. And then some acted like they were just hatched yesterday and were so resolute in their lack of awareness about what was going on and why they had to be there in the first place that it was simply appalling.

I can't help but think that when enlightened Americans watched these people in action—the people who were actually *elected* by us to be in office—that they recoiled in horror at the absolutely stunning lack of knowledge, awareness, sense of place, sense of, well, *anything* that was displayed by these senators yesterday. Is this really the best we can do? I certainly hope not.

At any rate, the message in that hearing room was clear: Detroit put itself in the shape it finds itself in by building bad, low-tech cars that nobody wants. That they were regurgitating the now-obligatory, woeful misperception of Detroit that has spread across the country—a Detroit that hasn't existed for the better part of a decade, by the way— was obvious. The fact that these senators weren't aware of the kind of ultracompetitive products that these companies have out now was predictable. And the fact that they weren't aware of the kind of leading edge technological development that Detroit is actively engaged in was predictable too.

Being clueless in Washington isn't all that uncommon, unfortunately, but when misconceptions, half-truths, and flat-out lies get hoisted up the flagpole as Fact, then it's no wonder that the leaders of these Detroit car companies were on the defensive and unable to score points with the judges.

Proof of that was on display yesterday when the senators in that hearing room kept talking about restructuring, as if it was a new-fangled idea that these Detroit CEOs weren't aware of. And they had to be reminded over and over again that Detroit *has* been restructuring and revamping since 2000, that Detroit *hasn't* been operating in a vacuum, that Detroit *does* build competitive and class-leading products, that Detroit *has* pioneered new technologies, that Detroit *is* a viable, relevant, strategic industry that's part of the crucial fabric of America's manufacturing base, that the worst financial crisis in seven decades *has* wreaked havoc on their ability to do business, and on, and on, and on.

Back when things were booming for the domestic automobile industry, the importance of lobbying in Washington and having a consistent and focused image strategy that presented these companies' positions and outlined their contributions to the American economy wasn't a top priority. Now that it is, and the Detroit Three are playing catch-up—while taking body blows and being backed up against the ropes—the Old Detroit is still slamming the New Detroit to the ground.

The perception gap that exists out there for the Detroit automakers isn't narrowing, it's actually growing wider. Because when Americans get what minimal news they're willing to digest—and only because it's prepackaged in carefully doled-out sound bites—then the Old Detroit will perennially overshadow the New Detroit, hands down.

Detroit may get help from Washington, but left to their own devices—and timetables—it's looking like the politicians will come up with something that's too little and too late to actually make a difference.

And that's a giant bowl of Not Good.

Chapter 22

Washington to Detroit: Drop dead

The glee with which the Washington establishment—and every two-bit instant car "expert" who decided it was high time to weigh in with his or her opinions —attacked Detroit and what's left of the U.S. car industry that week in November was a sight to behold. Everyone from chief knucklehead Michael Moore to Neil Young (Neil Young?) got on the "Detroit Deserves to Die" bandwagon, adding to the chaos with their naïvely crafted pop logic musings and "finger snap" solutions. It was truly pathetic.

STARTING WITH THE STUNNINGLY ill-informed members of the Senate and the House, led by that raging embarrassment Dick Shelby from Alabama, who heaped derision on Detroit and its CEOs for having the temerity to ask for a bridge loan to help them through the worst financial calamity to face America in seven decades—while he conveniently forgot to mention that he helped arrange for over $650 *million* in tax incentives and other prizes for Mercedes-Benz, Honda, Hyundai, and Toyota to build facilities in his home state—to the gang of idiots who followed him while falling all over themselves trying to demonstrate how little they knew about the car business or about the Detroit that exists today as opposed to the Detroit they once read about in the 1990s, it was a beat-down of epic proportions.

That actual facts about the U.S. automobile business and its role as an essential part of the manufacturing fabric of the country were in short supply in the rote speeches made by the representatives and senators—and except for exactly one, Representative Thaddeus McCotter (R-Michigan), they were totally predictable. And so was the piling on that ensued.

By the end of last week it was as if the domestic automakers were not only the scourge of the western hemisphere but responsible for all known troubles afflicting this country at this very moment. Their CEOs were idiots, we'd all be better off as a country if their founding city was just wiped off the American landscape along with the rest of the Midwest, and gangs of citizens were assembling with pitchforks demanding bankruptcy for the Detroit Three. The loathing was so far off the charts and unwarranted, I was actually surprised that the mob mentality stopped short of demanding the heads of Chrysler's, Ford's, and GM's CEOs—or anyone else representing Detroit—on sticks.

It would have been difficult to comprehend all of this if it had originated in any other city besides Washington, D.C. After all, this is a town whose very existence is based on cronyism, perks, earmarks, lobbyists, and professional self-absorption. But even that pales in comparison to the *real* pro sport in Washington, which is The Blame Game. The fact that these politicians made hay on the whole corporate jet angle was laughable, especially since one of their esteemed colleagues—Nancy Pelosi—caused a royal stink when she became Speaker of the House by demanding a bigger government plane so that she was able to fly nonstop back to California. That many of these politicians eagerly accept rides on corporate jets from various contributors and lobbyists was a story that was missing in the gathering chaos of the lynch-mob mentality aimed at the Detroit Three CEOs, as if they were the only heads of corporations on Earth who use corporate planes. And the establishment media, ever in search of a fifteen-second sound bite, found what they were looking for and dutifully reported that angle as the meat of the story.

Lost in all of this, of course, was the fact that the backbone of the U.S. manufacturing sector was on the ropes because of the worst financial crisis since the Great Depression. But nonetheless, the real issues at hand were instead drowned out by the verbal jabs and cackles about corporate jets, and the Detroit Three CEOs were sent packing, but not before they were admonished like little schoolboys and told to bring back a real business plan for their $25 billion, and to come back "better prepared," as President-elect Barack Obama chimed in on Monday.

Oh really?

This after Citigroup, which only a month ago received $25 billion, was blessed with another $20 billion this past Sunday evening, and, as part of the plan, Treasury and the FDIC will guarantee against the "possibility of unusually large losses" on up to $306 billion of risky loans and securities backed by commercial and residential mortgages.

What, no hat-in-hand journey to Washington for Citigroup CEO Vikram S. Pandit so he could receive a good old-fashioned live-television ass-whipping for bad management decisions, marketing risky financial instruments, failing to anticipate dramatic shifts in the market, and piss-poor planning in general?

No stumblebum senators and congresspeople tripping all over themselves to demonstrate their complete lack of understanding of the nation's financial system or to criticize the fact that Pandit used the corporate jet to fly down to Washington?

No recriminations for Robert Rubin—the most prominent member of Citigroup's board of directors and a former treasury secretary—who was one of the chief architects of the bank's risky investment strategy, and who pulled down $62.2 million between 2004 and 2007?

And what about the go-along-to-get-along dimwits on the Citigroup board? The gang that J. Richard Findlay, head of the Centre for Corporate & Public Governance, described for the *New York Post* thusly: "Citigroup's board of directors increasingly resembles a first-class sleeping car on a train wreck that just keeps happening. Almost whatever it does, it is too slow and too late. It can take months for Citigroup's directors to clue into what others in the real world have known for some time."

And why does Citigroup merit bailing out again with no explanation whatsoever to the American taxpayers other than President Bush saying, "We have made these kind of decisions in the past. We made one last night. And if need be we will make these kind of decisions to safeguard our financial system in the future."

Oh really?

What's going on is the activation of a New American Double Standard, one that goes something like this:

Washington to Detroit: Drop Dead.

Washington to Wall Street: Who do we make the check out to again?

Thanks to our representatives in Washington, an industry that powered this great nation into the future, which basically created a viable American middle class, and which created the Arsenal of Democracy so that the nation could be properly equipped to win World War II, has all of a sudden become a national punch line and a burden to the rest of the country.

An industry that's responsible, either directly or indirectly, for one out of every fourteen jobs in the nation, an industry that's inexorably linked with the manufacturing base of this nation and whose failure would send this nation's economy reeling, was basically sent packing in search of a "plan" while Wall Street and the banking system was given carte blanche just for showing up.

How do we know that Citigroup won't crash in a few more months and need even more money? And how will they handle their "emergency" need in the new "enlightened" Obama presidency? By email?

What's wrong with this picture?

Why is it politically more expedient to trash Detroit and the entire domestic automobile industry than it is to shine a harsh light on the glorified pyramid scheme that propelled Wall Street and the banking system to new heights—and now to horrific lows—while screwing over millions of Americans in the process?

The fact that President-elect Obama added to the criticism of the Detroit Three CEOs by echoing the same misinformation spewed by the senators and congresspeople last week in Washington was not exactly an uplifting development, either.

"We can't just write a blank check to the auto industry. Taxpayers can't be expected to pony up more money for an auto industry that has been resistant to change. I was surprised that they did not have a better thought-out proposal when they arrived in Congress," Obama said. "Congress did the right thing, which is to say, 'You guys need to come up with a plan and come back before you're getting any taxpayer money.'"

Oh really?

But we—as American taxpayers—can expect to keep writing blank checks to mismanaged banks and failed Wall Street conglomerates, and be expected to "pony up" more money to an industry that's resistant to change, with no thought-out proposals of any kind and no real "plan" in sight? How does that work, exactly, Mr. President-elect?

As if to backpedal a bit, Obama added that, "We can't allow the auto industry simply to vanish. We've got to make sure that it is there and that the workers and suppliers and businesses that rely on the auto industry stay in business."

Oh really?

Then why is it—Mr. President-elect—that you're endorsing the miserable performance put on by our so-called leaders in Washington last week? Why is it that you're regurgitating the same tired inaccuracies about Detroit that we were subjected to for two days last week? Do your homework, Mr. Obama. Stop listening to the media or the sycophants you've already assembled and dig deeper into this "Detroit thing" before you start sounding like all the rest of the less-than-gifted in Washington.

Memo to the old *and new* Washington establishment:

A large number of American citizens are painfully aware of the hypocritical double-speak that's currently festering in the halls of Congress and on the Senate floor.

A large number of Americans are tired of the now-tedious stereotypes and flat-out untruths being bandied about in Washington about an industry that's vital to the long-term health and well-being of the nation, an industry that actually creates and builds tangible hard goods, an industry that devotes $12 billion a *year* in advanced technical research that benefits the entire nation, an industry that is a fundamental part of the American industrial fabric, and an industry that employs millions of Americans all across this nation.

A large number of American citizens are tired of this New American Double Standard, where the financial well-being of millions is held hostage and put at risk for the benefit of a few—with no explanation, no "plan," and no accountability whatsoever.

Detroit may be Washington's whipping boy du jour, and our esteemed representatives may want to continue on with their witch hunt—will they demand that the Detroit CEOs bring their college transcripts with them next time?—but they won't be fooling anyone.

It's not about what's good for the rest of the country in Washington. It's not about nurturing the American fabric, or protecting the foundation of our manufacturing base, or taking care of a productive national industry that creates real American jobs, or keeping the nation as a vital player in the global economy.

No, not even close, as a matter of fact.

In Washington it's about whoever is greasing the skids or blowing in a senator's or congressperson's ear just right. And the Motor City finds itself on the outside looking in.

Detroit might as well start writing its own obituary right now, because even if some sort of bridge loan package is grudgingly bequeathed, the strings and built-in entanglements are likely to choke the life out of the U.S. auto industry once and for all.

Chapter 23

America speaks, and Washington is forced to listen

The battle drums were beating along the Potomac, and the message ringing unmistakably loud and clear in the ears of senators and congressional representatives was this: The U.S automobile industry doesn't begin and end with Detroit, southeast Michigan, and the Midwest—a city, a state, and a region that have apparently become expendable to the powers that be in Washington. But rather, its tentacles spread out across the union in a powerful network of small and large businesses alike, from the local auto dealer franchise in small-town America all the way to multibillion-dollar supplier corporations in the heart of Silicon Valley. And now that this essential part of the U.S. manufacturing base was on the brink of oblivion, the real story was finally being told, and the untenable realities and ramifications of a collapse of the domestic automobile industry were being put in stark terms that even our leaders in Washington could understand. That week the true value of the domestic automobile industry was coming to the fore, and people all across this country were starting to take notice.

THE *LOS ANGELES TIMES* reported on Monday about the huge portion of sales tax revenue generated by vehicle sales in California and its affect on the taxes collected by city, county and state governments. Using just one example—when Heritage Lincoln Mercury (among the largest Lincoln Mercury dealers in California and part of the Tustin

Auto Center) closed its doors in the city of Tustin in August—the *Times* reported that a crucial source of revenue for the city, which relies heavily on taxes from automobile sales to keep afloat, was devastated.

Of the city's $20 million annual budget, about $5 million comes from the local auto center, the city's director of finance, Ronald Nault, told the *Times*. And with sales of Lincoln and Mercury cars and trucks down by nearly a quarter nationwide through October compared with last year, the Heritage dealership was forced to fold. But it doesn't stop there, because many of the other dealerships in the auto center, although still in business, are seeing severe sales declines, which means even fewer sales taxes collected.

"It has definitely affected us," Nault told the *Times*, adding that collections from the auto center were on pace to be off 20 percent for the year. And with industry-wide vehicle sales falling even more sharply in recent months, the revenue shortfall could be substantially greater, forcing the city to consider spending cuts, a salary freeze, reductions in travel, and the possibility of layoffs for the first time in the city's history.

The *Times* continued by saying that "sales of new and used cars, as well as parts and service, are the single largest source of sales tax revenue for almost every state, county, and local government, ahead of gasoline sales, restaurants, and department stores. (Alaska, Delaware, New Hampshire, Oregon and Montana do not collect sales tax.) More motor vehicles are sold in California than in any other state; in the second quarter, nearly 15.5% of all sales taxes here, or $193 million, came from the automotive and transportation sector, compared with about $135 million from restaurants and hotels, according to HdL Cos., which compiles sales-tax data for government agencies."

But, the *Times* cautioned, California's second-quarter automotive sales-tax receipts were down dramatically—more than $30 million short in the second quarter alone from a year earlier—contributing to the huge budget shortfall that has led Governor Arnold Schwarzenegger to propose a sales-tax hike and spending cuts.

"This is very bad for states," Donald Boyd, senior fellow at the Nelson A. Rockefeller Institute of Government told the *Times*, while also pointing out that sales taxes are the first or second most-important revenue source in almost every state.

And to think there are people still out there who suggest that the collapse of the domestic automobile business somehow won't affect them.

Let's go on to another part of the state of California: Silicon Valley, a relative hotbed of anti-Detroit rhetoric and home to major corporations involved in the manufacturing of semiconductors.

The *Mercury News* reported in last Sunday's edition that "The financial crisis hammering Detroit's auto industry is sending shock waves to Silicon Valley, where a number of companies make the computer chips that have become increasingly vital components in cars and other vehicles. And if Ford Motor, Chrysler and General Motors go belly up, as some experts fear, the repercussions in the valley could intensify."

"As soon as the automotive industry coughs, a lot of other companies get a cold," Thilo Koslowski, who tracks that business for research firm Gartner, told the *News*. "That includes companies in the semiconductor industry and that includes a lot in the Bay Area. . . . It's a relatively big market for them in Silicon Valley."

For the record, the roster of South Bay companies that supply semiconductors for carmakers include Intel, Atmel, National Semiconductor, Spansion, Altera, Maxim Integrated Products, Xilinx, Linear Technology, and Cypress Semiconductor, according to the *News*.

And one more report about the U.S. automobile industry's role in the American economy. *Crain's Chicago Business*, a sister publication to *Automotive News*, did a deep dive on what the collapse of a Detroit automaker would do to Chicago—"from South Side manufacturers to northwest suburban dealerships to downtown TV studios"—and these are some of the staggering statistics they came up with:

*As General Motors, Ford Motor Co. and Chrysler LLC
seek a multibillion-dollar lifeline from the federal government,
many Illinois companies and workers are holding their breath.*

The state's stake in Detroit is huge: Illinois trails only Michigan, Ohio and Indiana in the number of auto-supplier jobs in the U.S. More than 80,000 jobs statewide are directly tied to the auto industry, government figures show, and one estimate puts the total number of workers with direct links to automakers at more than three times that number. The industry pumped more than $16 billion last year into the state economy through assembly plants, parts makers and car sales. If a Detroit automaker goes under, thousands of jobs will be lost, hundreds of businesses hurt and millions of dollars drained from the local economy.

"I would hate to imagine the trickle-down effects of the job loss if these companies are allowed to just close up," Greg Baise, president of the Illinois Manufacturers Association, told *Crain's*. "It would have a much broader impact than it would have had thirty years ago."

The reason for that is that the U.S. automakers have delegated much of their supply chain over the years, including crucial parts-making operations. *Crain's* reports that Illinois has about two hundred auto-parts manufacturing operations today.

"Those plants employ tens of thousands of workers; three auto assembly plants employ another 7,000," reported *Crain's*. "Total employment attributed to the auto sector—including related businesses such as those that supply or service parts makers—is about 267,600, or roughly four percent of the state's total workforce, according to a 2007 study by the Center for Automotive Research, an industry think tank in Ann Arbor, Mich."

Crain's reported about one dealer's fate: "Lattof Chevrolet of Arlington Heights closed its doors Oct. 10 after more than seventy years in business at the same Northwest Highway location. The company, which once had $30 million in annual sales, was in its third generation of family ownership. The closure put sixty-five employees out of work."

"It's a shame to see this," Arlington Heights Mayor Arlene Mulder told *Crain's*. "Lattof Chevrolet for years was synonymous with the town of Arlington Heights. Everybody bought their cars there. . . . It was a Lattof who helped us build a hospital in our town 50 years ago."

As in Tustin, California's case, the closure will hit Arlington Heights' budget too. *Crain's* reported that "In the first six months of this year, the village of 77,000 had tax income from sales of cars and auto parts totaling $730,000, down from $838,000 in the first six months of 2007 and $915,000 in that period in 2006. The village has an annual operating budget of $60 million."

The point of all of this?

The point is that the powers that be in Washington, D.C., are just waking up to the fact that the U.S. automobile business is so ingrained and intertwined with the nation's economy on the local and state levels that a collapse of the Detroit automakers would be a cataclysmic event that would send this nation—already teetering from a deep recession—into a full-on depression. And to pretend otherwise is just pure folly at this juncture.

This week, our lawmakers in Washington will be getting a double-shot of reality about the Detroit they were so quick to scoff at and criticize a couple of weeks ago. The fact that they spewed hoary stereotypes about the Detroit that existed more than a decade ago was painful to listen to and even more painful to watch.

But this time they will be introduced to the *real* American automobile companies.

American automobile companies that have been doing the heavy lifting and fundamental restructuring needed since 2000.

American automobile companies that are now on the cutting edge of advanced technological developments in fuel efficiency, safety, and environmental responsibility.

American automobile companies that are building an impressive array of class-leading vehicles in all segments, with more on the way with each passing quarter.

American automobile companies that have been part of the American industrial fabric for one hundred years.

American automobile companies that powered this nation's growth and propelled the development of middle-class, mainstream America.

American automobile companies that responded in the time of this country's gravest need and created the Arsenal of Democracy that helped win World War II.

American automobile companies that are an inexorable part of every village, town, city, and state in this great nation.

Washington will be forced to listen this week by the sheer momentum that comes from ordinary citizens speaking up all across America. People who understand what these American automobile companies mean to their local communities and to their livelihoods.

Ordinary people with extraordinary understanding that this whole issue concerning Detroit's future isn't a Republican thing or a Democratic thing, but an *American* thing.

Chapter 24

Queen LaGreena
and the
Dunderheads

It occurred to me after having been subjected to yet another painfully lame interview of Speaker of the House Nancy Pelosi, who had been doling out "haircuts" in Washington at a fevered clip in order to see to it that the Auto Industry Financing and Restructuring Act had real teeth in it—by her estimation — that the domestic automobile industry, at least as GM and Chrysler knew it, was going to be inexorably altered, and not in a good way either. As a matter of fact, if the auto companies actually survived Washington's "help," it would be a miracle of this new century. Pelosi—who would be henceforth known in the pages of Autoextremist by her newly minted sobriquet of "Queen LaGreena"—and her esteemed Dunderheads (I mean colleagues) on both sides of the aisle had been hell-bent on making Detroit pay for its countless transgressions—both real and imagined—affixing blame for whatever was currently ailing the U.S. in general to the domestic automobile industry in a masterful redirect of the anger of the citizenry at the piss-poor conditions of the economy. Not Good didn't even begin to cover it.

I NOW UNDERSTAND COMPLETELY what the term "skilled politician" actually means. It's the ability to mask your blatant incompetence and complete lack of understanding of the issues involved—*any* issue—by creating a fog of negativity and misinformation so impenetrable that the true sport of Washington—the Blame Game—can commence, unencumbered by accuracy, fairness, or reality.

And now, with a so-called deal on the table to provide GM and Chrysler with loans that will get them through to when President-elect Obama's administration takes over, the assembled incompetents in Washington continue to demonstrate that they *still* don't get it and still can't find the first clue about the industry and how it works. Nor are they likely to gain on it anytime soon either.

The evidence? Two hoary stereotypes remain in effect in Washington even after members of Congress have been exposed to reams of evidence and pound upon pound of facts and figures about this industry over the last month. And these stereotypes are:

1. Detroit is stuck in a time warp that seems to hover around 1995, and 2. "Fixing" Detroit and the problems facing the domestic automobile industry will take the sacrificing of a couple of executives, a dollop of more stringent emission regulations and fuel-economy standards, a couple of finger snaps, and *voila!* It will be just a matter of months before thousands upon thousands of shiny green cars will be marching out of shiny green factories built by Shiny, Happy people singing:

> *Hi ho, Hi ho!*
> *It's home from work we go!*
> *We did our part—we churned them out*
> *Hi ho, Hi ho, Hi ho!*

(While saluting pictures of Queen LaGreena and the Car Czar as they file out of the gates, no doubt.)

Right now the loan package "deal" for GM and Chrysler that's on the table in Washington is mired in partisan political infighting, and it's anyone's guess as to when this "deal" will actually materialize. Senate Republicans want to crush the unions and are threatening a filibuster, green-tinged Democrats want a provision that would force automakers to drop lawsuits against California's greenhouse gas limits on vehicles—something the White House is adamantly against—and operatives from the incoming Obama administration are in the mix, wanting to extract their pound of flesh from the deal too.

Add in the "Car Czar" provision to the deal—certain to be a Bean-Counter-in-Chief with no feel for the automobile industry whatsoever—and you have a political train wreck of incalculable proportions.

Never have so many people armed with so little knowledge been poised to do so much damage to the country and the American industrial fabric as Queen LaGreena and The Dunderheads are poised to do.

But it will all be good, according to what Queen LaGreena had to say during her various media appearances yesterday. In a display fraught with embarrassing wince moments, she careened around the morning news programs demonstrating her clear lack of understanding of the depth and breadth of the issues facing the industry. Not content with stopping right there, she then threw out her finger-snap solutions and the woefully unrealistic timetable she envisions for the shiny green auto factories of her new American automobile industry to come online.

No, Queen LaGreena. Left to the devices of you and The Dunderheads—the masters of obfuscation and pontification—it will all be bad.

It's absolutely horrifying to think that the fate of the U.S. automobile industry and the future of America's manufacturing base now hinges on the collected "wisdom" on display in Washington.

Chapter 25

It's up to you, Mr. President

The U.S. Senate voted against passage of a bill to give an emergency bridge loan to the Detroit automakers—specifically GM and Chrysler—paving the way for the eventual collapse of the domestic automobile industry and sending this country's already teetering financial situation to the brink of disaster. The inaction—a blatantly malicious display of placing political self-interests before the best interests of the nation— was orchestrated by Senators Richard Shelby (R-Alabama) and Mitch McConnell (R-Kentucky), two men who were pushing "the Southern Corridor"—a network of transplant manufacturing facilities operated by some import car companies—as the new American auto industry, even though it meant destroying the foundation of America's manufacturing base and ruining the livelihoods of millions of people— including autoworkers, dealers, and suppliers—who depended on the domestic automobile industry for their livelihoods, not to mention their healthcare and pensions. It was right about then that Detroit—or what was left of it, anyway—found out what being "politically expendable" really meant.

BESIDES SENDING A CLEAR MESSAGE to Detroit—yet again—that this industry doesn't matter, the senators behind the failure to get the bill passed reinforced the notion that too much of the rest of the country, for the most part, refuses to understand the ramifications of what a collapse of the domestic automobile industry really means, and that the attitudes of "it won't affect me" and "whatever" are the new dual mantras of the American people.

That we have become a Starbucks Nation of consumer zombies who have lost sight of the fact that this country's ability to manufacture things is more important to the future of our country than the convenience of another coffee shop is appalling enough, but the fact that this country has become a patchwork quilt of warring factions hell-bent on destroying each other no matter what the cost to our fellow citizens is beyond reprehensible.

Over the last three weeks I've watched as those miserable excuses for our "representatives" in Washington have spewed so much misinformation and flat-out lies aimed at Detroit and the domestic automobile industry that I've lost track in trying to tally all of it up, but suffice to say at this juncture it really doesn't matter.

What happened in Washington last night was one of the most egregious displays of selfish, narrow-minded thinking in the history of our nation. Facts were either misrepresented or ignored altogether and dire warnings were scoffed at, while our nation is in its most precarious financial state in seven decades.

The bottom line is that hardworking people involved in an industry that has tentacles in every state and accounts for one out of every fourteen American jobs are being punished today because of two self-righteous senators who think their view of things should be the country's view.

That an industry that supported the American middle class for one hundred years, that forged the Arsenal of Democracy during World War II, that has responded to every disaster and national crisis by giving endlessly of time, money, vehicles, and resources, that makes up the majority of our nation's manufacturing and research and development prowess—to the tune of $12 billion annually—has become expendable.

The anti-car, anti-Detroit cabal alive in Washington and in certain corners of the media has seized the opportunity to bury Detroit and the domestic automobile industry once and for all, and in so doing has set into motion the final erosion of the American industrial fabric, sending a message to the world that this nation has not only lost its will to fight and is incapable of protecting one of its essential industries, but that it has willingly set a course for long-term weakness and vulnerability.

Mr. President, countless American families are calling on you to keep this essential American industry going. We hope you see to it to do the right thing.

Chapter 26

Ninety days to nowhere.
Reality bites for Detroit

Two thousand nine opened for Detroit with what amounted to a thud, because in the cold days of early January, what had changed exactly? Not much. Yes, GM and Chrysler got their "bridge" loans, but consumer credit was still locked tight; vehicle sales were borderline nonexistent in too many places—meaning more dealers were on the brink of oblivion than ever before—and American consumers continued on with their no-spending holiday, a grim reminder that the final days of 2008 were still very much with us in 2009. But with a new president about to take office, and all the changes that may (or may not) entail, there were some key things to contemplate about Detroit and the automobile industry in general going forward in 2009.

PRESIDENT-ELECT OBAMA and his new administration will bring a different perspective to Washington, but that alone won't be enough to save Detroit. Not when there are southern senators and members of Congress who are hell-bent on destroying the Detroit Three in their quest to ultimately replace the nation's homegrown auto industry with a loose network of imported auto-manufacturing facilities based in the Southern Corridor. Not when there are members of the new establishment in Washington who are rabidly pushing for a huge green directional shift for industry and manufacturing in this country, with little concern about the realities or the ramifications of that kind of massive shift on America's manufacturing base or immediate economic future. Not when our leaders in Washington continue to give a free ride to countries and manufacturers who want to do business here, at the expense of our own industries and manufacturing base. And especially *not* when the nation's consumers are locked in this painful reduced-credit or no-credit holding cell that has paralyzed commerce across the country.

As I've said before, no matter how well-intentioned President-elect Obama is and how exuberant or visionary his agenda may or may not be, if consumer spending doesn't resume—allowing companies to generate revenue and putting this country back in business—then the rest of it won't matter for Detroit, or the rest of the nation for that matter either.

Getting American consumers to look beyond the negative perceptions and discover the positive reality about Detroit's competitive models might be the most daunting, make-or-break marketing challenge in history. Speaking of the American consumer, the most damaging byproduct of the lambasting that the Detroit CEOs suffered in Washington was that it seared a losing image for the domestic automobile companies—at least two of them anyway—in the American consumer consciousness. The people who hated Detroit to begin with found reassuring affirmation in what went on in those hearings, of course, but it was the consumers out there who really didn't have an opinion one way or another about the subject who were swayed against Detroit—primarily Chrysler and GM—because of the Grand Inquisition that went on in Washington. The entire fiasco laid waste to Detroit's hopes that a quick turnaround of the American consumer mindset was just around the corner.

In a world where Detroit has tremendous difficulty getting consumers to even *look* at their product offerings, let alone actually consider buying them, the debacle in Washington was devastating, which makes the task facing the Detroit Three's marketing mavens the most daunting, make-or-break marketing challenge in history. The majority of American consumers, even when presented with the facts and reams of evidence to the contrary, still don't believe that Detroit builds desirable or fuel-efficient vehicles, and that *must* change if Detroit is to survive in some way, shape, or form.

Despite the pronouncements and the table-pounding, Washington will find out little in ninety days. The ninety days given to GM and Chrysler to allegedly get their acts together reinforced how little Washington knows about the car business and the industry in general. The thread that Chrysler LLC is hanging by is on its last tendril, and the loans that the company received may only allow it to get out from under the debts owed to key suppliers. I said at the end of last year that I didn't see a future for Chrysler beyond the first quarter, and nothing I've seen has given me a reason to change my mind. As for GM, they can rearrange their brands, deemphasize their brands, ice some brands, or shelve some brands altogether, but that will have little or no effect on the company over the next three months, no matter how much foot-stomping and hand-wringing goes on in Washington. Short of a complete cessation of state dealer franchise laws and a wholesale shift of corporate emphasis to just two divisions—Cadillac and Chevrolet—GM's future will remain murky, at best, and well beyond the ninety-day "window" too.

What *will* Washington find out about Detroit and the U.S. auto industry in ninety days? Two things: 1. The crushing reality of the situation for the U.S. auto industry at this very moment in time is that at the current sales rate, only one Detroit auto manufacturer can survive long term (in this case, "long term" is defined as 2010), and Washington will either have to come to terms with what that will actually mean for America's economic future going forward, or it will have to take even more aggressive actions and measures designed to prevent the total implosion of the domestic auto industry and in turn the continued erosion of our manufacturing base; and 2. Without a coordinated and comprehensive economic stimulus program that not only restores consumer confidence and gets people spending again (while restoring order to the national banking system), but lays the groundwork for a sustainable, supportive, and reinvigorated future for the U.S. manufacturing base, then the U.S. automobile industry will be left reeling indefinitely.

Sobering words on the eve of the 2009 North American International Auto Show, but in this case, reality well and truly bites.

Part Four

The High Hard Ones

Chapter 27

A new "Green Gap" vexes the auto industry

I had written about the "perception gap" that had vexed Detroit often over the last three years, and that's the gap that exists between consumers' perceptions of Detroit—that they build uncompetitive, poor-quality, undesirable vehicles with poor fuel efficiency—and the reality, which was that Detroit is building highly desirable and, in some cases, class-leading offerings that are competitive in terms of design integrity, safety, quality, and fuel-efficiency, and which feature the latest technological advancements to boot. This gap had paralyzed Detroit and impeded its progress at every turn, contributing significantly to the domestic industry's image problems and creating a marketing challenge of unprecedented proportion. This same perception gap was evident for all to see in Washington, D.C., at the end of 2009, when U.S. senators and members of the House of Representatives regurgitated hoary notions about the Detroit they assumed they knew— which was the Detroit that last existed a decade ago—while pummeling the Detroit CEOs for hours on end for being symbols of everything wrong with corporate America.

THIS WEEK WASHINGTON, D.C., becomes the focal point for the industry again as the city's auto show takes center stage. A minor event by any measure up until about four years ago, the Washington Auto Show has now become a must-see/be-seen stop on the auto industry's traveling agenda, and for obvious reasons too. Dubbed "The

Automotive Seat of Power" (how's that for an arrogant auto show theme?), this is where the Washington politicos who didn't bother to come to the Detroit Auto Show last month (only Senator Corker of Tennessee flew in to check out the hardware at Cobo Hall, to his credit) will gather to see what's going on in the auto biz in terms of future products and technologies.

And Detroit and the rest of the industry are responding by displaying a kaleidoscope of extended-range electric vehicles, pure electric vehicles, hybrids, and plug-in hybrids to please even the most jaded tree-hugging senators and members of Congress. And therein lays the problem, because a new and potentially even more damaging "Green Gap" is emerging that's vexing Detroit and the rest of the auto industry.

Translation? What Washington and California politicians want in terms of emissions and mileage standards from 2016 on versus what the average consumer will buy and what the technology (i.e., the electrical grid, battery development, production, etc.) can support are such wildly divergent notions that a looming train wreck is developing between expectations and reality.

One unfailingly tedious trait that the Green Horde displays is the remarkable ability to trivialize the impact of technological development—and cost—while skipping right to their vision of The Future filled with Shiny, Happy people driving Shiny, Happy Smiley Cars that emit nothing but a wisp of a rainbow as they hum along the highway of life. It's a nice, idyllic pipe dream—akin to a giant bong filled with some of Humboldt County's free-range best—but it bears little resemblance to reality.

And reality suggests that consumers get all touchy-feely and spout the obligatory green-tinged buzz phrases in focus groups, but when it comes time to actually put real money down on this new technology (that car companies are working so feverishly away on) they balk, as in, "Wait a minute, I want to save the planet and reduce my carbon footprint and all, but I'm not paying $5,000 *extra* for it." Especially in this dismal economy. Not to mention the fact that there are severe technical and logistical limitations to creating a viable playing field ripe for the variety of electric vehicles that our politicians want to see on America's streets and byways.

Politicians in California and Washington give off the distinct impression that they view reality as an irritant. Let's take California Governor Arnold Schwarzenegger, for instance. Here's a guy who is presiding over a state teetering on bankruptcy largely because of its egregious, self-induced regulatory environment (movie production companies are even fleeing the state and moving some of their operations here—to southeast Michigan of all places—so what does that tell you?), and who is now pushing for even *more* regulation and *more* restrictive emissions policies for automobiles in the state in his quest to dictate to the rest of the nation what we should all be driving.

Was any consideration given to the real live consumers out there and what they'd actually drive, or better yet, what they'd actually pay for? No, because that would mean the concept of reality would have to be roiling around somewhere out in Sacramento, and as we all know, the words "reality" and "Sacramento" go together about as much out there as the words "reality" and "rational thought" do in Washington.

In other words, not so much.

This week the Washington Auto Show will be crawling with earnest Obama administration crusaders and California state operatives seeking evidence that the idyllic green vision that's hanging over Washington like a choking fog of denial is coming to fruition. And what they'll see is just what I described: a kaleidoscope of extended-range electric vehicles, pure electric vehicles, hybrids, and plug-in hybrids, none of which will make economic sense any time soon, or even six years from now.

The Green Horde likes to think that all of this planet-saving stuff will come down to simply giving the auto industry a swift kick in the ass while tossing in some technological development monies—plus some consumer incentives thrown in for good measure—and *voila!* We'll see a million plug-in electric vehicles on the road by 2016. But even the most optimistic players from the leading auto and energy companies don't see that happening because, given all of the evidence available—in terms of battery development and production capacity and the capability (or lack of same) of the electrical grids in cities and towns across America—and considering all of the projections, it's just not technically feasible. Not to mention the fact that when you throw in the consumer's ability or, more important, *desire* to pay for it, it adds up to a heaping, steaming bowl of Not Good.

Short of coming up with a national energy policy that sets a minimum price for fuel, which will dramatically and permanently reconfigure America's fleet of vehicles ($2 per gallon gasoline won't change anyone's habits or purchase decisions), then everything the politicos in Washington and California are doing is so much costly window dressing.

Do electric-oriented vehicles have a place in our nation's fleet of vehicles? Absolutely. Will they become the dominant type of vehicle in the future as some have suggested? Not even close. Electric vehicles will have a place in the nation's fleet, there's no question about that. But I don't see these vehicles taking more than a 20- to 25-percent piece of our transportation pie, and that's *way* down the road too.

Washington and California politicos are great at pushing agendas, making grand pronouncements, and then setting ball-busting targets, but they're not so good at figuring out who will bear the brunt of the cost of their decisions—on the corporate *or* consumer level—or if the technology is even there to fulfill their grandiose ambitions.

At least with the old perception gap Detroit could understand what they were dealing with. A combination of consumers holding on to obsolete notions and an industry that did a piss-poor job of explaining who they were and what their story was is pretty easy to digest—and a realistic appraisal of the scope of the situation. It doesn't make it any more palatable or solvable, but at least it's understandable.

This new green-tinged perception gap is another thing altogether, however, and it has the potential to be much more lethal. Not just for Detroit, but for the auto industry as a whole. When you have people with biased agendas and a blatant disregard for reality making rules, setting targets, and writing laws—with no rhyme or reason as to what is achievable or even remotely cost-effective—then you have nothing more than a recipe for total disaster. And needless to say, that's the very last thing this industry—or the economy—needs right now.

I'd like to believe that the Obama administration may actually see the light on some of this and be able to put things in proper perspective—as in no one is buying anything right now, so you're going to have to fix *that* before worrying about how green the future of the industry is—but then again I'm not so sure the politicos and policy wonks (of any stripe) are capable of that kind of understanding, no matter how much hope is involved.

Chapter 28

Two scenarios emerge for GM's future. Is it time for Precision Motors?

With the annual sales rate for the U.S. auto industry plunging to its lowest level in decades, GM proposed an accelerated downsizing program to the Treasury Department that went much further than the plans it had discussed in December in Washington. The dramatic moves included eliminating 47,000 hourly and salaried jobs globally in 2009, closing fourteen factories by 2012 (the previous number discussed was nine), and deleting its Hummer truck brand from its divisional portfolio. And if Saturn wasn't able to be revived, it would be eliminated in 2011. Some believed GM could need as much as $16.6 billion in additional loans from the U.S. government and could run out of money in March if it didn't receive at least some of that funding. GM also insisted that bankruptcy was not an option and that it would cost as much as $100 billion in lost revenue. The biggest news by far was that GM was unable to reach an agreement with the UAW in terms of accepting debt equity for half of GM's VEBA (voluntary employees' beneficiary association) obligations. GM was also unable to cut a deal with its bondholders to cut its massive debt obligation. As I said several times previously, this "deadline" date was never going to be about coming up with a hard-and-fast deal, because there were just too many loose ends in play. So now the real work began, and it would be one tough slog from here on out.

THOSE WAITING FOR SOME *voila* moment tomorrow (February 17) when GM brings its "Plan" for survival to Washington shouldn't hold their breath, because the plan will be incomplete pending many factors, including critical negotiations with bondholders and the UAW. Even *if* GM arrives at some sort of tentative agreement with these factions in the next twenty-four hours, there will be simply too many loose ends pending for GM to walk in and say, "Here it is, we're good."

It's common knowledge that GM is working on two plans to present to the government, however. The first one would involve taking more money from the government to continue its ongoing restructuring and contraction efforts, and a second one involves a bankruptcy-type arrangement—*without calling it as such*—which would have the government contribute funds to help GM pay off obligations and unwind existing entanglements in order to start over as a new company.

The first scenario is clearly the preferable one with many GM insiders because it allows for the gradual reduction of dealers, divisions, and employees (projecting out to 2013), which would be the least painful in terms of impact to its people and its dealers. It hinges on a lot of ifs, however, and judging by the acrimonious dealings between GM and its bondholders, not to mention the continued recalcitrance by the UAW to disband its longstanding existing agreements—in particular the so-called supplemental unemployment benefit, or "SUB" pay, which gives laid-off workers 95 percent of their net wages—reaching the goal is not going to be easy. And some would argue that achieving it is nothing more than a pipe dream at this juncture, which is why a second scenario has emerged as a viable option worth considering, at least within some corners of GM.

Now, how the government and GM would position such an arrangement—this "phantom" bankruptcy—so the consumer public wouldn't view it as such remains to be seen, because using the "B" word in conjunction with an auto company and unleashing the subsequent negative consumer attitudes that it would be sure to trigger is a scenario that no one wants to see play out. Especially considering that the negativity associated with GM (and Chrysler) since the debacle in Washington last December has already wreaked havoc on consumer attitudes toward these two companies and contributed dramatically to their precarious swoon in sales over the last three months.

Which is why some GM insiders are suggesting that the second option—a "government-assisted reconfiguration" or whatever they'd call it—would give them a much greater chance at survival over the long term, because it would allow the company to get out from under the cloud of negativity that is hovering over everything GM is trying to achieve and accomplish.

It would also have some other indirect consequences, too, and that is that it would mean the end of the United Auto Workers union for all intents and purposes, as most of its existing agreements with GM would become untenable and obsolete. This would obviously present some awkward challenges for President Obama, but no matter how noble and well-intended (and unrealistic) his administration is about things, reality has a way of rearing its ugly head even to the most touchy-feely of endeavors. If the ultimate goal is really to save the domestic automobile industry and shore up America's manufacturing base, then the biggest casualty may in fact have to be the UAW.

We already know one thing for certain, and that is that whatever scenario plays out for GM, a new company will emerge consisting of just four of its divisions: Chevrolet, Cadillac, Buick, and GMC. Pontiac will retain two and at the most three models to be sold at select GMC dealers, while Saturn, Saab, and Hummer will cease to exist in the GM solar system (that's not to say that Hummer and Saab won't find new owners somewhere out there because that remains a possibility, but Saturn is, in fact, done). This also means that the reduction in the numbers of GM dealers all across the country will not only continue, it will accelerate. Not good economic news under any scenario.

After writing since Day One of this publication that GM had too many models, too many divisions, and too many dealers, it pains me to see that after almost ten years GM is *still* grappling with this perennial problem. And the fact that they're now being *forced* to confront this issue once and for all—when they could have been reducing their redundancies for *years*—doesn't make it any easier.

However GM gets there, whether it's by the government allowing them more time—and money—to reorganize, or if it's by executing and funding some sort of a prepackaged reorganization that allows GM to terminate agreements and contracts without ever uttering the "B" word, the GM that will survive should hopefully be a leaner, healthier, and more competitive company.

And after all is said and done, if GM is able to emerge from all of this with a strengthening pulse, then I have a recommendation. Substitute the word "Precision" for "General" in the company title and then move on, burying the old company name—and the associated negativity—once and for all.

Chapter 29

PMD Unplugged:
The "Old Broken-Down
Piece of Meat" edition

By March 2009, the negative sentiment toward Detroit was beyond palpable. The degree of vitriol and bile being directed at the industry was staggering, and the incompetent gang in Washington masquerading as the Auto Industry Task Force was a sorry sight indeed. It was time for someone to tell it like it really was.

NOW THAT WE HAVE BEEN blessed with a visit from President Obama's auto task force, we can just feel the rush of Shiny, Happy adrenalin running through our veins. *Not.* Unfortunately, there's no amount of fact-finding and due diligence that's going to get these people up to speed in order to save the domestic auto industry, no matter how well-intended they claim to be.

With countless auto suppliers on the verge of total collapse, GM and Chrysler teetering on virtual bankruptcy, auto dealers closing left and right, and the car business veering close to coming to a complete standstill, it is difficult to see anything positive that we can grab on to, especially while we're waiting for a plan from people who are trying to compress thirty-five years of recent auto industry learning on top of a century of auto industry history in a little more than eight weeks' time in order to make an "informed" decision about the industry's future. In other words: notevenremotelygonnahappen.com.

Of course added to all of this is the growing national gloom-

and-doom offensive that's threatening to swallow this country whole. The relentless din of negativity in the media is infiltrating every nook and cranny of our society, and it is taking its toll, to the point that Brian Williams of *NBC Nightly News* has been getting slammed from viewers via email demanding that he come up with something—*anything*—positive to say about our country right at this very moment. (And to his credit, each night this week he's closing the program with a positive story.)

As for the doom-and-gloom thing, it's something that people who live around these parts are unfortunately very familiar with. This state and region have been in a serious recession for three years now, and I think it's safe to say at this point that we've now graduated to being in a full-blown depression.

The Motor City Meltdown and the ongoing economic calamity have absolutely decimated this region, with thousands upon thousands of people losing their jobs and their homes. And their minds are probably not far behind, too, for that matter. And in a state already widely known for its dangerously crumbling infrastructure—our roads are simply legendary around the country for their shocking state of disrepair—the reduced funds that go hand in hand with the declining tax revenues of a plummeting economy and the fact that there's no money to repair them have left the citizens of this state simply begging for mercy, or some kind of respite of any kind, even though there's no relief in sight. (How bad is it? Some major thoroughfares are approaching the impassable stage unless you have a vehicle with substantial ground clearance. Even the local traffic reports have switched from being primarily about the usual traffic tie-ups and such to a relentless stream of road-crumbling alerts. Grim doesn't even begin to describe it.)

Several years ago, I called Detroit and the declining U.S. auto industry the canary in the coal mine for the rest of the nation. The lack of a national healthcare program, the nation's growing uncompetitiveness in the face of a burgeoning global economy, the steady erosion of this country's manufacturing base, and so on were issues that were going to catch up to the rest of the country eventually. Add in the real-estate fiasco and the egregious and rampant Wall Street misbehavior, and it's no wonder "We the People" are finding ourselves in dire straits today.

But all of that being said, I say enough already.

I'm tired of the auto industry being treated like an old broken-down piece of meat or something that should be taken out back and shot. Our so-called leaders in Washington—particularly certain senators and representatives who should know better—have relegated an entire industry to the dust heap. And why? So a few idiot southern senators can tout their states as the "new" center of the auto industry? Or is it because Detroit and the center of industrial America don't quite fit into the new "Green" world that Northern Californian politicians want to shove down our collective throats?

I'm tired of this "Green" sickness that's spreading due east from California like an out-of-control virus that there's no known antidote for. With Nancy Pelosi and Governor Arnold Schwarzenegger— those quintessential manifestations of vapidity—leading the charge and insisting on projecting their relentless lack of common sense and glaring inability to differentiate facts from outright fiction as the environmental platform that this nation must adhere to going forward, even if it means prolonging the national recession and darkening this country's manufacturing future, it's no wonder the rest of the country is finding it difficult to be optimistic about the direction we're heading.

Memo to the Green Horde (and you, too, Mr. President, since you seem to fuel these blowhards): You will not have an auto industry to "reinvent" after you finish dismantling this country's manufacturing base and crippling its ability to innovate because of your Byzantine declarations and manifestos.

Do I want cleaner air? Of course I do. We *all* do. Believe it or not there are citizens all over the country—not just in California— who embrace the notion and want to get there for the well-being of *all* Americans. But it won't come by way of a simple *voila!* and a finger snap, or by cramming increasingly ridiculous rules into law that will turn huge swaths of this country into vast wastelands of unemployment and futility. If the "Green" vision for our nation—at least as brought forth by Pelosi, Schwarzenegger and Co.—consists of a so-called idyllic future featuring a Shiny, Happy populace peddling our way around in balsa-wood Smiley Cars while whistling our way to work that we can't find, well, then, *you can include me out*, as Sam Goldwyn once said.

The domestic automotive industry—much to the chagrin of its critics—is home to some of the most advanced technological expertise and innovative minds in the world today—yes, equal to, if not better than, any car maker from any other country, too—and I am absolutely confident that they have the talent and the know-how to move this country forward when it comes to meeting the goals of environmental responsibility. It will take a serious commitment and incredible amounts of research and development time and money to get where we eventually want to go, but we will get there.

We won't get there, however, if we leave it up to the people who have little or no understanding of concepts like production feasibility or the idea that a car company must deliver vehicles a.) that people actually *want to buy*, b.) that they can actually afford to buy, and c.) that the company producing it can actually make real money on in the process. That last part is the real kicker for the Green Horde. Not only is profitability a dirty concept to them—after all, someone might actually *make* money by taking risks and delivering a desirable product (how radical is that?)—but I get the idea that after all of their pronouncements and hard-and-fast rules that they're so quick to throw around, they'll feel "entitled" to paying less than ten grand for a car that will allow its passengers to walk away from a sixty-mile-per-hour crash into a bridge abutment while emitting nothing but the faint whiff of Pacific sea breezes going down the road.

For that and several other reasons I have zero confidence in the politicians from Northern California and other states and their green-tinged acolyte-activists when it comes to moving this country forward, and unless the din of misinformation that's emanating from this environmental cabal is countered with common sense and reality—and soon—then this country is in for a horrendous period of mediocrity and ultimately a second-rate future.

As for the rest of what's ailing this nation, not much of anything is making sense these days, frankly. Banks being gifted government money that they refuse to lend out; blatant, malicious dimwits with the title of "U.S. Senator" not even pretending to be "for the people" anymore while pushing their particular egregious agendas to the detriment of the rest of the nation; and our so-called government leaders standing around paralyzed, waiting for something to happen as the U.S. auto industry's infrastructure and supplier and dealer networks continue to crumble.

And now that we've all been brow-beaten and scolded for months for being bad, wasteful Americans for using our credit cards and living our lives—and we all actually listened for once and stopped doing *anything*—our esteemed leaders are now telling us *not* to go into duck-and-cover mode, that it's fine to spend a little bit of money, that it's all going to be okay.

Oh, *really?* When is *that* going to be, exactly? The end of the fourth quarter? When our Green Snuggies are aligned with Nancy Pelosi's emerald chakras just so? When the grand pooh-bah, a.k.a. Warren Buffet, declares victory and says it's okay for us to play outside again? When Arnold and Nancy do a two-step on the ashes of what's left of the domestic automobile industry? Judging by what passes for public discourse in Washington and around the country these days, let's just say the nation won't be collectively holding its breath.

While I'm at it, since when did Americans turning on fellow Americans become a sport in this country? The abuse that the domestic auto industry and the people who work tirelessly in it has received from the legions of two-bit pundits and instant auto "experts" out there over the last six months is unconscionable and despicable. Even those words don't come close to describing the kind of out-and-out hatred that has been aimed at our own automobile industry over the last twelve months. Hell, even Bernie Madoff has gotten more of a break than the U.S. auto industry, and that's just disgusting.

Why is it okay for thousands of Americans and their families to become expendable for being aligned with an industry that not only forged this country's manufacturing base and to this day is responsible for much of this nation's technical innovations, but fueled our country's ability to meet global military challenges throughout history while powering the emergence of the American middle class?

Why is okay to dump on an industry that still either directly or indirectly employs one out of every fourteen Americans?

Why is it okay for some asshole in a New York TV studio to pontificate about an industry he knows absolutely nothing about, and then have his unmitigated bullshit be taken as "gospel" by another hundred TV pundits who know even less?

I say enough. Enough to *all* of it. I say enough to this country's mass embrace of this collective "mope-a-dope" mentality, as I like to call it. And I say enough to the media's crucifixion of our own domestic automobile industry as if it and all of the hardworking people in and around it somehow deserve to be put on trial for war crimes.

We can do better. *Much* better. And we will get better, too, individually *and* as a country. As more Americans discover that fearmongering and negativity for negativity's sake is not a good look for us—and that waiting for our esteemed politicians in Washington to adjust our attitudes, or waiting for them to do *anything*, for that matter, is a fool's errand—I absolutely believe we will rise above this.

Chapter 30

GM's "duck and cover" strategy falls flat

In trying to convince the Obama administration that it was worthy of the billions of dollars in additional loans in question by Washington's March 31 deadline (now termed as an "arbitrary" date by Obama's troops), General Motors had been on a slash-and-burn offensive within the company to save dollars wherever it could, and in doing so had made some highly questionable decisions that could severely impact the company's ability to compete when the economy starts moving again. The evidence? GM had reduced its marketing offensive to "deal" advertising at a time when the American consumer needed more. Much more. And with the constant din in the national media along the lines that GM deserved to die, consumers needed to know "Why GM?" and they needed to know now. They needed to understand where GM had been, i.e., what the company had meant to this country over the last one hundred years and the essential role it had played in America's economic and strategic success, where it was now—what it was doing to get better and, oh, by the way, tout the excellent, highly rated products on dealer lots right now—and where it was going, as in, what did GM's future look like beyond the Chevrolet Volt?

WHILE GM GOING "DARK" in the media and missing out on major PR opportunities out of deference to the Washington politicos must have seemed like a good idea down at the RenCen, it's not playing out in a good way by any stretch of the imagination.

But there's more to GM's duck-and-cover mode than just marketing and PR missteps, because its "cut at all costs" mentality is now costing it product advantages that could have been keys to the company's future success.

The most egregious example of GM's misguided thinking? It has postponed its new, highly efficient, light-truck diesel engine (one of the most technically advanced engines from *any* manufacturer in the last ten years), which was originally scheduled to begin production next fall. This postponement will cost GM at least one year (the time it takes from a "go" decision to get the program up and running again) in a market where genuine product advantages are extremely hard to come by. GM also postponed the Cadillac CTS Coupe by a year, a can't-miss product "hit" and exactly the kind of car it needs in-market ASAP. Not Good.

And this is just the stuff we're hearing about today. There are rumblings from within GM that the cutting has gone absolutely off the deep end, with everything from silly, inconsequential, cover-your-ass-type sacrifices being made by executives running scared to blatant product planning screw-ups that threaten to squander all the hard-won gains that have occurred in the Lutzian era, and in turn threaten the company's fundamental competitiveness in the future.

Which brings me to GM's move last week of *not* taking the interim $2 billion in government funds. All of the cost-cutting going on within GM since January 1 has been geared to send a message to the Obama administration that the company is making meaningful progress in their "downsizing" efforts and that with additional funding from the government they will be poised to be a reconfigured and reinvigorated company. And that's why last week's maneuver was no last-minute decision or happy accident. But there was more to GM's motivation than just that.

It's no secret that GM has been seething about the fact that Ford has been able to put some serious distance between itself and GM (not to mention Chrysler) in terms of creating a more favorable public image by not taking government money. As a matter of fact,

Ford has gotten meaningful positive feedback from both consumers *and* Washington politicos alike for its stance, and this has rankled GM to no end. So GM's move last week was clearly calculated to blunt some of the PR hay that Ford has made in its campaign to distance itself from "The Old Detroit Two."

Whether or not it really matters in the giant scheme of things is debatable.

What *does* matter is the fact that GM has apparently chosen to ignore one of the oldest adages in this business—or *any* business, for that matter—and that is that you can't "cut" your way to prosperity.

"Duck and cover" does not constitute a marketing or PR strategy, or an advertising strategy, for that matter. And it certainly doesn't qualify as a strategically sound technique for product planning.

The bottom line in all of this is that GM needs three things more than anything else right now, and they are:

1. OUTSTANDING PRODUCTS THAT PROVE TO ANYONE WHO WOULD BOTHER TO LOOK BEYOND THE NEGATIVE HEADLINES THAT THE COMPANY INDEED DESERVES TO EXIST;

2. THE COLLECTIVE CORPORATE BACKBONE TO BE ABLE TO SAY TO ANYONE IN THE OBAMA ADMINISTRATION—OR TO ANY OF ITS CRITICS TOO—THAT IT IS WILLING TO GO TO THE MAT TO PROTECT THE ESSENTIAL PRODUCT PROGRAMS THAT WILL ENSURE ITS LONG-TERM VIABILITY AND COMPETITIVENESS, EVEN IF IT MEANS NOT LOOKING AS FINANCIALLY ROSY ON MARCH 31; AND

3. JUST AS IMPORTANT, THE GUTS TO SAY WHAT NEEDS TO BE SAID WITHOUT COWERING IN FEAR THAT THEY MIGHT OFFEND SOME FACTION "OUT THERE" IN THE MEDIA OR IN WASHINGTON.

GM's duck-and-cover offensive has swung the pendulum too far in the wrong direction, and the consequences of its actions could have far-reaching effects.

Will cooler heads prevail so that some of these product and image missteps get put back on track and on time?

At this point it's the biggest "wait and see" of the year.

Chapter 31

State of the Motor City Nation: The "Polishing of the Pitchforks" edition

Given the fact that President Obama found it funny that "the only thing less popular than putting money in banks is putting money into the auto industry" as he told 60 Minutes *one Sunday night, and the anti-Detroit furor in Washington was such that there were still custom-built chrome-plated pitchforks reserved for Detroit and lurking under the desks in the Senate and House that could be mustered at a moment's notice, it was no wonder that the mood around the Motor City leading up to the March 31 deadline for further payments to GM and Chrysler could only be described as grim.*

As we emerge from a particularly brutal winter with hopes that a warm and soothing spring will somehow lift the somberness around here, instead the region is faced with an unspoken reality that GM and Chrysler have already been written off by two-thirds of the media, two-thirds of the American public, and two-thirds of Washington, for an Ultimate Trifecta of Not Good. And that even with a substantial additional infusion of money, it will be a long and tedious road to a "recovery" that will amount to half of what the domestic automobile industry once was.

It hasn't helped matters, of course, that "Minimum Bob" Nardelli has all but hastened the demise of Chrysler with his constant bleating about how great things are and how Fiat will be the savior and the future product lifeblood of the company. It has been distressing to see some less-than-stellar members of the automotive media picking up on the whole Fiat-Chrysler link-up idea and running it into the ground before even stopping to carefully listen to what Sergio Marchionne, the CEO of Fiat, was actually saying, which was basically something like "we'll see what happens with the government loans, but thanks for giving us thirty percent of the company in the interim."

In other words, you can speculate about how *bella* the Fiat-in-fused product lineup will be and how it will transform Chrysler all you want, but the reality is that Fiat is doing a giant "let's wait and see" and everyone else is booking a few favorable comments as gospel. Not exactly what you want to base the future of a company on, especially one as busted flat by the side of the road as Chrysler is.

The wheels came off of Nardelli's glorified bait-and-switch act with a resounding thud last week when Chrysler insisted that Fiat was all good with taking on Chrysler's debt, followed by an empathic response from Italy suggesting that it was not only never a consideration but that that it was notgonnahappen.com (insert an Italian accent for emphasis). Needless to say, the timing couldn't have been worse for something like this to come out, and I can assure you that the moment that little tidbit was exposed, the polishing of the pitchforks commenced in Washington.

It's no secret that Chrysler has been teetering on the brink for months, even though they've been insisting all along that they're in better shape than GM (which is flat-out untrue, by the way). Add to this the fact that the Cerberus corporate bylaws won't allow the company to sink any more money into Chrysler (what, they can't change the rules, or is the reality that they will do anything to get out from under this mess without spending one more dime closer to The High-Octane Truth?)—the worst financial play in the company's entire history—and pretty much nothing associated with the Auburn Hills bunch is sitting too well with anyone in Washington these days.

Which brings me back to Nardelli. Remember, this is the guy who stated upon being tapped to run Chrysler that "the New Chrysler has the opportunity to prove that private business models can thrive in this industry." How is that working out for you and the Cerberus brain trust so far, Bob? I'll answer that for you: Not so much.

Nardelli brought his "don't let the screen door hit you in the ass on your way out" exit strategy from Home Depot with him to Detroit. The only problem is that no one at Cerberus bothered to do due diligence to see if he was equipped for the job or not. (Not that anyone at Cerberus actually had the first clue about running a car company to begin with.) And guess what? He wasn't. And there's no amount of Jack Welch/GE-tinged business school mumbo jumbo bullshit on the planet that can cover up that fact. The wayward Welch acolytes at Cerberus weren't just ill equipped for the task at hand—they had no business even going near it. And it has been such an unmitigated disaster of incalculable scope that even Jim Press's once-golden reputation has been destroyed in the process.

If Chrysler gets any money next week it will only be in preparation for a Chapter 11 bankruptcy that will quickly become Chapter 7 liquidation by summer. And then we'll see if Sergio or Carlos or whoever makes deals to pick over the carcass of what was once—at least at certain moments intermittently sprinkled throughout automotive history—a pretty damn good car company.

As for General Motors, the media firestorm that has been unrelenting since last December's Washington fiasco has decimated the company's sales, in spite of the slew of fine vehicles on the ground at its dealerships across the country. And GM's new "let's get everything on the table" posture has talked the consumer right out of the brands it said it would phase out in time—Saturn, Saab, Hummer, and, to a lesser extent, Pontiac—and that has just killed showroom traffic—and its dealers—too.

GM's too many models/too many divisions/too many dealers conundrum that I began writing about in the very first issue of this publication ten years ago has finally collapsed under the strain of an economy that's in unprecedented freefall. To exacerbate matters, GM's bondholders are being uncooperative in reconfiguring its debt out of fear the company's projections about a turnaround in the economy—and how a newly downsized GM will be ready to take advantage of it—are too bullish and unrealistic. And let's not forget the pitchforks waiting for muster in Washington—where certain dimwitted senators are ready to bless us all with their stupendous stupidity again—and in California, too, where the environmental lobby is poised to pounce on even the idea of a viable GM, because it means the prolonging of an industry that they want dead, buried, and forgotten.

How bad is it? It's bad enough that the Winds of Not Good are blowing so strongly around GM's tubular spires hard by the Detroit River that you don't want to leave your overly full coffee cup unattended on the upper floors out of fear the liquid caffeine might just slosh out in waves.

Did GM make a convincing case with the instant auto "experts" in Washington? I believe they did, but if only it were that simple. Even with Saturn, Hummer, and Saab on the way out, GM still has too many product mouths to feed. Pontiac will go away simply because GM can't afford to do it justice, and if that's the case, then I'm all for letting it slumber.

As for the rest of GM, if it's going to still be around in North America by 2012, then I see the company configured this way:

Chevrolet: mini car (Spark), compact (Cruze), mainstream sedans (Malibu, Volt, and TBD), crossovers (Traverse and Equinox), sports cars (Corvette), sporty cars (Camaro, along with other performance variations of the lineup), and pickup trucks.

Cadillac: CTS lineup (coupe, sedan, sport wagon), as well as high-performance V-Series versions, a crossover (SRX), an eventual full-sized sedan, and one larger SUV (Escalade).

Those two divisions—Chevrolet and Cadillac—will be the primary focus and future of GM. Buick will be reduced to two sedans (LaCrosse and Regal) and a crossover (Enclave) sold at Buick-GMC dealers, while GMC will retain larger SUVs and luxury pickups only.

That all sounds well and good, but there are far too many question marks floating around to count on anything, exactly to the bondholders' point, by the way. When will the economy turn the corner? And will it happen soon enough for GM to pull itself off of the mat? How quickly will GM's dealer count get reduced? And will the newly downsized GM be able to survive at a 15 percent share of the U.S. market? Because that could very well be the number down the road, even though no one wants to think about it. And when will the Green Posse acknowledge that GM (and Ford) actually has some very competitive green entries, with more on the way, instead of dismissing everything Detroit has to offer as "yester-tech"?

And on and on and on.

Will GM get the money? Yes. Will it be enough? See those questions above. Will Chrysler get the money? Yes, but it won't be for ultimate survival, but rather to ease the process of winding down.

And what about Ford?

Except for the clear and unmistakable signs that the emergence of Ford as America's car company ascending is real and something to be cautiously optimistic about, the winter of Detroit's discontent has turned into a gut-wrenching, pothole-infested, cold, and gloomy spring.

Not really much to go on—especially when the fate of an industry and an entire region is in Washington's hands—but at the moment it's all we've got.

Chapter 32

A Pandora's Box of Not Good

On March 29 President Obama was expected to announce that GM (and Chrysler) would get additional emergency funding, while giving each company more time to achieve additional cuts with, in GM's case, its bondholders and the UAW. The president would also seize the moment to chastise the American automobile industry yet again, as if that would somehow make up for the missed opportunity that blew right by him when he failed to take swift enough action on the AIG mess. (By Monday morning, Obama's plans were emerging. GM would get sixty days to get its situation in order; Chrysler would get just thirty days, but only *if it made a deal with Fiat. It's clear that the Obama administration was pushing for a "quick-rinse" bankruptcy with government protection for consumers who buy vehicles from these manufacturers as part of the package.) And as part of his "shared sacrifice" mantra that he's so good at relentlessly pounding into the American public while framing the domestic automobile industry as some sort of national scourge, Obama demanded and received a body—in this case GM chairman and CEO Rick Wagoner—so he could hold it up to the American public on one of his administration's custom-built chrome-plated pitchforks and say, "See, I'm doing what I promised! I am slaying the evil dragons of American corporate greed! I will reshape America into a kinder, gentler nation of group hugs while creating a more realistic and caring set of common corporate goals!"*

And not only had an ugly precedent been set, but America's future had just been turned dark by the realization that our government would not hesitate to reach into every available orifice—corporate or otherwise—and put their stamp on it if it didn't quite conform to the Obama administration's Shiny, Happy vision of what this country was supposed to be.

CONTRARY TO THE HORDE of instant pundit-experts out there who don't have the first clue as to what this industry is all about—or what it's like to actually *work* in this industry—Rick Wagoner was by no means the evil architect of GM's current predicament. Yes, Wagoner made some mistakes, and I have documented them long before the "Rick Wagoner Must Go" train left the pundit station. The Fiat adventure was disastrous, and Wagoner's initial reluctance to wrestle with GM's bloated structure proved costly. But Mr. Wagoner's most glaring failing really wasn't his at all, but rather it was that he was a product of GM's long-corroded and obsolete cultural ideal that the people who run the company should only come from the financial office. This is nothing new, it should be pointed out, because it has been part of the GM *raison d'être* since the Alfred Sloan era. But it was Rick Wagoner's—and GM's—reality.

But there was another side to Rick Wagoner's tenure that the instant pundits out there either refuse to acknowledge—out of their out-and-out hatred for anything to do with GM and Detroit—or that they simply couldn't fathom because of their abject lack of experience or, what is probably closer to the truth, their complete lack of under-standing of how this business actually operates. And that is that if Rick Wagoner hadn't taken the aggressively decisive actions that he *did* take, GM would have been out of business years ago.

Wagoner's move into the Chinese market (a continuation of the doctrine laid out by his predecessor, Jack Smith) proved to be pivotal in providing a road map for the company's future. And Wagoner's in-sistence on utilizing and exploiting the global capabilities of GM's far-reaching corporate empire, with forays into Korea, Brazil, Mexico, and Eastern Europe, laid the groundwork for a completely modernized and globally competitive endeavor.

But Wagoner's most impressive move during his tenure was to recognize his own limitations as a financially oriented leader, while at the same time setting his own ego aside in order to bring Bob Lutz into the company. Wagoner handed Lutz the keys to GM's woefully moribund product-development system and said "Fix it," while giving Lutz carte blanche to do it. And the results were magnificent. During Wagoner's tenure—while benefiting from the vision, passion, and sheer will to succeed that Lutz brought to the table—GM saw its greatest design, engineering, and product era since its glory days of the '60s.

Down the road, long after the lynch-mob hysteria subsides—and this administration's pitchforks have been hopefully melted down into brand-spanking-new American-made automobiles—Rick Wagoner's tenure will be judged more fairly and with the proper perspective. But until that time it must be said that the economic catastrophe that overwhelmed this country conspired to bring an entire foundation American industry to its knees, and there was no leader—socially "approved" or otherwise—who could have prevented GM and the rest of the domestic automobile business from collapsing.

Rick Wagoner and I had our run-ins (he didn't take too kindly to my early writings in Autoextremist.com, to put it mildly), and we've never had more than a passing conversational relationship at the countless car events over the years, but he's far from the ogre that his critics make him out to be. On the contrary, he is an exceedingly bright, gifted, and personable executive who has ended up taking a bullet for the company that he has been a part of since 1977. And he did it in order to appease the overlords in the Obama administration so that the company he loved would live to fight another day. That says a lot about the measure of the man, in my book.

A pity I can't say the same for Mr. Obama and his posse. When I say that an ugly precedent has been set by the administration's blatant and meddlesome actions into corporate America—resulting in an executive actually losing his job—that is the understatement of this or any other year.

President Obama and the overlords in his administration have opened a Pandora's box of Not Good by this action.

And by far the ugliest part about it?

No one has even the remotest of clues as to where or when it will stop.

Chapter 33

Obama weighs in, telegraphs bankruptcy for GM

President Obama made it very clear in his address to the nation the morning of March 30 that he and his team had no intention of running GM and that they only had the best intentions in mind when it came to the future of the American automobile industry. He then went on to say, of course, that he had ordered the sacking of GM's Rick Wagoner and that a "quick rinse" bankruptcy could be the best way for GM to emerge a stronger and healthier company. Why he bothered to say that they had no intention of running GM while they in fact were running the company at that very moment was a little hard to understand, but the net-net of his message wasn't. And that is that he and his administration's brain trust were moving GM toward bankruptcy, but that it would be the "good" kind, meaning that the government would take the onus off of the word "bankruptcy" by guaranteeing people's warranties. He also made a pitch for how good current American cars are, which was all very interesting.

AFTER ARGUING VEHEMENTLY against bankruptcy for GM since last December, the president's speech this morning got me to shift my thinking. Why wait sixty days at all? Given that Obama and his crew are basically telegraphing the fact that they are going to move GM toward bankruptcy anyway, I recommend GM cut a deal with the Obama administration to go to bankruptcy *immediately*, with the following conditions: 1. Obama becomes "Car Salesman-in-Chief" and he and

146

his wife participate in a one-hour infomercial that will tout American cars complete with proof points as to why they're worth buying; 2. The government guarantees warranties for all GM cars and trucks and makes sure every American knows it via "live" read advertisements at the end of Obama's weekly radio addresses; and 3. Offer $5,000 to every American who purchases a car assembled in North America (domestic or import).

Why screw around sixty days and miss the heart of the spring selling season? The Obama administration has made it very clear that they will not rest until GM resembles exactly their vision for an American car company, even though, beyond the usual smarmy platitudes, they haven't exactly been forthright in delineating what that is, but so be it. This way GM can go right down to two divisions—Cadillac and Chevrolet—with a couple of Buicks and GMC trucks thrown in for good measure, and we can get on with the future of the American automobile business, whatever form that takes, without the Obama administration hovering over GM's shoulder at every turn.

As for the Fiat-Chrysler-Cerberus deal, let's not get carried away here, because there's a *l-o-n-g* way to go before we see a concrete plan emerge. I am quite certain of one thing, however, and that is that Chrysler is dead and buried one way or another, which is exactly what I've been saying for many months now, much to the chagrin of the Chrysler nostalgia buffs out there who equate me with being the antichrist. But the problems for this deal are deep and ugly. Chrysler is over-dealered by two-thirds, and that one issue alone is so fraught with peril that it could derail this deal right out of the blocks. Short of total capitulation—meaning an Obama-ized "clean" bankruptcy— Fiat-Chrysler doesn't have a snowball's chance in Hell of surviving, no matter how good the linguine tastes.

And so it goes.

Chapter 34

China set to redefine the global automotive industry

We didn't normally mark April Fool's Day with any special coverage, but that week in April I was ready to shift gears, so I concocted a fanciful—albeit too close to reality—scenario that had two secretive Chinese billionaires sweeping in and buying GM and Chrysler, lock, stock, and barrel. And with the news constantly churning and the fate of the U.S. automobile industry hanging by a thread, I felt it was time to do something completely different. Thus, Fu-King Motors was born, and it was done with such authentic detail—right down to the real sounding names of the reporters—that some people were fooled right up until the point I was named as CEO.

NEW AUTO CONGLOMERATE BASED IN CHINA SET TO REDEFINE THE GLOBAL AUTOMOTIVE INDUSTRY; SECRET NEGOTIATIONS RESULT IN STUNNING DEAL TO BUY BOTH GENERAL MOTORS AND CHRYSLER.

SHANGHAI (AP) – Capping off a tumultuous week, the global automobile market is set to be turned upside down yet again after a stunning move to consolidate the auto industry has been announced by Endless Green Horizon, a newly formed global automotive conglomerate based in Shanghai, China.

"We are pleased to announce that our initiative into the global automobile market is progressing rapidly and that we're being welcomed with warm greetings," said Co-chairman James "Jimmy" Fu.

"We look forward to redefining the automobile industry and intend on being a significant player for decades to come."

Mr. Fu's partner, S. L. "Sonny" King, added, "We live our lives to achieve this goal. This is no pretend moment. Our reality will become the industry's reality shortly."

INITIAL SKEPTICISM FOLLOWED BY GRUDGING ACCEPTANCE

Coming hard on the heels of President Obama's bludgeoning of GM and Chrysler this past Monday, including the forced removal of GM CEO Rick Wagoner, the secret negotiations and subsequent deal were announced abruptly overnight Tuesday, after rumors began to emerge late yesterday in Shanghai.

GM released the following prepared statement this morning: "When first approached by Mr. Fu and Mr. King, we weren't able to ascertain the seriousness of their intentions early on, and admittedly, we were dismissive of the overture," said CEO Fritz Henderson. "But over the last few weeks the complexion of their offer changed, as did the tone from the Obama administration, obviously, and it was clear that this whole thing with Washington was going nowhere good. Given all that has transpired in the last six months, culminating in the chaos of the last few days, we feel Endless Green Horizon's offer was in the best interest for GM, its employees and retirees, our dealers, our suppliers, the United Auto Workers union and all interested stakeholders, including our bond holders and most important, the American taxpayer."

Jason Vines, the executive vice-president and director of global communications for the new automotive endeavor, said in a statement that a special media briefing would be held on Thursday morning, April 2, in Detroit, in the Wintergarden lobby of the RenCen. "As you can imagine, given the global impact of these developments, it is imperative that we give everyone enough time to digest what has just happened. The press conference is scheduled for tomorrow morning at 10:00 A.M., and it will be broadcast live around the world for media sources unable to get here on such short notice."

Steve Harris, GM's PR chief, said there would be no additional comment forthcoming from Mr. Henderson or GM until the joint press conference scheduled for tomorrow morning.

A statement was also released by Robert Nardelli, the CEO of Chrysler LLC this morning: "We were first approached by Mr. Fu and Mr. King a month ago, and we too were unable to muster the energy to take them seriously. That of course changed over the subsequent weeks. After long hours of consideration fraught with soul-searching and hand-wringing, we believe this is the best deal for Chrysler, its employees and retirees, our suppliers, our dealers, the UAW and for our corporate parent, Cerberus. It is the end of an era for the American automobile business, but the beginning of a new chapter for the global automobile industry."

Mr. Nardelli was approached for a comment as he got into his car at the main entrance to Chrysler's headquarters, but he waved off reporters' questions with a brusque "I really don't give a shit anymore. Buh-bye." Last seen, his car was peeling out of the driveway, heading to whereabouts unknown.

Ron Gettelfinger, the head of the UAW, refused to comment after his arrival this morning at Solidarity House, the labor union's headquarters in Detroit. "I can assure you that I'll have plenty to say later tomorrow when we have our own press conference," Mr. Gettelfinger said.

SECRET NEGOTIATIONS CLIMAX IN 15 MINUTES THAT WOULD CHANGE THE AUTOMOTIVE WORLD FOREVER

Negotiations began in late February, according to sources, the timetable of which was later confirmed by Mr. Vines. "Initial overtures were made to GM and Chrysler in late February by Mr. Fu and Mr. King," Mr. Vines, a longtime industry PR veteran with notable stints at Ford and Chrysler, said. "It was made clear from the outset to both automakers that the offer being made by Endless Green Horizon was serious, legitimate and substantially funded," Vines continued. "After GM and Chrysler leadership demonstrated their initial skepticism, actual common parameters emerged over a very brief period of time. This deal didn't come together until it was made quite clear by President Obama and his administration this past Monday afternoon that these two automakers were just north of being expendable, or, as I carefully explained to Mr. Fu and Mr. King, they were toast."

Mr. Henderson made his first appearance in front of the assembled media as GM's CEO yesterday at the company's headquarters in Detroit. He talked about the car business and his plans to reinvent the company, a new customer assurance plan, how much he respected the Obama administration's automotive task force and the president himself and other topics. There was no indication whatsoever that this deal was in the works. But things would soon change.

The dramatic moment came just after 9:00 P.M. EDT last night (9:00 A.M. this morning in Shanghai), when Fritz Henderson called Mr. Fu at the end of a hastily called emergency board meeting led by newly minted nonexecutive chairman of the board Kent Kresa and said, "We're done here. Let's do it." Thus ended 100 years of U.S. industrial history as the American corporate icon finally acquiesced to a complete takeover.

Mr. Henderson then had Mr. Nardelli informed of GM's decision immediately, and Mr. Nardelli called Mr. Fu and accepted the conglomerate's offer 15 minutes later.

The financial details of this historic agreement were not released, but Mr. Vines made a point to a small group of reporters gathered in front of the GM building at 5:00 A.M. this morning that the debt issues that were strangling both companies had been addressed by the Chinese conglomerate. "Complete financial details will be forthcoming at the press conference tomorrow morning," Mr. Vines said. "But I can safely say to you that the massive debt of these companies, something that's of primary interest to all of the parties involved, has been covered, in *cash*."

SHADOWY BACKGROUNDS

The details of how Mr. Fu, 61, and Mr. King, 59, accumulated their staggering wealth are, as a kilted Angus McPherson, the notably acerbic Scottish journalist stationed in Shanghai put it, ". . . missing in action, a wee bit sketchy, I would say," as he stuffed his notebook back in his sporran. The two figures have operated in the shadows of the burgeoning Chinese industrial machine for years. Mr. Fu started manufacturing model cars in the late '70s and is now rumored to control every toy-making concern in China, though none of this has actually been confirmed after years of investigations. Mr. King became partners with Mr. Fu after initially supplying the elaborate wheels and carefully detailed tires on Mr. Fu's model cars. The two have been partners ever since.

Said to be fond of younger women, fast American muscle cars, Knob Creek Kentucky Straight Bourbon and Gulfstream jets, Mr. Fu and Mr. King nonetheless pride themselves in avoiding the limelight. Both men were married and divorced in their 30s, but little is known about that part of their life stories. It is known now, however, that Mr. Fu is trying to push the career of a budding 26-year-old Chinese pop star, his current girlfriend, while Mr. King seems to be addicted to an endless succession of young female gymnasts nearing the end of their competitive careers.

Mr. Vines provided no details other than to say, "Mr. Fu and Mr. King are reclusive, talented workaholics who also enjoy life to the fullest. Other than that, I really have no further comment.

Shock in Washington

President Obama's press secretary, Robert Gibbs, clearly caught off-guard when asked by reporters of the development early this morning before a press briefing, said "Huh?" to the news. "We know nothing about it, but, uh, er, you're kidding, right?" When assured the news was genuine, he cut off the media briefing and raced out of the press room.

A statement was released by the Obama administration just one hour later. "President Obama has been assured by the new owners of General Motors and Chrysler that all existing pension obligations will be met and that their crushing debt burden has been addressed. He looks forward to meeting with the new owners to hear of their plans to contribute to America's industrial fabric and help lead us to a sustainable, green-driving future. The president is also pleased to announce that the additional money discussed for both GM and Chrysler on Monday will no longer be needed, and that the money initially borrowed by the two companies since last December has been paid back in full."

When pestered for more details on what the president knew and when he knew it, Mr. Gibbs said, "I got nothin'."

Mouths agape in Detroit

The mood in Detroit was one of resignation when the news emerged. "People are walking around in a daze, looking like that '1984' Apple TV commercial," said one high-ranking GM executive. "First there was Monday's shocker and now this."

One administrative assistant who did not want to be identified was found at the Starbucks in the RenCen (GM's headquarters) staring off into space, pouring Kahlua in her Grande Iced Chai Soy Latte Triple Dirty. Asked about the news, she shrugged her shoulders and said, "GM, Endless Green Horizon . . . what's the f***ing difference?"

Another GM employee commented as he was leaving the building, "At this point, I'd prefer a couple of Chinese cowboys owning this place over those numb-nuts in Washington."

A homeless man, queried on the street corner in front of GM headquarters, muttered, "Monica Conyers for president" as he walked away.

A UAW member speaking on condition of anonymity added, "That's fine, man, but what's in it for me?"

Stunning choice for CEO

In another stunning development, Peter M. De Lorenzo, a longtime industry marketing veteran, was named to be the chairman and CEO of the new company's North American operations—to be renamed Fu-King Motors—which will include the remnants of GM and Chrysler. Mr. De Lorenzo, capping off a controversial 10-year run as the man behind Autoextremist.com—the highly influential industry publication—was a surprise choice by Mr. Fu and Mr. King to lead its new venture.

Mr. De Lorenzo got the call moments after the deal was consummated, according to Vines. "It turns out that Mr. Fu and Mr. King stumbled upon Mr. De Lorenzo's website when they first became familiar with the Internet. As a matter of fact, both gentlemen learned English by having Mr. De Lorenzo's 'Rants' columns translated for them. They also learned to say some of Mr. De Lorenzo's patented sayings phonetically, like 'notgonnahappen.com,' 'halle-frickin'-luja,' and 'the Answer to the Question that Absolutely No One is Asking.' And when the two gentlemen used some of Mr. De Lorenzo's sayings in the negotiations with GM and Chrysler, the blood drained out of the faces of the Detroit executives, to put it mildly. Mr. Fu and Mr. King have been in contact with Mr. De Lorenzo for six years, after they first approached him at the Los Angeles Auto Show. When they first contacted GM and Chrysler about their interest, Mr. De Lorenzo became part of the behind-the-scenes team orchestrating this deal. Mr. Fu and Mr. King said that Mr. De Lorenzo was their clear choice for CEO from the very beginning."

"Mr. De Lorenzo will bring years of experience leading our company," said Mr. Fu. "He puts pedal down hard, no B.S.," Mr. King added, as they addressed a small group of reporters gathered in Shanghai. "And if he doesn't like something, NOTGONNAHAPPEN. COM!!!" they shouted in unison to the bemused expressions on the faces of the reporters, who clearly had no clue as to what the two men were talking about.

Mr. Vines said that Mr. De Lorenzo would not be available to the media until tomorrow's meeting.

COMMENTS FROM AROUND THE WORLD POUR IN

The development was so swift and stunning that comments were just starting to pour in as we were completing this story. Volkswagen released a joint statement from VW's Ferdinand Piech and Porsche's

Wendelin Wiedeking moments ago: "We look forward to hearing more details about what appears to be a fanciful quest to remake the automobile industry. We know who we are and what we do best. We will crush them."

Ratan Tata, CEO of Tata Motors, was equally dismissive, saying, "It won't make a Nano-bit of difference to us."

Sergio Marchionne, the Fiat CEO, was apparently stunned at the news: "I do not understand, this can't be true. I mean, we kinda had a deal." And then he slammed down the phone.

Toyota released the following statement from CEO Katsuaki Watanabe: "We find this to be a perplexing development. We have no idea what this means, or why this is happening. We want the auto world to go back to the way it was, when we dominated everything. And it's not happening. Why?"

When contacted by cell phone for a comment about the choice of De Lorenzo, Robert Lutz, the vice-chairman of GM, who was on the roof of the RenCen, said, "Oh, hell yes. That's an inspired choice. He'll shake the rafters, kick ass and *will* that company to greatness. I might just re-up to work with him!" Mr. Lutz then got into his helicopter to fly home.

And finally, Keith Crain, the publisher of *Automotive News* had this to say: "It's a wonderful time to be in the automobile industry."

By Wang Liu for the Associated Press, with Vikram Bhan in Mumbai, Thurston Chesterton IV in London, Tammi Sue Jenkins in Detroit, Heather Elizabeth Wellesley in New York and Masami Katsuta in Tokyo

Chapter 35

"Defeatist-in-Chief" or "Salesman-in-Chief?" What's it going to be, Mr. President?

It's clear now that President Obama's speech to the nation that week in April about the dire situation facing this country's automobile industry was meant to send a very strong message to General Motors' bondholders to come to the table and be ready to get serious about how much of a whacking they were going to take in order to reach a settlement that would help ensure the company's viability. The president used the word "bankruptcy" to make his point loud and clear. Since the president's speech, Fritz Henderson, GM's newly minted CEO, had been highly visible on the news-talk circuit, flaunting the "B" word at every opportunity—as in all parties should come to the table and be prepared to make a deal, or else face the consequences—seconding the president. Unfortunately, every time President Obama or one of his handpicked team of auto "experts" mentioned the word "bankruptcy," GM's sales erosion continued and more of its dealers were pushed to the brink of extinction. Traffic had slowed dramatically at GM stores over the last three months since the pundits came out of the woodwork (after the hearings in Washington, D.C.) touting the "B" word as a safe and sane option for GM, and the media cacophony in favor of the idea had only grown in intensity since.

Now that the president and his Auto Industry Task Force have touted the concept of bankruptcy for GM as an idea not only worth considering, but one that actually has myriad merits, it has framed the discussion and skewed the attitude of the entire country against the company. And Fritz Henderson's embrace of the word as a talking point—to show that he's aligned with the president's thinking on the subject—hasn't really helped, either. After all, if the new CEO at GM is talking about bankruptcy as a viable alternative scenario, then it must have a chance of actually unfolding that way, right?

The problem is that just the hint of the "B" word and the media's unrelenting obsession with it has tainted the American consumer's already extremely negative perceptions toward American cars, *especially* GM. And not just the "damaged" or expendable brands like Saturn, Hummer, and Saab, either. No, GM's *entire* product lineup, including some of the best and most competitive products on the market today— exactly the kinds of products GM needs to succeed—has been tainted by the talk of bankruptcy.

People who have been arguing vehemently all along that bankruptcy is the best scenario for GM and that it would have no effect on consumer attitudes toward the company or its products have been proven emphatically wrong over the last few months, as GM's sales continue to tank. When the American consumer hears the constant din of bankruptcy talk in the media and from the president's own Auto Industry Task Force, why wouldn't the idea begin to sink in? And why wouldn't sales continue to erode at an alarming rate? And why wouldn't the American consumer begin to wonder about spending money with GM, or at least wait for the fire-sale deals that are sure to be just around the corner if they just hold on long enough?

Some would argue that our Supreme Green Leader's "vision" for a newly sanitized and streamlined American auto industry, one that would only build "acceptable" products—of course whether American consumers would find them acceptable or not is another notion entirely—is behind this administration's headlong rush into bankruptcy for GM. That the president would then get his wish to create a Shiny,

Happy auto industry churning out Shiny, Happy green-tinged Smiley Cars that the American public would have absolutely zero interest in is certainly one scenario that has crossed more than a few observers' minds (mine included).

I hate to break it to the president, our touchy-feely friends out in California, and the anti-car, anti-Detroit "intelligentsia" in the national media, but short of a national energy policy—a concept that Washington has been resolutely unable to embrace for decades—which would set gasoline pump prices at a higher plateau in order to gradually wean American drivers away from high-consumption transportation choices, then Americans don't buy Shiny, Happy green-tinged Smiley Cars. Instead, they buy cars and trucks that, remarkably enough, fit their needs as they see it. And there's no amount of cajoling and arm-twisting from Washington, or Sacramento, or from the *New York Times* that is going to change that.

The problem with the president's idea for a new "green" American automobile industry is that his view is woefully short on reality (big surprise) because he and his esteemed minions are talking about an auto future that is a half a decade or more down the road, *at best*. And when, how, and *if* he gets this country to the Emerald Green City at the end of the Yellow Brick Road, he will leave a legacy of bankruptcies, regional depressions, and a devastated industrial heartland in his wake because of his naïveté and his steadfast refusal to wallow in the facts long enough to understand what's actually achievable, as opposed to what's on a wish list.

The more immediate problem for President Obama, and the one that he and his group-hugging, corporate-law-bending, reality-flaunting acolytes should be concerning themselves with? If Americans don't start buying cars in the very near future there won't be an American auto industry to re-create, no matter how wonderfully amazing his emerald green–colored glasses are.

If the president wants to do this industry and America's industrial heartland a huge favor, he should suspend his defeatist, "bankruptcy will make it all better" plan for the imminent destruction and fanciful rebirth from the ashes of a business that he and his followers know absolutely nothing about, and instead figure out a way he can actually *help* an industry that desperately needs it.

He can continue his negative, Defeatist-in-Chief posture, or he can be truly productive and become the Salesman-in-Chief while touting America's competitive products every chance he gets.

Rather than giving American consumers more reasons to walk away from Detroit and the domestic automobile industry, he should be giving American consumers concrete reasons to buy, *right now*.

It would be a start, at least, and it would certainly be more productive than having to listen to yet another reason why bankruptcy is the only solution for this mess.

What's it going to be, Mr. President?

Part Five

A Yellow Brick Road
to Nowhere

Chapter 36

Turn out the lights, the party's over for the "old" General Motors

The article that appeared in the New York Times *that April was telling in that it reported how the product presenters working the display stands for GM and Chrysler were being heckled and harassed by showgoers at the New York Auto Show because the two companies had received government money and were asking for more. One female show attendee even accused GM of being responsible for the death of American soldiers in Iraq, according to the* Times, *because "if GM made more fuel-efficient cars, the country would not need so much oil, and if the country did not need oil, United States troops would never have invaded." Yes, it was getting uglier by the minute.*

IT'S CLEAR TO ME THAT the constant din of negativity that has swallowed these two companies whole since the end of last year has effectively killed their futures (although as I've said repeatedly, Chrysler didn't really have one to begin with). And that, combined with President Obama and his auto team's telegraphing of bankruptcy for these two companies—while pounding the notion into American consumers' heads that these two corporate entities would be better off euthanized so that they can emerge as healthier, better and of course greener companies—has hastened their demise.

Let's forget about Chrysler for now, because whether the Italians can convince the government that a link-up with Fiat would be just what Chrysler needs for survival is nothing but pure speculation at this point. Chrysler would still have to jettison almost two-thirds of its dealers and wring additional concessions out of the UAW and its bondholders before it has a clear shot at a future, and that's a tall order by any stretch of the imagination. And it won't happen by the deadline.

GM, on the other hand, has tremendous product on the ground and in the works, and the "good" or eminently salvageable GM—which includes Cadillac, Chevrolet, Buick, and GMC—as opposed to the "expendable" GM (Hummer, Pontiac, Saturn, and Saab) can and should be a worthwhile automotive entity for years to come.

But the fundamental question at this point is will the "good" GM get the chance, or is the American consumer consciousness so corroded about the idea of GM—*any* GM—that it's just too late?

GM is teetering on the brink of permanent "unacceptable" status with the American car-buying consumer right now. Yes, there are enlightened consumers walking around who are very aware of GM's "must consider" list: the Cadillac CTS line; the Chevrolet Malibu, Camaro, Corvette, Traverse, and Silverado; the Buick Enclave; and even some of the outstanding GMC products.

But for the majority of consumers "out there," the overriding message that has been hammered home since the end of last year is that GM is not only over, dead, and buried, it's a company with no redeeming value whatsoever and the country would be better off without it.

Even though GM's marketing and PR operatives are well aware of just how difficult a challenge this is going to be—hot products, or no—the task at hand, to get consumers to embrace whatever shape the "new" GM takes, will be monumentally daunting.

And I'm not so sure it can be done, either. A relentless cacophony of GM = Bad coverage in the media has enveloped the company in a shroud of negativity emphatically punctuated by the president of the United States getting up in front of the American public saying, for all intents and purposes, that GM was damaged goods.

I *am* sure, however, that it can't be done with the General Motors name attached to whatever this new "good" GM entity is. The GM name is that far gone. One hundred years of accomplishment and historic value to the American industrial fabric has been decimated in a matter of months. Once one of America's corporate icons, GM has now been reduced to a punch line for a running national joke, and this new car company will have to be unburdened of the GM name, pronto.

Will a name change be the magic elixir for this "good" version of GM's new automobile company? No, of course not, but it won't be the focal point of negativity, either.

The endless train wreck that the GM bankruptcy scenario has become will creak and groan right up until June 1. But after that day, the "good" automobile entity made up of the worthwhile remnants of the company formerly known as General Motors better have a new name attached to it if it's going to have the slightest of chance of survival.

Chapter 37

GM bankruptcy is a certainty. What happens next isn't

With the Obama administration's Auto Industry Task Force flexing their muscles with each passing day—they had ordered Chrysler to cut its marketing budget in half for the duration of the nine-week bankruptcy period—it was clear that lessons learned and actions undertaken by the group entrusted with executing Chrysler, I mean, uh, executing the bankruptcy for Chrysler would be enhanced and fine-tuned for the General Motors bankruptcy, which was as good as a done deal on June 1. That the task force would finally get into marketing decisions was no surprise because marketing was not only a huge expenditure for an automobile company, in many respects it was the very lifeblood of a company. But once you start messing with a car company's marketing, the "trickle down" effect is considerable, and that's why when outsiders start determining marketing spending, the wince factor grew exponentially for people in the business with a fundamental understanding of what was actually involved.

WHAT WILL THE Auto Industry Task Force learn by playing in the marketing arena? Probably not much about marketing, but there's a real good chance they'll learn some very painful lessons in "Managing an Auto Company 101."

Cut a car company's marketing budget and what happens? You reduce that company's presence in the media. Cut its presence in the media, and you directly and negatively affect its presence in the

166

market. Cut a car company's presence in the market, and you directly and negatively affect its dealers who are trying to retail cars and trucks in that market. Take actions that directly and negatively affect a car company's dealers, and you start losing sales. Start losing sales, and you start cutting back the number of vehicles being produced at the plants, translating into plants that are either running at reduced capacity or worse, idled completely. Not to mention an immediate reduction in revenue for the company.

Keeping up this train of thought and given the fact that Chrysler's plants are already idled, once a car company has idled plants or plants running at reduced capacity while in turn generating reduced revenue or, in this case, zero revenue, then it directly and negatively affects the funds available for the company's long-term product planning and reduces the kinds of competitive vehicles the company can eventually bring to market. Once that happens, then research and development funds are curtailed and the whole scenario starts feeding on itself in a swirling maelstrom of Not Good.

Everybody is still talking about how great the Fiat partnership will be for Chrysler, but no one is talking about the fact that the first Fiat likely to hit Chrysler showrooms—even *if* everything goes perfectly—is a good twenty to twenty-four months away. What, pray tell, are Chrysler dealers going to do in the meantime, besides close?

With the Obama administration's Auto Industry Task Force telegraphing what's going to happen when GM pirouettes into bankruptcy by way of the steps it's taking while handling Chrysler, the upcoming scenario for GM is a thousand shades of grim.

Once the announcement is made on June 1, plants will be idled, marketing will be drastically curtailed, suppliers will file for bankruptcy en masse, and GM's dealer body will implode. In effect, GM will go "dark" for the entire summer. What happens next isn't likely to be pretty.

As I said a few columns ago, the constant din in the media associated with both Chrysler and GM for the last six months has been the two B's: Bankruptcy and Bad. In Chrysler's case, having Fiat to lean on is its only hope, but they don't have any product to speak of for two years—except for a new Grand Cherokee—so where does that leave that enterprise, besides stalled at the side of the road?

GM *does* have some very capable and highly competitive products, however, both on the ground now and in the pipeline, but if the company goes dark this summer while the dealers who are left busy themselves moving existing inventory—at least that's the plan anyway—what, if anything, will be left of GM after months of being in bankruptcy?

The thought that a "new" GM will be able to emerge from bankruptcy, flip a switch, and start selling 2010 models on Labor Day like nothing bad ever happened is incredibly naïve at best. That a leaner, meaner company emerges from bankruptcy with just four divisions to worry about—Cadillac, Chevrolet, Buick, and GMC—is a noble plan, but that doesn't guarantee success by any stretch of the imagination.

It's easy for people to say that the "GM" moniker will be pushed to the background and that the divisional offerings will be the focus of the new company, but does anyone out there really buy into the notion that it will fly with the U.S. consumer? After months of negativity associated with GM, do you actually believe shoppers will say, "Oh, they're all fixed now, I'm good with it" when it comes time to consider a GM product?

The GM loyalist customers out there might buy into the "new" GM, but I'm afraid that's as far as it will go, even if the company *does* have some of the best products available in the market. The rest of America's car shoppers will have that negative formula of GM = Bad roiling around in their brains every time they go so far as to even *consider* a GM product.

And that's a Mount Rushmore of Not Good.

With its stock tumbling to its lowest level since the Great Depression, a GM bankruptcy filing is a certainty.

The assumption that it will emerge from bankruptcy and actually *survive* isn't, unfortunately.

Chapter 38

The darkness
before the dawn

The new national emissions limits and fuel-economy standards announced by the Obama administration that May and endorsed by environmentalists as well as both domestic and import auto companies would eventually alter the American motoring landscape permanently. The short story is that the deal accelerated by four years—to 2016—the timetable for requiring automakers to meet a fleet-wide average of 35.5 miles per gallon, which meant passenger cars must average 39 miles per gallon and light trucks 30 miles per gallon by then. To say this was a significant development was the understatement of the year, but was it a surprise? Hardly. The writing was on the wall the moment President Obama was sworn in. That the tail wagged the dog in this matter could not be disputed either. It was clear that the will of legislators with environmental agendas in several states—led by California—had prevailed over the rest of the country, and we now had mileage standards that were effectively dictated by a few. Was it right or fair? It simply didn't matter anymore. It was what it was.

THAT THE ENVIRONMENTAL FACTION in California won this war is the reality that the global automobile industry will have to deal with in order to compete in the U.S. market. Will these standards be adopted globally? That remains to be seen, but with the importance of the U.S. market diminishing in the face of the looming Chinese market, it certainly will not be an automatic. It would be wonderful if there was one global standard, but that is so far beyond comprehension and requires so much rational thought that it isn't even worth discussing at this point.

But the scope of the compromise reached *is* definitely worth talking about. This deal finally eliminates the threat of California and thirteen other following states from setting their own emissions standards, which would have sent the industry into chaos and which was fought vehemently by both domestic *and* import manufacturers alike. (Yes, even Toyota was against the patchwork quilt of standards pushed by the saintly California-led Green Posse.)

The new regulations force the Environmental Protection Agency and National Highway Traffic Safety Administration to work together to set the new tailpipe emissions limits and mileage standards for the first time—a provision that the automakers absolutely wanted and needed in order to make a deal—because it will take the states out of the emissions-regulation business, at least until this deal runs out in 2016, which is why the auto company executives were visibly represented in Washington at the announcement.

(What happens after that is anyone's guess. Chaos could resume and California-led environmentalists could demand that individual transportation options be eradicated altogether—finally becoming The Blissful State powered by a fleet of Shiny Happy, flatulence-powered balsa-wood Smiley Cars—or rational thought could reign and we might just continue moving forward on the same page and in a reasoned manner.)

But what does it mean, ultimately, for the cars and trucks we drive and the vehicle choices we will have?

First of all, the rationalizations given by the apologists in the Obama administration that the increase in costs of the extra emissions equipment will be offset by the mileage gains consumers will get is unmitigated bullshit. They insist that the $1,300 additional dollars added to vehicle emissions equipment (including the $600 already required) will be a wash. This is based on a $3.50 per gallon gasoline price. Uh, sorry, but I'm not buying it. (They also insist that these new requirements will save 1.8 billion barrels of oil and eliminate 900 million metric tons of greenhouse gases, the equivalent to removing 177 million cars and trucks off the streets and byways of America, but that's another column entirely.)

But the fact of the matter is that these new cars will be *notably* more expensive, no matter how this new technology is amortized, or how this administration's minions spin it. Pickup trucks, in particular—the vehicles still needed by the people who actually do real work in this country, by the way—will be hammered, price-wise. And the argument that over the six-year run-up to 2016 people will get used to it and it won't be such a big deal by then? We'll see about that.

Secondly, consumer choice will be curtailed. This is all part and parcel of the Green Posse's "vision" for us going forward. After all, the idea that we live in a country that is all about the freedom of choice is anathema to these zealots, and the sooner they can eliminate that evil train of thought the better we'll all be. So get ready for fewer choices, and those in need of larger or specialized vehicles or vehicles that don't fit inside the Green Window of Happiness will pay dearly for the privilege of driving what they want. That's just the new way of doing things in the good old R.S.A.—the Regulatory States of America.

Finally, the idea that these regulations will reduce our dependence on foreign oil—a noble goal, indeed, especially oil derived from hostile regions, which is just about everywhere oil is found these days—is somewhat true. But finagling CAFE standards is a dumb way of going about this, although it's certainly in keeping with the seething cauldron of regulation that this country has become.

I would have preferred a national energy policy instead—something that the Obama administration was allegedly going to give hope to—but instead we continue with a CAFE program that has been woefully ineffective and ludicrous almost from its inception, and that was made painfully obsolete with the record high gas prices of a year ago. Those stiff gas prices back in the spring and early summer of 2008 did more to get this country's mind "right" about the vehicles we drive and the choices we make than any CAFE standard during the entire existence of the CAFE program. And yet when gas prices dropped, people started drifting right back to driving larger vehicles again, to no one's surprise.

But imagine if we had a national energy policy in effect that wouldn't allow the price at the pump to fall below a certain level? This country's fleet would be transformed in no time.

That bottom line in all of this discussion is this: Do we need to use less fuel whenever possible while reducing greenhouse gas emissions, and do we—as a country—need to make smarter choices about our transportation needs?

Absolutely.

There are certainly different ways of achieving these noble intentions, but for now and the foreseeable future we're doing it this way.

I think it's very important to remember that a little perspective is a very good thing to have at this point in time. This era reminds me very much of the early '70s, when auto industry experts and auto enthusiasts alike believed that the looming switch to unleaded gasoline and the onset of even more stringent regulations would have an adverse, if not fatal, effect on the entire industry.

And make no mistake, at the beginning of that time it *was* exceedingly grim for the industry with horsepower numbers "adjusted" downward and anemic engines becoming the norm (the 165-horsepower Z28 Camaro seemed to encapsulate that era). As a matter of fact, some of the worst cars in history were built back then.

But then things progressed. The electronics revolution transformed what the industry was able to achieve with engines in terms of making them cleaner, more efficient, and, lo and behold, even more powerful, and a great new era in automobile engineering began, culminating in today's machines, which are arguably the finest cars and trucks ever built.

So is this the darkness before the dawn?

This administration is certainly hoping so, and I do too, frankly. But it's not going to be smooth, and it's not going to come easy. There will be no "finger snap" engineering miracles or breakthroughs that appear overnight, either. This will require serious long-term invest-ment, tireless work, and a realistic set of expectations from all sides of the equation.

And it's going to cost all of us who like to drive more. A *lot* more.

If you would like a sneak preview of what the mainstream American sedan of the year 2016 will look like, a machine that's eminently capable, comfortable, and remarkably efficient, a machine that is the embodiment of where these new regulations are taking us, and a machine that surprisingly enough isn't Japanese, German, Korean, or Chinese, but an American design from an American car company, take a good long look at the 2010 Ford Fusion Hybrid.

America, welcome to your driving future.

Chapter 39

Going, going, gone

It wasn't just another company, no, far from it. It was, at its peak, the mightiest corporation the world had ever known, a juggernaut among mere mortal companies and a shining beacon of American industrial strength, resolve, and leadership envied around the world. Now, General Motors, after an incredible slide to oblivion that no one could have predicted, was officially bankrupt. How we had gotten to that point had been dissected, discussed, and downloaded for years. I had founded the Autoextremist website ten years prior on the premise of telling it like it is about this industry—as someone who was both lucky enough to be around and experience GM up close and personally in its heyday and one who was also around to witness the abject futility and stupidity of the "bad" GM while mired in the marketing trenches, attempting to make a difference. All that being said, this was still a difficult column to write.

AT ITS BEST GM WAS A monolithic corporate dynamo bristling with brilliant personalities and talent so deep that its bench could have easily led the other two domestic car companies in their spare time. From the late '50s through to the late '70s, GM set the tone for the entire automotive world. It had some of the finest designers, the most gifted engineers, the most savvy marketing and salespeople, and, without question, the sharpest financial minds in the business.

GM dictated the operating cadence for the entire industry—from design to engineering and pricing to content—right down to the market segments created and even the color palette choices favored.

GM was so dominant that if it was analogous to a professional sports team it would be akin to the New York Yankees in their glory years. It didn't just win championships—it won the championship *every year*. It was so successful as a corporate entity that at one point long ago, elected officials in Washington were seriously talking about breaking up General Motors, because it had become *too* big, *too* powerful, and *too* dominant.

But the world changed, and what worked for GM in its era of dominance became woefully obsolete and untenable in a new automotive world that didn't put much stock in the past "glory days." Detroit's market share eroded right along with each new competitive entry from Europe and Asia that arrived on these shores, but GM, steadfast in its refusal to acknowledge that the world was changing dramatically around them, stuck to a game plan that was simply unworkable.

And at that point the "bad" GM took over, and we got to see the company at its worst.

GM took its eye off of the ball for the better part of two decades as its management became more and more complacent, unable to take their focus off of their painfully narrow-minded thirty-day sales reports. And when they weren't doing that, they were building— except for a very few exceptions—bland excuses for automobiles that were engineered to the lowest common denominator and that were religiously benchmarked to their competitors' *previous* generation models, so that they fell further and further behind the curve with each subsequent year.

And while lost in their own little world, pretending things would get better—and that a turnaround was "just around the corner"—an entire generation of customers who were turned off by the mundane choices and the shoddy, or better yet, *nonexistent* workmanship, combined with a relentlessly piss-poor dealer experience, simply walked away in droves, never to return.

On top of it, the timeless adage of this business—*It was, is, and always will be about the product*—somehow got lost in the shuffle, and GM and the rest of Detroit simply either forgot about that simple premise or even worse, pretended it really didn't matter anymore—while the import manufacturers handed them their lunch, month after month, quarter after quarter, and year after year.

And because of it, traditional automotive reputations were destroyed for good and new reputations were created overnight and the entire domestic automobile industry became unglued.

And even still, GM—while grappling to slow the inexorable downward spiral of its plummeting market share—clung to its hoary divisional structure despite all evidence and rational reasoning to the contrary. The classically ingrained Alfred E. Sloan concept of "a vehicle for every purse and purpose" was brilliant when GM controlled 50 percent of the U.S. market, but it was flat-out disastrous with a market share that was deteriorating with each passing year.

I wrote about GM's burden of too many models, too many divisions, and too many dealers from Day One of this publication, but it was such a fundamental part of GM's *raison d'être* that the company's paralyzed upper management and entrenched bureaucracy could never deal with it with any permanence or make even a substantive attempt at retuning its structure for a radically altered automotive landscape.

And it absolutely killed the company.

Even with this constant swirling maelstrom of negativity, there was more than a glimmer of hope for GM when former CEO Rick Wagoner hired the brilliant product guru Bob Lutz just after the turn of the century in a desperate attempt at fixing the moribund company once and for all. As I predicted, Lutz completely transformed GM's product-development function and reenergized its design staff, and he *willed* GM to greatness again. Under Lutz's tutelage a GM product renaissance began in earnest and a series of concept and production cars was unleashed that were simply some of the greatest the company had ever produced, even rivaling the very best from its illustrious history.

But in the end, it was simply too little, too late. The spike in gas prices a year ago killed off demand for large SUVs and trucks and that in turn destroyed GM's last vestige of profitability. And that, combined with the global economic meltdown last fall, put paid to any chances of GM surviving as a thriving, independent company.

And so here we are.

Despite a glittering historical legacy that will never be duplicated again, the greatest American industrial icon of the twentieth century is now flat broke and busted, a listless hulk smoldering by the side of the road.

General Motors, the once-majestic American symbol of success that in its glory days was a source of intense pride to its employees and dealers, even eliciting grudging respect from its most bitter of rivals, has been relegated to a punch line, staring at an ignominious future that has the UAW—of all things—owning 20 percent of the company and the U.S. Treasury owning as much as 70 percent of the rest.

A living, breathing corporate entity of some note may emerge from the wreckage at some point down the road—although I for one have *very* serious doubts about that—but the General Motors that once was has now officially been relegated to the history books.

An inglorious end indeed.

Chapter 40

Cash for Clunkers: A yellow brick road to nowhere

Judging by the splash of coverage at the time and the boost in car and truck sales, you would have thought that the frenzied "Cash for Clunkers" program was akin to finding a cure for all known afflictions affecting mankind and achieving world peace. Oh, if it were only that simple. Yes, it had undoubtedly made an impact. People were swarming the showrooms, dealers were happy, manufacturers were (quietly) thrilled, and politicians were shouting from the rooftops that this was exactly the kind of "for the people" stimulus program that the American economy had needed. Were there positives? Absolutely. Newer cars and trucks with better fuel economy were on our roads, local businesses were busy playing a supporting role in the execution of the program (even though the incompetence of the government-run program had been beyond laughable), and most important, a listless car market had been temporarily energized, which, except for that word "temporarily," was a really good thing. But it's that word "temporarily" that was bothering me. It had a foreboding feeling about it that could very well spell another round of trouble for this industry.

AFTER ALL OF THE *Sturm und Drang* expended over the fate of the domestic automobile industry over the last nine months, after all the talk about Detroit needing to build the kinds of vehicles "Americans want," that deliver the kind of fuel economy "America needs," after all the public thrashings of Detroit in Washington and all the taxpayer money spent, and after all of the hand-wringing about Detroit needing to focus on building great products, here we are in the midst of yet another program that focuses on "the deal" over and above everything else.

When GM jumpstarted the auto business—and the nation's economy—after 9/11 with its "Keep America Rolling" campaign, it was a boon to the industry *and* to the economic mood of the nation. And it worked well. *Too* well when it came right down to it. Invigorated by the awe-inspiring sales numbers, GM marketers adopted a strategy that would use the artificially compelling aura of "the deal" to crush its competition in the market, move the metal, and grab points of share.

But that noble gesture after 9/11 turned into a nightmare in short order. After that, when consumers thought of American cars, their thoughts turned only to the size and scope of the deal. Whether or not the products were actually desirable or not rarely entered into the equation, because for the American consumer, domestic cars and trucks had officially become commodities attached to deals, not image-enhancing conveyances attached to hopes and dreams. Those kinds of thoughts were now reserved for imported brands, except in a few instances.

And to this day America's car-buying consumers for the most part associate "the deal" with American cars, and nothing else.

Short term, yes, Cash for Clunkers is an undeniable boon. *Halle-frickin'-luja* and all that. Long term? Not so much. Because the hangover after this program could be severe, with consumers sitting on the sidelines waiting for the next sales gimmick to get them off of their couches. And if that's what the future holds for the Detroit automakers—conjuring up the next sales gimmick to generate showroom traffic—then this Yellow Brick Road paved with Cash for Clunkers is going nowhere good.

If Detroit is ever going to have a shot at long-term survival, then consumer attention must be shifted to the integrity and inherent competitive goodness of the products themselves rather than the deal. Consumers have to understand *why* vehicles like the Cadillac CTS and SRX, Chevrolet Equinox and Malibu, Ford Fusion, Flex, and Taurus, etc., etc., are worth consideration on their own merits.

And until that happens, I'm afraid that this inexorable commoditization of the domestic-sourced automobile will continue.

Chapter 41

That rumble you're hearing? It's the slow-motion train wreck unfolding in Auburn Hills

According to a report by Luca Ciferri in Automotive News, *Chrysler-Fiat executives at the Frankfurt Motor Show had hinted at a "grand" brand plan in the works for the floundering automaker and said that "the plan" would be unveiled sometime in November. That was good news, because everyone in the auto business genuinely hoped that CEO Sergio Marchionne and Co. had something up their sleeves. After all, they'd gone "dark" out in Auburn Hills—with little news emanating from the Chrysler headquarters hard by the northbound lanes of I-75—and we were all eagerly awaiting some signs of life from this new enterprise. But even so, my gut told me something different. To me it looked like Sergio Marchionne was making it up as he went along, and I sensed things were much more precarious out in Auburn Hills than anyone realized, or was willing to admit.*

WITH THE VARIOUS CHRYSLER executives talking of late, that microscopic pinpoint of light at the end of the tunnel started to reveal itself as something completely different, more like a freight train bearing down on the whole endeavor at great speed.

The most ominous statement came from Peter Fong, the former

midlevel Ford regional executive who was plucked from virtual obscurity to become Chrysler brand CEO and head of sales for all of the company's brands. Fong told *Automotive News* "We're going to have to offer a broad array of products across every one of the segments."

Uh-oh, there's that dreaded "being all things to all people" mantra rearing its ugly head again—the one that has waylaid plenty of other car companies in this business—some even having much more going for them than the "new" Chrysler does at this point in time, as a matter of fact.

So how does that, ahem, "train" of thought work, exactly? Is this the best foot forward for a company that's on life support? A company that even *with* all of Fiat's resources working overtime couldn't cover all segments in any given—and wildly optimistic—scenario in *five years* let alone in twenty-two months? Does it even make any sense at all?

I'll answer that one for you—it doesn't.

But Fong didn't stop there, oh no. Next up was his declaration that Chrysler would be taken "a notch above Lincoln, a notch above Cadillac." Again? *Really?* After all, it has taken Cadillac seven long *years* and well over $5 billion with a "b" to get to the point it occupies now. And that's just to a level of respectability, mind you, nothing more. Does Chrysler-Fiat have that kind of investment money on hand, even if they do shortcut the process by employing Fiat technology?

And besides, *Chrysler?* Let's think about that for a moment. Chrysler, the brand known more for its cool concepts at various auto shows—and the recently successful though fading 300 sedan—is suddenly going to vie with Cadillac's renewed mojo for American street cred? Not. So. Much.

And if Cadillac doesn't sit well with you as an example for whatever the reason, let's take a look at Audi. It has taken Audi *ten years* to get to the point where it's now a legitimate contender for mainstream luxury superiority over BMW, Cadillac, Lexus, and Mercedes-Benz. Ten *years*.

And yet Chrysler-Fiat is just going to snap its fingers and somehow come up with a magic formula that will shortcut the time it will take to establish the Chrysler brand as a *real* contender in the luxury segment, as opposed to a *mo-faux* pretender bristling with the usual assortment of European luxury design and engineering "cues"?

It's just notgonnahappen.com, folks. Certainly not soon enough to make a difference in Chrysler's immediate fortunes.

The rest of the Chrysler brand "plan" was hinted at, too, with Dodge becoming a "driver's" brand, complete with Michael Accavitti, the new Dodge marketing honcho, telling *Automotive News* that Dodge will go "from a middle linebacker to Lance Armstrong." Uh, okay, but where does that leave its current car status as the police interceptor brand?

The Chrysler brand team is doing at least one thing right by all accounts, and that is that they're keeping Jeep, *Jeep.* I guess one for three isn't bad in the big picture of things, especially given everything we know so far about the "new" Chrysler.

The bottom line here is that Sergio Marchionne's grand "plan" for this new Chrysler-Fiat enterprise leaves a lot to be desired by early indications. But then again there has been a surplus of delusional thinking up in Auburn Hills ever since Sergio and his troops took over, and the fact that it's apparently still running unfettered and free doesn't bode well for Chrysler at this juncture to say the least.

What does a car company like Chrysler—on the ropes and desperately needing a way out—need to focus on right now?

Build *fewer* class-competitive or, better yet, class-*leading* vehicles that will resonate with consumers rather than blanket the market with mediocrity just to be represented in a segment, for starters.

And memo to the Chrysler brain trust: Forget about what you dream to be on some idyllic planet in some galaxy far, far away and concentrate on what you can realistically accomplish over the next twenty-four to thirty-six months.

Redirecting Dodge car? You might have a legitimate shot of making progress in that direction at the *end* of that timeframe, but that's only if everything goes just perfectly. But reinventing the Chrysler brand? Three years won't even get you half the way there, so you better pump that phrase "realistically accomplish" repeatedly over the public address system just so you guys don't get caught up in the euphoria of "What if?"

It's not going to go well for you if you don't.

Oh and one more thing? Whatever you do, *don't* screw up Jeep because if you do that, crafting a "new" Fiat North America is the only thing that you'll "realistically accomplish."

Chapter 42

Et tu, Toyota?

At one point Toyota was the most dominant automotive enterprise on Earth, a monolithic juggernaut that swallowed markets whole. So dominant in fact that it could dictate the tempo of this business with impunity, right down to taking over any segment it chose to compete in with a cunning mix of marketing guile, laser-focused pricing, remarkable product content, and a rock-solid reputation for nearly flawless quality that preceded itself with legions of customers across the country. Specializing in terrifically competent but relentlessly bland machines that never offended, never broke down—and never failed to elicit yawns from the enthusiast community—this car company was nevertheless on an upward trajectory that was undeniable and unstoppable, a brash rocket soaring into the stratosphere unimpeded by capable rivals or even the whiff of real competition. Oh, how times had changed.

A FUNNY THING HAPPENED to Toyota and its overlords on their way to world domination of the automobile business. They got greedy, pure and simple. They became obsessed with surpassing GM as the No. 1 global automobile manufacturer, and in doing so they took their eye off of the proverbial ball. While they added new factories at a dizzying rate in their quest for more capacity, their heretofore unimpeachable quality ratings slipped and recalls mounted.

All of a sudden dealers that were used to being on cruise control while busily filling orders had to get back in the actual business of *selling* again, something they hadn't had to do for the better part of a decade at least.

And the final blow? In the midst of a global recession Toyota's mojo disappeared, leaving its formerly glowing image flat broke and busted by the side of the road. So much so that even the squeaky green, holier-than-thou Prius couldn't make up for the dramatic swoon in the company's rapidly declining fortunes.

And the most amazing thing about all of this? It all happened in just the last thirty months.

Toyota now finds itself scrambling in an intense effort to extricate itself from this swirling maelstrom of mediocrity that has seemingly swallowed the company whole overnight.

Akio Toyoda, the fifty-two-year-old grandson of the company's founder, has taken over a company that suffered its first operating loss in seventy years for the fiscal year ending last March. His task is huge because he not only has to get Toyota refocused and reenergized, he has to decide what Toyota will be in the future.

Will it be the benevolent Jolly Green Giant of a car company that will spread its goodness around the world like the touchy-feely, Shiny, Happy minions worshiping the sun in the TV spots for the Prius?

Or will it be the "back-to-basics" car company that returns to its roots and humbly goes about the business of restoring its reputation in the automotive world through hard work, diligence, and attention to detail?

I don't envy Mr. Toyoda, because the landscape has changed considerably for Toyota, especially here in the U.S. market. Yes, Chrysler is a nonentity and GM is still reeling from its bankruptcy hangover—despite its stellar product lineup—which should give Toyota a running start back to its leadership role here. But all of a sudden Ford is a serious player, complete with something Toyota used to take for granted, and that is big-time momentum.

Whereas, before, Toyota could just blithely count on delivering its usual gangbusters sales numbers in the U.S., now it's a real battle, and Ford is very capable of giving Toyota all it can handle, and on several market segment fronts too.

But the real obstacle standing in the way of Toyota returning to its position of dominance?

Hyundai.

The Korean manufacturer is Toyota's biggest threat in the U.S. market, hands down. Boasting the quality numbers that Toyota used to deliver on a regular basis, and a rapidly-expanding lineup of ever more impressive models, Hyundai is more than yapping at the heels of Toyota—it's about to take a nice big chomp out of its reputation and market standing.

Hyundai is the new force, while Toyota is out to recapture the magic. Hyundai bristles with new model after new model—each more impressive than the one before it—while Toyota struggles to find its sense of self once again.

Needless to say, it has been fascinating to watch as Toyota dances about the rim of mediocrity and Hyundai cranks it up.

Is Toyota going to shrivel up and shrink away from the challenge from Hyundai or anybody else? Of course not. Toyota will be a formidable player for the foreseeable future.

But there is a pronounced difference now that wasn't there before. Toyota isn't the invincible, infallible player that it once was. Everything Toyota management touches doesn't necessarily turn to gold, like the old days. As a matter of fact, Toyota has become so frighteningly ordinary that it's threatening to become—heaven forbid—just another car company, a dreaded fate previously reserved for only the most mundane and mediocre car companies that exist in the world.

Yes, Toyota, *even you* are susceptible to mediocrity and turmoil.

Even you can be caught wildly flailing away, hoping that something, *anything* sticks.

If this was a horse race, it would be easy to bet on Toyota to place or to show.

But the days of picking Toyota to win automatically are long gone.

Chapter 43

On Mystical Wizards, Marketing "Geniuses," and Blithering Idiots

There was no real let-up in the swirling maelstrom of news, conjecture, rumors, and innuendo going on those days, so it was a perfect time to take a lap around "the biz" and see what was happening, and better yet, to see if we could make any sense of it.

JOURNALISTS RECEIVED A formal invitation last week from the Chrysler Group to finally get the much-speculated lowdown on the company's plans from 2010 out to 2014 on Wednesday, November 4. Chrysler Group chairman Robert Kidder will give the welcome remarks, followed by a strategic overview from CEO Sergio Marchionne—who was finally going to come out from behind the curtain—followed by presentations from the various members of the management team. All well and good, because the growing cacophony from the media corps was starting to definitely turn from "let's wait and see what they've got" to "there's no 'there' there." Except, that is, for the little notation in the invitation that said that the session "will begin at 11:00 A.M. EST and is expected to last approximately six hours."

Huh? *Six hours?* A six-hour presentation to a group with an attention span akin to a bunch of high school seniors waiting for the last bell of the school year to ring? This is so wrong on so many levels that I can't even believe that they're going there, or actually believe it's a good thing. First of all, let's get this out right up front: There is no way that Chrysler's plans for 2010 to 2014 should take six hours to explain. They just don't have that much going on, and to believe otherwise suggests a level of looming arrogance within their management ranks that adds up to a giant bowl of Not Good.

And it's not enough to say in explanation that it's the way that Sergio likes to do it, either. Wrong. What Sergio likes at this point is not really the issue. The issue is that two-thirds of the assembled media don't give Chrysler a snowball's chance in hell of survival, and they want to know the who, what, when, where, how, and why of things. Bang. *Right now*. And that better take ninety minutes, tops.

And then the media wants what they're *really* going to the meeting for, and that is to be able to grill Sergio Marchionne without all of the filters or the flacks running interference, or the calculated PR bullshit pronouncements explaining that "it's just Sergio's way" because that's not going to cut it, and besides, the journos grew tired of that act months ago.

Memo to Chrysler: Reconsider the orchestration of your big media rollout. Get the hard details out in the first sixty to ninety minutes, and then immediately after that you better make Sergio available for ninety minutes of questioning in what will be the giant media scrum of this new century. The days of Sergio hiding behind the curtain like some Mystical Wizard of Auburn Hills are over. We're paying attention to the man behind the curtain. And he better be damn good.

And from the "Marketing Genius" file comes word that Olivier Francois, Chrysler's new marketing chief, likes to take risks and court controversy. Oh, *swell*—yet another marketing "genius" ready to weigh in on automotive advertising and make us all see the light. Francois, who is also in charge of the Chrysler Group's brand development and marketing strategies, and is the CEO of the Chrysler brand itself and head of Fiat's Lancia brand, likes to shake things up, apparently. I've got some advice for you, Olivier: Before you start shocking the world with your genius vision you better make damn sure your boss provides the substantive products to justify all of those smoke-and-mirrors ideas percolating in your head. We've been down this "Emperor's New Clothes" road before, and let's just say it's not going to be pretty if your advertising is so out front of the actual product that people begin to wonder and ask, "Why?" I'm just sayin'. . . .."

Speaking of marketing geniuses, there's much ado in this town right now because GM is shaking up its advertising agency roster, something that even the most casual of observers would acknowledge has been *long* overdue. It seems that despite Bob Lutz saying—wildly prematurely, I might add—that it wasn't the ad agencies' fault, instead suggesting that it was the poor direction they were getting from less-than-competent marketing leaders within GM 's marketing ranks, all bets are suddenly off and the agencies are all under the gun.

Why the change of heart? It may have something to do with the fact that certain individuals on the board began noticing that some of GM's ad agencies have been on the same account for *one hundred years* and started thinking that maybe the company ought to take a look at what else is out there. Or it may be the fact that a certain giant black raven whispered in Maximum Bob's ear that it's time to finally start making changes to GM's ad agencies. Or it may be because GM needs to move the needle and take risks and court controversy, just like Mr. Francois's rep. Whatever the reason, Modernista, which had the Cadillac account, has been tossed overboard in favor of a creative jump ball involving several agencies. The assignment? The new CTS Coupe launch next spring. And Campbell-Ewald, one of my advertising alma maters and the steward of the Chevrolet account for almost a century, has been put on notice that an assignment for Chevy car—the crucial "all-in" launch for the new Cruze compact—will be turned over to a jump-ball situation too.

Campbell-Ewald, unlike other agencies put in this situation of late, is going to fight for the Cruze launch, which is commendable. Some are saying that this is a precursor to C-E eventually losing all of Chevrolet car and just keeping Chevy truck. And some are suggesting that C-E will retain the nuts-and-bolts aspects of servicing Chevrolet but that *all* of the creative will be placed elsewhere. However this scenario unfolds, it's clear that it's not the rank and file of C-E that's to blame—because there *are* some tremendously talented and capable individuals at work there, I might add—but instead it's an upper-management structure that has been moribund and notoriously stagnant to its core for years. And it's finally catching up to them.

Speaking of Marketing Geniuses, Part II, the other aspect of this story is that Brent Dewar, one of Fritz Henderson's pals—they served at GM Brazil together—was brought back from GM Europe to run Chevrolet and significantly was the only divisional head to be given a VP title right off of the bat. It is said that he is the chief instigator of the Chevrolet account review, but that's not completely true, as previously noted. It is clear, however, that Dewar—a legend in his own mind and, if a contest were staged, would be hands-down winner of the GM executive least likely to engender any love for his arrogant, reactionary, and at times nonsensical behavior and rigid view of the world and his place in it—is the heir apparent to Lutz's CMO title whenever Bob is ready to hang up his spurs. And in case any of you analysts out there are paying attention, this is a *very* bad thing and at the very least should give one pause about GM's marketing future, "A.L." (After Lutz.) Needless to say, this is a developing situation that will bear watching.

And finally, from "The Blithering Idiots" file comes word that the California Air Resources Board, those blithering idiots who are absolutely relentless in their "we know what's good for you and you will do what we say and like it" attitude, are pushing a proposal for "cool cars"—but not the kind of "cool" that the average automotive enthusiast would understand, mind you, but a proposal that would limit solar energy entering vehicles beginning in 2012 (requiring new vehicles weighing 10,000 pounds or less to prevent 45 percent of the sun's total heat-producing energy from entering a vehicle by 2014, and 60 percent by 2016), which would in turn require less use of air conditioning, which would in turn reduce greenhouse gas emissions, etc., etc.

As you might imagine, this proposal is not going over too well with the auto companies, or anyone who happens to live in the real world, which at this point constitutes everywhere but Sacramento and its immediate environs (and Washington, of course). As David Shepardson reported for the *Detroit News* Washington bureau, the Association of Automobile Manufacturers—the trade association whose members include Honda, Hyundai, Nissan, Toyota, and other foreign automakers—asked the California Air Resources Board (CARB) to reconsider its plans, with association president Mike Stanton saying in a letter released yesterday that the cool cars' standards "would do exactly what we are trying to avoid: force automakers to build vehicles solely for California."

This thinking is in line with other auto manufacturers around the world, who when not putting out politically massaged letters like the one released yesterday are privately saying that the CARB is frickin' crazy, per usual.

Not that such things as name-calling or common sense ever bothered the California Air Resources Board. After all, this celestial body has operated in its own solar system for years with impunity, not really answering to anything but the dulcet tones of their own delusional thought balloons.

The same thought balloons that suggest that only *they* have the vision and wherewithal to save the United States—and the planet in its entirety for that matter—from certain environmental death. This, of course, while developing nations like China and India embrace rampant pollution at such a prodigious rate that CARB could order the citizens of California to immediately switch to Shiny, Happy pedal-powered rickshaws and it wouldn't make one iota of difference in the big picture of things.

I've said it before and I'll say it again: The strident minions at work in the government of California and their blind ardor for regulating everything that moves has done more to create the economic disaster that currently paralyzes that state than any global or localized economic calamity could have.

But until the people of the state of California start electing officials who are responsive to the needs of the people instead of delusional bureaucrats who are hopelessly in love with their own blue-sky—and relentlessly unrealistic—agendas, then this situation will continue until the whole damn state comes to a screeching halt.

Chapter 44

The UAW's true colors exposed again for all to see

Well, that was special. Just when the new "kumbaya" era of management-union cooperation looked to be actually taking hold of the domestic automobile industry after years marked by, at times, sheer lunacy and flat-out idiocy, we were once again being reminded that common sense and "big picture" thinking are two concepts that continued to escape the United Auto Workers union.

THIS WEEK, with the Ford Motor Company trying to reach a tentative agreement with the UAW on a series of concessions that would put the company on par with Chrysler and General Motors—two companies that were bailed out by the American taxpayer and that now have built-in competitive advantages over the Dearborn-based automaker that need to be addressed—the union membership is balking, insisting that they've already given too much and, besides, Ford is doing better and they don't really need the union's help.

This past Monday, over 80 percent of the rank and file voting at Ford's Sterling Axle Plant deep-sixed the proposed contract changes, a shocking result by any measure since the facility stood to gain around one hundred more jobs if the new contract terms were ratified. One hundred more jobs in a city and a region so desperate for any positive signs of life that it just boggles the mind that these relentless boneheads would even deign to think that it was even remotely a good idea to turn down such a deal.

But that wasn't all. Oh, no, it never is with the UAW. Last weekend an incredible 92 percent of the union's workers at the Ford assembly facility in Kansas City rejected the new agreement too, according to the *Detroit News*.

What has led the UAW to do an about-face on the only company that didn't take a government bailout and that is just now showing signs of palpable momentum in this market with a slew of excellent, competitive new products?

The agreement in question has the temerity to suggest that there be a freeze on wages and benefits for new hires and changes in work rules that would allow Ford more leeway in how it deploys workers in factories. Shocking, no? But the real crux of the matter is that the deal would include limits on the union's right to strike over wage and benefit increases, which would throw a monkey wrench into the union's favorite negotiating tactic—pattern bargaining. In other words, if the proposed contract is ratified, Ford workers—like GM and Chrysler's workers—would not be able to race for the picket lines if they can't reach an agreement on any increase to wages and benefits during the next round of national contract talks slated for 2011.

Wait a minute, wasn't it the rampant wage and benefit increases over the last three decades that contributed immeasurably to the domestic auto industry's demise? And yes, it took two parties to make those deals, but really? After everything that has transpired in the last year the union is *still* clinging to the notion that they actually have a dog in this hunt when it comes to getting this industry off of the ground again? That somehow, some way, when things get all back to normal again, they can go right back to the M.O. that helped bring this industry to its knees in the first place?

I've got one word for the UAW and its behavior: Reprehensible.

Remember this is the entity that for the most part escaped any serious grilling from the senators and congressman just over a year ago when the domestic auto industry leaders were taken to task—for sins both real and imagined—by a squadron of blowhards spewing their

Foghorn Leghorn–like stylings at those hearings in Washington. Lost in the shuffle of the Detroit = Bad, Imports = Good pontifications by pompous carpetbaggers like Senator Richard "There's a Reason They Call Me Dick" Shelby and others of his ilk—the UAW basically got a free pass while quietly listening as "management" was repeatedly taken to the woodshed.

It wasn't our fault, the union quietly—and not so quietly—suggested. The leaders of these companies put us—and this industry—in jeopardy, they insisted. Yes, that's right, it's never the UAW's fault for *anything*. After all, when this organization's fundamental negotiating premise for years revolved around the doctrine of less work for more pay—no matter what the cost to the companies involved or from what direction the ominous ill winds of a dramatically changing global automobile industry were blowing—why would we expect such a noble concept as accountability to suddenly become part of their mission overnight?

This week, despite the crushing realities surrounding the lingering ugliness associated with two-thirds of the U.S. domestic auto industry having to be forced into bankruptcy, despite the looming crisis facing the nation as we watch the continued erosion of our industrial base decimate this country's ability to compete in the global industrial future, and despite the fact that far too many people in this country are without jobs and desperate for help, the UAW has decided that it's time to remind everyone why its premise and purpose long ago grew out of step with the future needs and goals of this nation. That when it comes right down to it, this union would rather bring down an industry and cripple this country when it least can afford it, in order to protect their warped view of what the world should be about.

Reprehensible.

Ford is being taken to task by these pinheads in the UAW because of the most evil word in their limited vocabulary, apparently: Profitability. It's a terrible thing that the Ford Motor Company mortgaged the future of its very existence in order to survive a looming global economic downturn, according to the warped UAW mentality.

It's a terrible thing that Bill Ford, Jr., in a desperate move to save his company and his family's legacy, hired the most gifted leader to come to this industry since Alfred Sloan—Alan Mulally. It's a terrible thing that Mulally then led his troops on a mission to save the company and ensure its profitability for years to come by putting the organization's collective noses to the grindstone in order to develop new, efficient, and desirable cars and trucks that could sell on their merits alone.

And it's a terrible thing—at least according to the virulent union mentality, apparently—that because of those ahead-of-the-curve and costly sacrifices, the Ford Motor Company is just now on the verge of better-than-expected earnings, and that there's a fiber-optic pinpoint of light at the end of the tunnel. Not halcyon days by any stretch of the imagination—because Ford is still haunted by massive debt—but at least a shred of optimism can at least be seen off in the far distance.

And now that Ford has done the heavy lifting, the bottom line is that the UAW wants its cut. It wants to be "rewarded." For what, exactly, I have no clue.

UAW President Ron Gettelfinger—the so-called enlightened leader who has gotten a free ride for far too long for being a "nice" guy, but who has continuously allowed this kind of nonsensical behavior and bad attitude to fester in his union—has basically lost control. Whatever it is he's saying doesn't matter anymore. Whenever we hear the usual platitudes about "unity" and "responsibility" and that the UAW has "the best interests of this industry and this nation in mind" come out of Gettelfinger's mouth, we can all safely assume that it is—and has been—total, unmitigated bullshit.

The UAW's true colors have never, *ever* changed. It is a wildly irresponsible entity that has crippled the U.S. auto industry time and time again with its demands and its insistence on its fundamental "rights."

"Rights" to what, exactly? The "right" to continue to contribute to the erosion of America's industrial base? The "right" to put its selfish, totally unrealistic and woefully out-of-touch goals ahead of what's best for the rest of the nation? The "right" to relentlessly scoff at basic logic and the bigger picture? The "right" to shirk accountability and responsibility in order to further their whacked-out vision of a utopian future that will never happen?

The bottom line here is that the UAW has squandered every last possible opportunity to talk about its "rights." It is a misguided, malicious relic that exists in a parallel universe expressly created for the warped vision of its members, and it is simply out of touch, out of time, and out of step with the sobering realities of America's economic future.

Reprehensible, indeed.

Chapter 45

They came, they saw, they bored us to death

Okay, I must say right up front that the much-anticipated unveiling of Sergio Marchionne's five-year reinvigoration plan for the "new" Chrysler-Fiat was special. So special, in fact, that I was falling asleep twenty minutes in to it. If the organization of that death march was any indication of the kind of organizational "synergy" these guys were employing going forward, well then, watch out. Overwrought and overindulgent, it was by far the worst media event I'd been to in ten years of doing this publication. Imagine beyond-category tedious and then go sharply downward from there and you'd have at least somewhat of an inkling of what it was like. Today, the jury is still out about Marchionne and his plan.

AFTER CHRYSLER BOARD CHAIRMAN Robert Kidder kicked off things by saying a few words and then Sergio came out and gave his introduction—thankfully brief, I might add—the whole thing fell off a cliff. Imagine the wonderfully talented and engaging Ralph Gilles with a Shiny, Happy lobotomy, and you get the idea. Who knew that being all things to all hip people would constitute a "new" marketing plan? By the time he was finished, I not only didn't care about Dodge, I never wanted to hear about the brand ever again in my lifetime. Not that any of it wasn't earnest and well intentioned, but *really*, was there any real news going on here? Uh, not so much. (Okay, well maybe the seven-passenger CUV for Dodge was news, but after that, wow.) And then there was Fred Diaz. Oh my. At least Paolo Ferrero—the Fiat power-train guru—had his proverbial shit together and had a sense of humor.

How about the nuts and bolts of the new Chrysler-Fiat? Are there going to be shared technologies and synergies—and reduced costs—throughout this unified company? Yes, of course, but then again, I would certainly hope so. And are there going to be shared powertrains and vehicle architecture consolidations? If they have a snowball's chance in hell of competing in this global automobile market there better damn well be. Is there going to be quality? Well, they say there will be, and it *is* the minimal price of entry in today's automobile market, but given Chrysler's dismal quality reputation of late, it's all going to be fixed by 2010? Really? I'm all of a sudden from Missouri.

Let's talk about the real *raison d'être* for this meeting. The Fiat overlords—led by Sergio and his brain trust—had to show the world that the "new" Chrysler was going to be a revitalized player in the auto biz and that they had a Plan, enough of one to justify their existence, anyway. And on some level they achieved at least a modicum of that. But then again, there were no great revelations and no stunning, jaw-dropping, let's run through the wall *voila!* moment that made me believe that any of the hype was justified in the least. Frankly, there were enough obvious stumbles and displays of business-as-usual thinking in the presentation to give me pause—a huge pause, as a matter of fact—and I am not totally convinced that this enterprise can survive the next two to three years on manufactured hype alone.

Let's talk about those next two to three years because that's the real crux of the issue here. Chrysler dealers are damn near on life support, hoping against hope that these guys know at least enough about what they're doing to help them stay in business until the reinvented Chrysler really gets it together in 2012, 2013, 2014. And I didn't see anything today that would lead me to believe that these dealers are going to have anything close to smooth sailing.

The bottom line in all of this?

Chrysler is a car company still very much on the mat with a plan to get off it, but that's *it*. It's only a plan. The painful reality for

Chrysler is that it is far behind its domestic competitors, which means it is behind every other car company too. This in a global market that has no time for laggards and excuses. Chrysler sales numbers are pitiful, and its quality performance is flat-out inexcusable.

Chrysler has a reputation of being a perennial loser, thanks to gross mismanagement by Daimler and Cerberus compounded by a very publicly financed bankruptcy that *cannot* and *will not* be fixed overnight. Yet Sergio and his troops actually believe all of this is going to get fixed with a creative five-year plan?

I'll put it succinctly for you: *No frickin' way.*

Part Six

The End of an Era

Chapter 46

It's time for a True Believer to run GM

The rumors had started weeks before—that GM had put out feelers to replace CEO Frederick "Fritz" Henderson—so it was frankly no surprise to me when it was announced that the board had accepted his resignation. In other words, Fritz was forced out, a.k.a. fired. Throughout his career, Fritz was the quintessential company man, loyal to a fault and a specialist at being dropped into GM hotspots and doing yeomen duty as a "fixer" of GM's financial problems. But it was for exactly that reason that Fritz's tenure was destined to be short. With a new makeup of its board of directors, and with new board chairman and industry outsider "Big Ed" Whitacre demanding action, there was no way Henderson was going to survive the year. Was there a ridiculous set of expectations imposed on Henderson? Absolutely. And it was time to comment on what GM should do next.

ED WHITACRE'S PAINFULLY limited knowledge of the task at hand and general naïveté about this business was prominently displayed when he announced that he wanted to see results "in ninety days," a little less than three months ago. It was patently absurd that GM was going to see a meaningful turnaround in ninety days, and everyone in the business knew it, not the least of whom was Fritz Henderson, so when Whitacre got up and said it I winced, because it was the quintessential example of notgonnahappen.com.

But the bottom line in all of this was that Fritz Henderson was a GM "lifer" and GM wasn't going to change fast enough—or at all, frankly—under his watch. The buzz among the analysts and the media over the last few months has been that the "new" GM looked a lot like the "old" GM, and it was more than obvious that this was the case. As much as we all heard that things were "different" and that the GM "culture" had been turned upside down, the people saying it were all GM lifers, and the lingering scent of "same as it ever was" was hovering over the entire enterprise like a cloak of mediocrity.

The legendary arrogance was not only still present and accounted for—it seemed to be actually *growing*, which was absolutely astounding, given the spectrum of perilous circumstances facing the company. Where was the meaningful progress within the organization to mirror the stellar products either here or due to arrive? It was missing in action, because the reality was that legions of GM lifers were being rearranged and reassigned, but the look, feel, and *reality* of the place wasn't changing one iota.

WHAT'S NEXT?

It's clear that Whitacre and the GM board have had their fill of reading about Alan Mulally and his success with turning around Ford, and right now the marching orders to the search firm assigned the task of finding the next GM CEO are specific and they go something like this: *Get us an outsider with vision and perspective, someone with a proven track record of success in whatever industry they come from, someone who commands respect and demands—and gets—results.*

Simple, right? *Wrong.*

First of all, if they're smart, they won't move too far afield from a candidate with heavy industry experience, preferably in the automobile business, or one very similar to it, because I don't care what the intelligentsia in the business community says, the automobile business is unlike any other business in the world, and to suggest otherwise is just plain silly. Don't forget that Alan Mulally had heavy industry experience in building airplanes, and he also has an engineering background, so it's not as if he was plucked from obscurity and dropped into a business that was completely foreign to him, or that he didn't have a fundamental feel for.

The other important fact to remember about Alan Mulally is that he's a singular figure in this business, and Ford happened upon a once-in-a-lifetime leader to guide it into the future. And for GM to expect that there will be another candidate like Mulally out there in terms of talent and ability is ridiculous. Even if they identify someone who seems to have the same qualifications as Mulally on paper, that doesn't mean that the all-important intangibles of chemistry, personality, and leadership will be there too.

That you cannot predict, and that is why GM's search for an outsider is a crap shoot, at best.

But the one thing that Whitacre and the GM board are forgetting about in this situation is that the lifers and the lifer mentality run so deep inside GM and are so entrenched that even if they do manage to stumble upon a Messiah-like figure who apparently can lead them out of the wilderness, I firmly believe that the bureaucratic paralysis that has powered the "GM way" for so long has to be addressed.

As in blown to smithereens.

The legendary GM arrogance has to be dealt with at the source. That means that many of the upper-level executives and the layer of executives just below them have to be exited from the company. In other words, a rearranging of the deck chairs will *not* suffice, and a whole new management crew is needed if GM is ever going to pull out of its perpetual two-steps-forward-and-three-back operating cadence.

I've often said that the True Believers within GM—meaning the tremendously talented individuals in design, engineering, and manufacturing who have delivered outstanding products time and time again despite the corrosive GM system and against all odds—and who are some of the most capable people in this business—will be the ones who will have to lead the company out of the wilderness.

That means the people behind machines like the Corvette ZO6 and ZR1, the Cadillac CTS-V and new Cadillac CTS Coupe, the Buick Enclave, etc., etc.—outstanding products by any measure—are the ones who will bear the burden of delivering GM's future success, or failure.

As I've often said, it's all about the product, it has always been about the product, and it always will be about the product in this business. And in GM's case, the company has some of the most competitive products in this business, either here or on the way. But the systemic cancer fueled by the go-along-to-get-along mentality that's still alive and well within GM and that still fights against its progress every single day will have to be eradicated in order for these new products to shine.

GM needs to identify a candidate with a scintillating track record in this business, a product-focused True Believer with the guts and the guile to blow up the GM system and shake the company to its very foundation, while marching the company out of the wilderness of organizational mediocrity and unjustified arrogance that has dominated the company for the last thirty years.

"Big Ed" Whitacre and the GM board better do their homework and choose wisely in their search for someone to lead the company into the future.

Anything less will be unacceptable.

Chapter 47

GM's classic "two steps forward, three back" dance of mediocrity is alive and well

Some of my colleagues in the media had been quick to canonize Ed Whitacre, characterizing the new "interim" GM CEO as some sort of visionary for his latest management shake-up. And judging from what I had been reading, "Big Ed" seemed to be getting a huge pat on the back for making the most rudimentary executive moves he could have possibly made— some of which were highly suspect, at best—and for using the words "accountability" and "responsibility" and phrases like "taking risks" as examples of GM's new mantra? Please. If coming up with a new set of corporate buzzwords was all it took to get GM back on track then we could have all breathed a sigh of relief and booked that loan payback ceremony at the White House for sometime in early March.

BEFORE I GET INTO Ed Whitacre's executive moves, you're probably gathering I'm not buying "Big Ed's" act, and you'd be right. After doing some digging around Whitacre's previous executive life at AT&T, it's easy to come away with a highly unflattering portrayal of GM's "interim" CEO. First of all, the "Aw, shucks, I'm just a country boy who has a few good ideas" persona is total bullshit. In his previous executive life, Whitacre was known as an arrogant know-it-all who was never wrong, never listened to reasoned advice, and who brought absolutely nothing to the table of his own on a day-in, day-out basis. Shocking? Hardly. Anyone who thinks *The Peter Principle* isn't alive and well in corporate America today is kidding themselves.

The fact that Whitacre was plucked from semi-obscurity after a lukewarm career punctuated by abject mediocrity at AT&T to lead what was once one of America's greatest corporations out of the wilderness was not only puzzling, but immediately makes the entire "new age" GM board suspect right along with him.

Let's take a microscope to some of "Big Ed's" so-called "visionary" moves, shall we, starting with Bob Lutz's new "advisory" role. This announcement was made in preparation for Bob leaving the company at the end of this month. Lutz was originally going to leave at the end of this year but then last spring he and Fritz got to talking about what he'd like to do when he did leave, and that's when Bob mentioned that he'd like to keep his hand in product development and design, but that he'd really like to take a shot at revamping GM's marketing, which he viewed as one of the company's weakest links (he was right, of course). One thing led to another, and all of a sudden Bob was vice-chairman in charge of marketing for GM.

Bob was slated to stay in that capacity at least through the end of 2010, but it was no secret that he has become less than enchanted with developments down at the RenCen of late, so he has decided that now would be a good time to end his day-to-day involvement in this business. But Bob isn't going away by any means, so no premature career sendoffs need to be written. He will continue to advise GM on product development and design, and—seeing as I consider him to be the top product guy of the last forty years in this business—that will be a very good thing for GM, or at least it *should* be if they continue to listen to him. But remember what I said about "Big Ed's" listening skills?

And what about Susan Docherty being promoted to run all of GM's sales, marketing, and service? Yes, Docherty's young, which the media latched on to as some sort of signal that Whitacre was shaping things up in a positive direction, but upon closer review, what exactly has Docherty accomplished over her career other than just being there?

Two words for you: Not Much.

As a matter of fact, this has been the unfortunate career path for a lot of GM executives over the last thirty years. What I mean by that is that longevity in the GM system does not necessarily mean that there's a dimension of success involved, it just means that an executive has survived long enough to make it to the next level on the Big Magic Wheel of executive job assignments.

A classic example of what I'm talking about? Docherty has just benefited from the latest spin of the Wheel—and been entrusted with the toughest task in automotive marketing history—and that is to somehow break through the black cloud hovering low over the "new" GM and to gain consumer consideration for GM's excellent new vehicles through laser-focused marketing and advertising.

Really? This from the person who green-lighted the embarrassing "Take a Look at Me Now" campaign for Buick, the one that she tried to defend to Lutz when he first took over marketing and that he immediately killed? And now Docherty is going to ride herd over awarding ultra-crucial new advertising agency assignments for Cadillac (the launch of the CTS Coupe) and Chevrolet (the launch of the all-important Cruze)?

Just off the top of my head, that isn't shaping up to be a good scenario for GM.

I've said it before and I'll say it again: GM marketing has a long history of being stocked with people who have no business making these kinds of decisions. They don't get it, they've never gotten it, and they're unlikely to get it anytime soon. They lack a solid frame of reference and a measurable track record of success in the advertising/marketing game, and it shows, time and time and time again. (As if to make matters worse, Docherty's replacement named to run Buick-GMC is Michael Richards, an ex-Ford marketing guy who brings absolutely nothing to the table. I mean z-e-r-o. Talk about perpetuating the mediocrity.)

And to think that "Big Ed" and the board are entrusting the very future existence of the company—betting the whole damn rodeo on it, as a matter of fact—on the idea that somehow, some way a miracle will transpire within the GM marketing ranks and that it will all come right for once?

This is a seething cauldron of Not Good, folks.

One positive development at GM in the past week, however, was the elevation of Mark Reuss to become president of GM North America. Mark—who just completed a less than two-year stint running GM's Holden operation in Australia, and who was brought back to head engineering—will now have more of a direct say in what happens down at the RenCen, and believe me that's a *very* good thing. *If* they let Mark run, that is. The other is that Stephen J. Girsky, who's already on the GM board, will become another personal adviser to Whitacre (along with Lutz).

The positives I've mentioned are all well and good for GM, but anyone who thinks Ed Whitacre is the answer—short or long term—is sadly mistaken. You either have a feel for this business or you don't, and "Big Ed" Whitacre clearly doesn't. And there's no amount of schooling on the fly by Lutz and Girsky as to the "whys" and "wherefores" of this game that's going to make a damn bit of difference either. Certainly not in the timeframe that's required, which is like yesterday.

But the most crucial issue facing GM is the fact that a highly skeptical American consumer public is finding it hard to be impressed with GM's excellent new vehicle lineup. And until that consideration needle is moved in a dramatically positive direction, the company will literally and figuratively be nowhere.

And it's the one crucial issue that has *not* been addressed by Whitacre's changes.

Why is that do you suppose? I'll answer that one for you: 1. He doesn't have the first clue at to how to go about it, and 2. Even if he did there's no one currently in the building in the post-Lutzian era capable of taking them where they need to go.

There continues to be a massive disconnect between GM's excellent new products and the ability or, more accurately, the *inability* of the company's marketing minions to communicate their strengths in compelling fashion to an entire nation of consumers who are all of a sudden from the "Show-Me" state of Missouri.

And until this company figures it out—or somebody is brought in to figure it out for the board and "Big Ed"—then this company will continue chugging along in time-honored fashion, lost in its classic M.O.—the "two steps forward, three back" dance of mediocrity—indefinitely.

Chapter 48

Blue-sky pipe dreams with a side of whimsy, and Nancy Pelosi, too, oh my!

Ah, yes, it was another January in Detroit. As I wrote this column the temperature was 21 degrees with "light" snow (this after a particularly nasty cold snap had slammed the region with single-digit temps). No, I hadn't joined The Weather Channel during our annual year-end break, but if we were talking temperatures, I figured it would be a good time to take the temperature of the auto industry as it prepared for the first big international automobile show of the brand-new year, which fired up at Cobo Hall the following week.

THINGS ARE—HOW SHALL I SAY—*mixed* to put it mildly. There is a shred of optimism lurking about because December car sales were more upbeat than expected. In the Ford Motor Company's case, this is very much a good thing because it continues to underline the positive sales performance and palpable product momentum that the Dearborn faithful delivered all last year. And 2010 is only going to get better as Ford launches a newly energized Mustang, the Fiesta, heavily reworked Edge and Lincoln MKX crossovers, and more good stuff—a much anticipated high-performance package for the standard 305-horsepower V-6 Mustang, for instance—throughout the year. I expect "the big MO" to continue for Ford in 2010.

But speaking of those same kinda-sorta upbeat December sales numbers, they were not so great for the Government Two (GM and

Chrysler) because there was big cash money being strewn about by these companies that jiggered their results. In GM's case it meant huge sums spent on closing out its Pontiac and Saturn inventories, and they spent heavily to move the rest of their product lineup as well. So despite having one of the most competitive new product lineups in the industry, GM still has to resort to cash-money incentive marketing to keep things afloat. That will have to change if GM is ever going to get out of the gate in 2010.

As for the Sergio Marchionne–led Chrysler, reality is hitting home hard for the Auburn Hills bunch. As I've said repeatedly in this column, it's the short-term future of this company that will ultimately determine its long-term fate. Marchionne can talk all he wants about the glowing future of Chrysler for 2014 and beyond, but if the company can't survive the next twenty-four months it won't matter.

Case in point? Chrysler is playing with fire by jettisoning almost half of its inventory into fleet sales and dumping big cash on the hood for the rest of its sales gains. This is a strategy that just cannot continue if this company plans on being around in 2014.

Next week's Detroit Auto Show at Cobo Hall—oh, yes, I forgot, the *North American International Auto Show*—will, of course, be a hotbed of Green activity as well. Every automaker—both real and imagined—will have its Green goin' on in some form or fashion in order to placate the Green Horde. You can bet that everything from real, substantive efforts to blue-sky pipe dreams with a side of whimsy will be on display.

And make no mistake—the national media will be all over the Green aspect of the Detroit show, especially when Nancy Pelosi tours the show on her bike. Okay, so maybe Madame Speaker won't be touring the show on her bike, but you can bet the headlines will be heavily green-tinged surrounding her visit, even though most of the products on display will not make a damn bit of difference to the bottom lines of any of these companies anytime soon (except in the severely negative direction, of course).

As much as our newly minted auto "experts" in California and

Washington want to believe that the kind of game-changing seismic shift in our nation's transportation fleet is only a finger snap away due to electrification and the populace's mass adoption of glorified rickshaws, etc., the reality is that we're still going to be driving predominantly piston-powered vehicles for decades to come, no matter what the P. T. Barnums, er, I mean Fiskers and Teslas of the world would have you believe.

Chapter 49

A disastrous move for General Motors

The news that "Big Ed" Whitacre would shed his "interim" title and become GM's new CEO was no surprise, or at least it shouldn't have been for those in this town and this business who had been paying attention. It was clear to me from the get-go that GM's board wasn't exactly beating the bushes to find the "right" person for the job. Yes, GM's recruiter contacted several potential candidates, but there was no real effort to go after the kind of game-changer that the company so desperately needed. After all, there was only one Alan Mulally walking around, and quickly realizing that they couldn't duplicate his perfect combination of outstanding leadership ability and solid, engineering-based credentials—or lure him away from Ford—the search became internally focused, as in, "Why don't we just give 'Big Ed' a shot?"

I'VE SAID IT BEFORE and I'll say it again: Don't allow yourself to be confused or fooled by "Big Ed" Whitacre, because if you're looking for something substantive beneath the veneer of his "Aw, shucks" demeanor and carefully managed "I'm just a nice guy trying to help this country out" earnestness—the kind of something that would warrant the CEO-level credibility and gravitas he instantly expects to be anointed with in this business—well, you're going to be searching for a long, long time, because there's simply no "there" there.

If running a car company hinged on being approachable and saying all of the right things, then just about anyone could do it. And if that truly was the extent of the credentials needed, then "Big Ed" would do just fine.

Oh, if it were that easy.

But when you have a company that was once one of the icons of America's industrial fabric, one that has subsequently been forced—embarrassed and humiliated—into bankruptcy and is in the midst of clawing and scraping its way back to respectability and credibility, being approachable and a nice guy counts for exactly nothing and is the very last thing GM needs.

Carefully scroll through Whitacre's tenure at AT&T, and it won't take much to discover that he accomplished little. Sure, he went on an acquisition spree—"It's all about scale and scope" as he used to say when acquiring Baby Bells and putting them together to build the "new" AT&T, but the net-net of all of his business meanderings was a company that delivered a very mediocre financial performance. (And mediocrity was indeed bliss in this case, as Whitacre walked away from AT&T with an exit package worth around $160 million.)

Not that Whitacre's career gives him the least bit of leg up on understanding anything about the automobile business, or GM's place in it for that matter. And any analysts out there who are suggesting that there are similarities between Whitacre and Alan Mulally—because of Whitacre's "outsider" credentials—and that he is *exactly* the kind of guy GM needs right now are simply delusional.

The differences between Mulally—an engineer who was intimately involved in the intricacies of leading a multifaceted team in the mass production of highly complex machines at Boeing—and Whitacre—a corporate bureaucrat enamored with the "art of the deal"—are so pronounced that any comparisons are simply misguided and wildly inappropriate.

Combine that with the fact that Whitacre is an arrogant know-it-all who has a difficult time listening and who doesn't cotton to being corrected when wrong, and you have a recipe for disaster. After all, it is one thing for a Bob Lutz to give off more than a hint of arrogance—because he's probably forgotten more than the up-and-coming executives of the "new guard" will ever accumulate in their lifetimes—but for "Big Ed" to harbor those kinds of tendencies? Not Good.

GM's present situation cries out for a true leader. Preferably an industry veteran who has, if not direct experience in the business of designing, engineering, and building cars and trucks, a background in heavy industry. Someone who has been directly involved in the business of manufacturing real, substantive *things*. Not air. And not "deals." But making products that actually contribute to this country's manufacturing base.

This leader has to eat, sleep, and breathe the nuances of the business and understand where GM once was, how far it has fallen, and what's needed in order to get it back on track.

And this leader would do well to display a take-no-prisoners attitude and a willingness to do anything and everything in order to slap GM out of its corporate slumber, blow up all of the hoary constituencies, pull the perennially and notoriously weak marketing function up by its lapels, and finally *force* the rest of the organization to be worthy of representing the growing number of excellent products the company is bringing to market.

"Big Ed" Whitacre isn't the guy. Not even close, in fact. Armed *without* an innate understanding of this business—or even the faintest of notions as to what it's all about—Whitacre's go-along-to-get-along life up until now as a corporate bureaucrat and deal maker is simply irrelevant to the task at hand.

"Big Ed" Whitacre is simply the wrong guy at the wrong time at the wrong company. The True Believers at GM deserved better. The American taxpayers deserved better. And this business deserved better.

Chapter 50

The Toyota implosion . . . what it really means

A corporate image for a company directly involved with consumers is a very fragile thing. A savvy company can carefully cultivate and nurture an image over a period of years. It can forge an identity by exploiting its nuances and crafting its effectiveness, and it can even create an aura for itself that may or may not be completely true, but if done expertly enough can convince legions of consumer/believers that you are who you say you are. Over the past thirty-five-plus years Toyota had burnished one overriding message into consumers' minds in this country, and that message revolved around the idea that Toyota-built cars and trucks were the highest quality vehicles on the road, and that if consumers adhered to by-the-book maintenance schedules, they just did not break. Ever. And Toyota had enjoyed considerable success in this market by riding that reputation for all it was worth, as more and more consumers bought into the idea that—though bland transportation conveyances for the most part—Toyotas just wouldn't let you down. Until the events of one week in February, that is.

LAST WEEK WAS THE culmination of a series of negative events having to do with quality—or the lack of same—that has vexed Toyota for years now. There was the oiling-sludge problem in a brace of their engines. And there was the severe rust problem in Toyota pickup trucks, to the point that the spare tire carriers would simply fall out and onto the road, just to name a few of the most noteworthy examples.

But Toyota skated through these "hiccups" as they quickly and, for the most part, quietly addressed consumers' problems and moved on, escaping the harsh light of a frenzied media too busy holding the domestic manufacturers accountable for myriad transgressions, both real and imagined. For years and years, if there was ever a Toyota recall the news of it would quickly come and go, while in comparison, if there was ever a recall from a domestic manufacturer it was the top story on Internet news sites and leading the evening television news for *days*.

As I wrote about it in *The United States of Toyota*, there was a blatant bias at work in the media that fueled the notion that Toyota = Good and Detroit = Bad—not that Detroit didn't contribute to its atrocious quality reputation, because it emphatically did—and Toyota's heretofore impenetrable and unimpeachable reputation for quality could never be sullied by a few rusted pickups here and there. After all, its cars and trucks—and its reputation—were bulletproof.

That attitude also came across in spades when the executives of the Detroit Three ended up in Washington, D.C., begging for financial help at the end of '08. In those disastrous hearings it became crystal clear by the intensity of the bile spewed against the Detroit executives that the "notion" of Toyota = Good, Detroit = Bad wasn't a notion at all, but a fact that had not only burrowed into the American consumer consciousness, but into the gaping maw of the Washington political establishment as well.

Until the events of last week, that is.

Last week the automotive world as we know it became unequivocally and irrevocably altered when Toyota was forced to admit that not only did they have a severe problem with sticking accelerator pedals—or sudden unintentional acceleration incidents in their vehicles—but that they didn't really have a grasp of the scope of the issue or just how they were going to fix it, either.

Toyota plants were idled and dealers were ordered to stop selling the vehicles in question immediately as the severity of the problem blew up into the American consumer consciousness. Rental car companies removed Toyotas from their fleets. Automotive auction houses ordered an immediate cessation of all activities involving the affected Toyota models. And the media of all stripes went absolutely crazy.

After all, this just wasn't another auto company recall—no, it was the end of everything great and wonderfully righteous about a brand that had basically enjoyed a free pass with consumers and the media for years.

Don't forget that as part of Toyota's orchestrated image offensive its U.S. marketing and public relations arms had purposely gone after something that no import automaker had ever attempted to do—or even *thought* about doing, for that matter—and that was to capture the hearts and minds of the American consumer public and convince them that Toyota was indeed an American company, by any measure.

Toyota absolutely believed that they could become part of the American fabric, and they were hell-bent on doing so.

Toyota sponsored everything from local ball teams to NCAA football, PGA golf, Major League Baseball, and NFL telecasts. As a matter of fact, wherever there was a quintessentially American sporting event going on, you could bet that Toyota was present and accounted for. But Toyota's calculated largesse didn't stop there. The company also promoted high-visibility educational scholarships and charitable initiatives, while its exceedingly slick lobbying efforts laid waste to any sense of objectivity left in the halls of Congress, and particularly in the states in which they built plants.

And its jolly green, Prius-driven, holier-than-thou persona as the Greenest Entity on Earth was just the icing on its self-righteous proverbial cake, as legions of consumers and legislators bought into the fact that that not only was Toyota an American company, it was, in fact, *America's Car Company* in every possible way. (Except, of course, when it pertained to where Toyota's profits went at the end of the day. Ah, those niggling little details.)

But now, with last week's massive recall and the burgeoning fallout from it, Toyota has become something it had so desperately wanted to avoid over the last thirty-five years: *just another car company.*

Don't believe it? Up until last week Toyota had managed to stay above the fray by operating as if it was in another solar system, one not subject to the vagaries of the business or such sordid, untidy, image-killing episodes as the kinds of recalls that other auto manufacturers had to deal with. Toyota believed—and had managed to convince a great number of others, too—that it was immune from such nonsense. That it really was above all the rest.

But last week changed all of that.

In this media-intensive frenzy that we all live in today—fueled by the Internet and exponentially multiplied by social media outlets—Toyota's one-word alter ego—"quality"—was eradicated. I was going to say it became something else, but what has really happened is that there's now a void, as if the one-word descriptor that once defined Toyota has blown away with the prevailing media-driven firestorm.

This Toyota debacle isn't just another car company recall, because the "Toyota Way" that used to perfectly encapsulate the mindset behind Toyota's success has now become "Toyota Has Lost Its Way." And other than the usual assortment of company apologies and platitudes, the company doesn't have the first clue as to how it will get its mojo back.

A few years ago, when Toyota management embarked on its now disastrous (and now quaintly ludicrous) quest to become the world's largest automaker, finally dethroning GM from the top spot, little did anyone know that—consumed by its mission—it would walk away from everything it had stood for up until that point in time.

The slow but ploddingly sure Toyota method of incremental sales increases year over year, followed by a correspondingly gradual increase in capacity—while accounting for its usual high quality standards—gave way to a frenzy of plant-building and a complete abdication of what it once stood for when it came to quality.

The Toyota implosion marks a definitive shift in the American automotive landscape. After dominating the hearts and minds of the American consumer public for the better part of three decades, we are now witnessing the end of Toyota's reign over this market.

With Toyota unable to avoid the kind of national and now international scrutiny—and notoriety—that has humbled lesser companies, we will see Toyota eventually fall back from the top tier in this market, eclipsed by a host of savvy competitors led by a dramatically rejuvenated Ford and an increasingly aggressive Hyundai.

It took thirty-five years of intense focus for Toyota to get to the top of the industry in this market and around the world, but in just one week Toyota's masterfully calculated image and hallowed reputation is now in tatters, decimated by a swirling maelstrom of its own hubris and unbridled greed.

It has been a devastatingly painful lesson for Toyota.

And it will be a worthwhile case study for the rest of this industry too—as in how even the best can get caught up in their own delusions and lose focus—for decades to come.

Chapter 51

Baseball, Hot Dogs, Apple Pie, and Toyota? Not anymore

I really wasn't going to write about Toyota again so soon, figuring that I had said all that needed to be said the previous week about the situation, but it was obvious that the story of Toyota's quality implosion and subsequent image freefall wasn't going away anytime soon. Not when the vaunted Prius—the sainted darling of the Green intelligentsia—had now joined Toyota's never-ending recall list. You could almost hear the Prius acolytes in California and across the country going face down in their bowls of edamame with the news that their glorious, supposedly guilt-free machines actually weren't infallible after all. Oh, the horror. No, this story— the classic tale of a company's intransigent arrogance and unbridled hubris—was going to play out in the days, months, and years to come.

FIRST ON THE AGENDA are the hearings scheduled for today in Washington—where congressional committees stocked with lawmakers who have been courted, schmoozed, and massaged by Toyota and its lobbying efforts over the last twenty-five years—will allegedly "get to the bottom" of the Toyota recall story.

Oh really? Let's review, shall we?

In an absolutely devastating piece from the Associated Press released this past Monday and reported by Sharon Theimer (with

225

contributions by Ted Bridis, Alan Fram, and Ken Thomas) Toyota's cozy relationship with Washington politicos was documented in riveting detail.

To wit: The Senate's lead investigator is none other than West Virginia Democrat Jay Rockefeller, whose ties to the Toyota family go back to the 1960s and who was so personally involved with the site selection for Toyota's Buffalo, West Virginia, factory that he "slogged through cornfields with Toyota executives scouting locations and still mentions his role in the 1990s deal to this day," according to the AP story.

Then there's California Representative Jane Harman, who represents the district of Toyota's Torrance, California, U.S. headquarters and who serves on the House Energy and Commerce Committee, which is also investigating Toyota's recall.

It's not so much that Harman and her husband, Sidney, held at least $115,000 in Toyota stock according to her most recent financial disclosure report. It's the fact that the company to which the couple owes much of their multimillion-dollar fortune, Harman International Industries (Harman/Kardon anyone?), founded by Sidney Harman, sells vehicle audio and entertainment systems to Toyota. The two companies even teamed up on a charitable education project in 2003, according to the AP, when Sidney Harman was Harman International's executive chairman. He retired from the Harman board in December 2008.

The AP also reported, "When leading Toyota engineer David Hermance died in a 2006 plane crash in California, Rep. Harman took to the [House] floor to pay tribute, calling Hermance the 'Father of the American Prius.' 'It was David's passionate approach and commitment to the environment that helped persuade a skeptical industry and auto-buying public to appreciate the enormous potential of his work,' Harman said at the time. 'In fact, Madame Speaker, my family drives two hybrid vehicles—one in California and the other in Washington, D.C.'"

Then there's always Senate Republican leader Mitch McConnell. You remember him, right? He was one of the leading bashers of the Detroit automobile company executives when they appeared before

Congress seeking loans in December of 2008. He was the same sleazeball who appeared at the Detroit Athletic Club three years earlier with his hand out, asking GM, Ford, and Chrysler for political contributions for his reelection campaign. And yes, he's the same guy who said, "Kentucky is still reaping the rewards of its twenty-year partnership with Toyota, and we hope to continue to do so for years to come," when he spoke at the 2006 anniversary of a Toyota plant there, according to the AP. They don't call him Mitch "Whichever Way the Wind's Blowing" McConnell for nothing, I suppose.

No, political lobbying efforts are nothing new, but Toyota's lobbying effort (estimated to cost $5 million annually) is led by a squadron of Washington politicos with deep ties to senators and representatives on both sides of the aisle, the same senators and representatives who will be asking questions of Toyota on Wednesday. The same lawmakers who also represent states with Toyota factories, including Indiana, Michigan, Mississippi, Missouri, Texas, and Kentucky.

Will our representatives directly and indirectly on the Toyota dole stand up and do the right thing on Wednesday? Or will they swiftly sweep all of this recall nastiness under the rug so as to minimize embarrassment to the company and so everyone can get back to the "business" at hand?

It will be very interesting to watch how this plays out.

The bottom line here is that Toyota's American executives have calculatingly crafted a plan over the years that revolves around one unwavering premise, and that is to convince the American consumer public that Toyota is not only part of the American fabric, but that Toyota *is* in fact an American company, and that to think otherwise is simply misguided and wrong. Never mind where the profits ultimately go, Toyota's PR wranglers are quick to point out. Instead, focus on the fact that Toyota is inexorably involved in countless American charities and employs thousands of American workers at factories, dealers, and suppliers.

That's all well and good, but as I've said before, this image-wrangling business can be treacherous.

The blatant obfuscation of the seriousness and scope of the problem by Toyota's Japan-based leadership only served to exacerbate the issues involved, which in turn prevented their American counterparts from getting out in front of the story, which in turn caused countless hand-wringing and negative stories in the media, which in turn exposed customers to a side of Toyota heretofore never imagined, which in turn caused a carefully cultivated image built up over the better part of three decades to blow up literally overnight.

And now every move Toyota makes, the new TV advertising, the public mea culpas, president Akio Toyoda's announced visit to the U.S. in order to take the pulse of its employees, dealers, and customers—to *genchi-genbutsu*, which is Japanese for "go and see" and is part of "The Toyota Way" business philosophy—seems forced, disingenuous, and very, *very* late.

On this frigid February day in 2010, I can actually begin to see the media rhetoric shift away from the Toyota = Good, Detroit = Bad mantra that has dominated this market for years.

Now it's Toyota = Incompetent, Toyota = Untrustworthy, Toyota = Unsafe, or worse, Toyota = Just Plain Bad.

And here Toyota was *this* close to having American consumers actually believing that it was as American as Baseball, Hot Dogs, and Apple Pie.

Not so much. Not anymore.

Chapter 52

Oh, Toyota's got trouble alright ... Trouble with a capital "T"

It would have been very easy to pile on Toyota at that point, because it had certainly brought most—if not all—of its current problems upon itself. Though I had been an ardent and vociferous critic of Toyota in the past because of its relentlessly bland transportation appliances; its borderline sick obsession with foisting itself off as an American car company while attempting to weasel its way into the American fabric at every opportunity; its smug air of superiority while coldly and calculatingly courting the Green intelligentsia—and their patron saint, Tom Friedman—in order to be viewed as the environmental savior that will solve all of our problems if only we—as a nation—would just acquiesce and hand over the keys to the American market; the blatant manipulation of the Washington political establishment through a shrewd series of lobbying maneuvers that go well beyond the pale, even by D.C. standards, in terms of the depth and breadth of its efforts; and its home government's willful manipulation of its currency to help Toyota exploit every advantage while competing in this market—just to name a few things that stick in my craw—it was clear to me that the Washington ass-whipping that week was eerily similar to the one that took place in December 2008, when the top executives of the then Detroit Three were called on the carpet for a plethora of sins, both real and imagined.

NOW THAT TOYOTA finds itself caught in this swirling maelstrom of out-of-control Washington, D.C.–fueled hysteria—which admittedly has been compounded by its own hubris, bad or non-decisions, and its failure to get out in front of this image-wrangling thing—I feel almost the same way I did back when the Detroit executives were hammered, pummeled, humiliated, and generally dumped upon by a posse of wimps and twerps masquerading as our country's Best and Brightest.

To say that Washington politicos thrive on the circus of it all above absolutely everything else—including objectivity, facts, etc.,—is stating the obvious. When they comfortably operate, connive, and cajole in the relative obscurity of their own friendly confines, I imagine it's real nice to get out in front of "the people" and flex their muscles now and again. After all, when the majority of your waking hours are devoted to justifying your existence, how could you possibly let the intoxicating opportunity for some good old-fashioned, self-righteous chest-thumping pass you by? Especially when it comes at the expense of corporate America, er, Japan?

The Washington political establishment is frighteningly aligned with the mentality that drives the geniuses down in Daytona Beach who rule over NASCAR, as in, it's all about "The Show." Start with some controversy, mix in some pathos, work the David (the "little people") vs. Goliath (the "evil" corporate empire) angle, and *voila!* Ladies and gents, you've got yourself a show!

I am reminded of Robert Preston's brilliant portrayal of Professor Harold Hill in *The Music Man*, when he exhorts the townsfolk of River City about the trouble that's about to befall them if they let their young people hang out in a pool hall:

> *Ya got trouble, Right here in River City!*
> *With a capital "T"*
> *And that rhymes with "P"*
> *And that stands for Pool.*
> *We've surely got trouble!*
> *Right here in River City!*

Remember the Maine, *Plymouth Rock and the Golden Rule!*
Oh, we've got trouble.
We're in terrible, terrible trouble.

Toyota has trouble alright, with a capital "T" and that means
that a lot of ill-qualified hacks in Washington are going to step up
to the microphone and expound on all the things they *don't* know, or
understand, or even have the faintest of clues as to what they're talking
about, for that matter.

But the grandstanding and public hand-wringing in Washington is not going to solve anything. Not even close. Oh, it will help our
attention-starved politicians get their TV on, but that's about it.

The harsh reality for Toyota is that it went too far overboard in
striving to become the biggest, baddest car company on Earth. And
in the course of their quest they literally abandoned damn near everything that got them to the point of being a true corporate juggernaut
to begin with.

"The Toyota Way"? It went right out the window as soon as they
started planning new assembly facilities at the same time they were
still finishing plants that weren't even up and running yet. The "old"
Toyota would never do that. The old Toyota would take their sweet
time in making sure that a new facility was every bit as focused and
dialed-in as their best facilities. If it wasn't, it simply didn't open until
it was.

But the "new" Toyota started skipping steps and compressing
timelines. And the details started slipping through the cracks.
People—engineers, managers, manufacturing types—were schooled
in The Toyota Way, but in the company's breakneck, accelerated pace
to eclipse GM as the world's largest automaker it didn't sink in. There
simply wasn't enough time to let it sink in either.

Communication broke down, both internally in Japan and
externally to the troops in the U.S. The Toyota Way wasn't the focus
of the organization any longer. Classic Toyota descriptors such as
"quality," "reliability," and "durability" were replaced with words like

"units," "volume," "production plan acceleration," and "domination" of markets.

Pretty soon the citizens of the new Toyota outnumbered the experienced and historically reverent citizens of old Toyota, and the whole thing veered off track in a horrendous train wreck now being picked over by our illustrious representatives in Washington.

Yes, Toyota brought this down upon itself. They made mistakes, and then they made *more* mistakes when they compounded their *original* mistakes by their calculated obfuscation, their corporate insularity—their utter lack of understanding and grasp of this image "thing" as it applies to the media-saturated U.S. market and how their stonewalling PR tactic wasn't a tactic at all but a self-destructive act of dumping fuel on the fire—and finally their almost manic unwillingness to realize that the vacuum they are comfortable operating in isn't necessarily one that will fly in the wider world.

Does Toyota have a problem with their electrical systems? I don't even pretend to know. But it's too bad that no one, and I mean *no one*, in Washington—whether they are senators, congresspeople, self-proclaimed "expert" witnesses, or anyone else for that matter—can admit that they don't know either.

And all the table-pounding, strident "yes" or "no" questions, mealy-mouthed soliloquies, teary storytelling, blatant political pontificating, and nonsensical mutterings aren't going to get us any closer to finding out, either.

Oh, Toyota's got trouble alright . . . Trouble with a capital "T."

But a witch hunt is a witch hunt, in any language.

Chapter 53

Time keeps ticking, ticking away for America's "forgotten" car company

By now we had seen the sale results for February—with Ford up a stunning 43 percent—its fifth straight monthly sales increase and the first time since 1998 that it had eclipsed GM in a month of sales action. And Subaru was up a whopping 38 percent, Nissan up a strong 29 percent, BMW up 14 percent, Honda up 13 percent, GM up 11.5 percent, Jaguar Land Rover up 11 percent, Hyundai Kia Automotive Group up 10 percent, and Toyota—in the midst of the recall crisis—down just 9 percent, an impressive performance given the fact that they were the whipping boys du jour. And the majority of those numbers were easy to explain. Ford's momentum was growing by the month, and consumers who were turning away from Toyota were giving serious consideration to Ford first, and it showed. But Ford's upward trajectory was not confined to disgruntled Toyota intenders, because its market reach was spreading wide across all spectrums. GM's product offensive began to register with consumers too—although these numbers were heavily influenced by sales to fleet—but there was room for a shred of optimism down at the RenCen. Subaru continued its meteoric performance, while Hyundai Kia impressed again. Even Nissan showed signs of real life. But then there was Chrysler.

WITH SALES FLATLINING in February—Chrysler says its sales were up 1 percent, but for all intents and purposes they were flat even against a year ago—Chrysler is stalled in the market *again*. But then it has been mired in this perpetual state ever since it emerged from bankruptcy. Chrysler is in a holding pattern, treading water as it struggles to stay afloat in a sea of much more formidable competitors. Adding to its woes, Chrysler has sunk to the bottom in the *Consumer Reports* 2010 Automaker Report Cards rankings.

Even though I've applauded Chrysler for coming out swinging with cleverly written ads for its Dodge Charger (the work even provoked a searing female-oriented rejoinder that's a hit on YouTube), it's clear that time is running short for the gang in Auburn Hills.

I've written repeatedly that despite Sergio Marchionne's track record in rescuing Fiat, the Chrysler situation is dramatically different, and to assume that because he did it once he can do it again is wildly optimistic and woefully off-base, because it's impossible to overcome years of product neglect with a finger snap and a curt "We know what we're doing" dismissal of the facts.

And the facts are these:

1. We're talking about a company desperately bereft of new product, thanks to the almost criminal malfeasance of Cerberus—the bloodsucking greed posse that gutted the company and left it for dead—and the previous Daimler-led regime, which pulled up stakes on their investment after they realized they had embarrassingly overpaid by a bunch, leaving Chrysler flat busted and broke by the side of the road. Now Chrysler is on the outside looking in with an array of shockingly "yestertech" products in a market that even in these depressed times remains driven by the "buzz" about the latest and greatest new products available.

2. Chrysler cannot play in this new "product buzz" arena, at least not yet. Why? Because they're busy running around tweaking and fixing products that never resonated with the consumer to begin with. Yes, the new Jeep Grand Cherokee with its all-new Pentastar V-6 should be ex-

cellent, but we're talking midsummer for any sort of in-dealer stock. And the new Charger and Chrysler 300 makeovers should be worth considering, too, but they're slated for the late fourth quarter, which means, in reality, next January at the earliest. But trying to resurrect the Sebring with new front and rear clips, some suspension tweaks, and a new name? A new *name*? Really? You mean a change in zip code might help that rolling monument to mediocrity? Should we expect another Florida-themed name this time? Something like the "Tampa" or the "Boca"? Yeah, that should make a *huge* difference in the outcome of things.

And there's more. Maybe I missed the memo somewhere along the way, but is there really a crying need for a large Dodge Durango crossover based on the new Cherokee? How about no? Or similar tweaks to the Dodge Avenger like what's being done to the abomination formerly known as the Sebring? Ugh. There's always the minivan franchise at least, and we're being promised dramatically different styling on the Chrysler Town & Country, to differentiate it from the Dodge Grand Caravan, so there's that. And Ram Trucks, of course . . . ..

But the reality in this situation is that the huge gap in time between its "new" and "reinvigorated" products, combined with the dismal day-to-day sales performance—or lack of same—of the current products, is not working in Chrysler's favor.

Product cadence is the new mantra in this business, and you either have it or you don't. And Chrysler doesn't have a lick of it right now. A bunch of redos and a few serious product makeovers all crashing into the market by the first quarter of 2011 does not constitute product cadence. Not even close, as a matter of fact.

And to those who would suggest that it will all work out, that all of Chrysler's frantic moves now will set the table nicely for the great Chrysler-Fiat product renaissance coming in 2012, I'm not buying it, because it looks to me more like a slow-motion train wreck that's unfolding with one sickening thud after another.

3. On top of Chrysler's myriad product program problems, the other ugly reality for Chrysler is that it has almost completely fallen

off of the American consumer public's radar screen. Of the two post-bankruptcy companies, GM is just barely scratching the surface with its herky-jerky marketing efforts, but at least it can be argued that its products are finally gaining recognition for being at least in the game, whereas before, only minimal consumer consideration would have been expected.

But Chrysler? Even with a few catchy ads popping up, it's barely moving the needle in this market. Serious consumer consideration? It's nowhere to be found, certainly not with any momentum behind it. The only thing keeping the whole enterprise afloat for Chrysler—at least for now—is the deal. Rebates and incentives, and lots and lots of 'em, too. But that, of course, isn't a marketing strategy—it's only a desperation ploy to tread water. And the incentives aren't going to make a damn bit of difference once Toyota cranks up its scorched-earth sales push that began today, ironically enough.

No, right now Chrysler is America's forgotten car company, with products too old and too stale to make a difference in its short-term future, and product promises that are *way* too far down the road to matter, especially with an economy that's slowly, make that *excruciatingly* s-l-o-w-l-y, getting back on its feet.

Time keeps ticking, ticking away for Chrysler, and at this point Sergio & Co. are going to need a miracle for a shot at survival.

Chapter 54

The End of an Era: The Ultimate Car Guy takes his leave

The news came over the Internet that Monday morning like a bolt of lightning. Bob Lutz, GM's vice-chairman of global product development, was retiring at the end of the year. Lutz, who had turned seventy-seven on February 12, was the straw that stirred the drink for GM and the man most responsible for GM's product renaissance over the previous seven-plus years. Lutz had dropped hints all along that the debut of the production Chevrolet Volt—due at the end of 2010—would be his crowning achievement in this business, so the suddenness of the news reverberated around this town and throughout the industry, coming much sooner than anyone had expected. I had gotten to know Bob quite well over the years. I had first worked with him in the mid-'80s when he was one of the top executives at Chrysler and I was the executive creative director on the Dodge advertising account for BBDO Detroit. I used to relish presenting our creative work in the boardroom through the cigar smoke generated by Lutz, Lee Iacocca, and others, and even though Bob took umbrage with some of my casting choices for the various commercials, we seemed to always have a good rapport. Bob and I really gelled when he was about to return to the business at GM and he admitted to me that he read all of my columns to date so he could "get my head back in the game," as he told me. We kept in pretty close touch during his tenure at GM, and he quoted from my columns frequently in his meetings, to great effect, from what I understand. Lutz was one of a kind, and it was not only a privilege for me to know him, it was a privilege to say I had worked with someone whom I consider to be one of the greatest industry executives in automotive history.

FROM THE DAY HE WAS HIRED by CEO Rick Wagoner back on September 1, 2001, Lutz set GM on its ear and turned it back into a real car company again after it had languished in Brand Management Hell for years. Up until the Lutzian Era, GM had been at the mercy of an endless succession of so-called marketing gurus led by John Smale and his acolyte Ron Zarrella, two guys who contributed immeasurably to GM's product and market share slide, almost running the company right into the ground. But all that changed when "Maximum Bob" arrived. For the first time since Ed Cole retired in the early 70s, the Product was well and truly King again at General Motors.

Rick Wagoner deserves all the credit for having the smarts to know back then what GM needed. After decades of fumbling and floundering, after dealing with various Messiahs of The Week who turned out to be the Bums of the Year, after countless bad decisions on top of non-decisions, and after suffering from years upon years of non-car mercenaries running rampant over the corporation for their own personal gain, GM finally got one very big thing right when they brought Bob Lutz on board.

This is what I wrote back in 2001 upon the news that Lutz was coming to GM:

> *For the True Believers at General Motors who thought this day would never come, the "Bob Lutz Effect" will be nothing short of a miracle. Make no mistake about this fact: GM still has a lot of very talented men and women toiling away inside its halls. They're everywhere too—in every department and from every discipline. These are the kind of people who fight for every last inch of product integrity. These*

are the people who have had to watch in recent years while the good ideas got sidetracked or killed, and the mediocre or just plain bad ideas got into production. These are the same people who have had to stand by and watch as non-car people basically did everything in their power to run this once-proud corporation right into the ground. Yet these same people are the ones who still bring the fight with them every single day. The same ones who have done stunning design concepts and who have managed to get some pretty respectable cars and trucks to the street—against some unbelievable odds. You stumble upon these people every once in a while at a racetrack or at car shows or at press previews, and it shocks you, because when you continuously read about the problems that plague GM at the top, you forget that these people are out there, still fighting the good fight, still being True Believers. These are the people who will benefit most from the presence of Bob Lutz. These are Maximum Bob's *people. These people can now look at the top of their company and see someone who "gets it," someone who has fought the battles and won the wars, someone who understands what they've been up against, and someone who they can finally believe in—because* he is one of them. *When Bob Lutz hits the ground running, these are the people who will be required to burn the midnight oil and do everything in double and triple time, but they will relish every moment of it because for the first time in a very, very long time they have someone at the top whom they can respect.*

Bob Lutz's first order of business when he hit the ground running at GM? To restore the swagger of the design staff. Working with Ed Welburn, GM's gifted design chief, Lutz returned GM Design to its rightful place as the showpiece for the corporation. In GM's heyday, GM Design ("Styling" back then) was the soul of the company and it rocked the automotive world with one design hit after another. But even with a rich design legacy powered by two of the most legendary figures in the business—Harley Earl and Bill Mitchell—GM Design had fallen on hard times, struggling mightily under the chokehold placed on it during the Brand Management Reign of Terror. And even though GM Design was showing signs of life a couple of years before Lutz arrived, Bob pulled the design function up by the lapels and gave them free rein to create, lead, *and* inspire—the three ingredients that propelled GM Design—and GM—to such heights in its glory days.

And it worked magnificently. All of a sudden GM Design was the talk of the industry, dominating car shows with adventurous, exuberant designs bristling with swagger and passion. And Bob Lutz, along with Ed Welburn's inspirational guidance, made it all happen.

The other crucial thing Lutz did for GM was undertake a massive reorganization of its moribund product-development system, the "behind the curtain" dimension to this business that few outside it understand, but one that is absolutely crucial to its success *and* profitability. Lutz cajoled, prodded, demanded results, and kicked some ass when he had to, and the result was that the company was able to translate GM Design's conceptual brilliance into a series of outstanding production vehicles—like the Buick Enclave, Chevrolet Malibu and HHR, Cadillac CTS and CTS-V, Saturn Aura, Pontiac Solstice, Pontiac G8, Saturn Sky, Corvette ZR1, and the briefly resurrected Pontiac GTO—while doing it on a global scale for the first time in the company's history. Lutz turned GM's old-school product-development system into a global powerhouse brimming with impressive expertise and capabilities and it simply transformed the company, a historic achievement unto itself.

I can't imagine what shape GM would be in right now if Rick Wagoner hadn't brought Bob on board seven years ago. I would venture to guess that GM might not even have made it this far without him; he has been *that* instrumental to the company's well-being.

Was Lutz able to save GM all by himself? No. Market conditions and the worst economic calamity in this nation's history conspired against him. But if GM *does* manage to survive, it will be due in large part to the absolutely superb job Lutz did during his tenure and the rich legacy of achievement and excellence he left behind.

Bob's impending exit is a serious blow to GM, make no mistake about it. He galvanized the entire company, got everyone on the same page, and forced them to aspire to greatness, at times by the sheer force of his will and personality alone. His departure not only marks the end of an era for General Motors, it marks the end of an era for this business, and, frankly, I hate to see it because Bob is truly one of a kind and we will not see the likes of him again, unfortunately.

Sadly, without Lutz this business will continue to be overrun by politically correct bean counters and slick corporate willies who have little or no feel for the product, no sense of automotive history, and even worse, no sense of humor.

Bob Lutz's accomplishments in this business are legendary, and even though there's no need (or enough space) for me to recount all of them here, suffice to say he's had one of the most glittering careers this industry has ever known.

In terms of his relentless vitality, his legendary wit, his unquestioned knowledge of the business, his passion for the product, his uncanny "gut," and his unerring feel for what the *essence* of the product is all about, Bob Lutz is simply second to none.

Having spent enough quality time with Bob over the years, I can safely say that he is, in my estimation, *the* greatest product guru of the last thirty-five years and he will leave the stage as one of this industry's all-time greats.

Part Seven

Brave New World
or same as it ever was?

Chapter 55

Clueless in the Motor City

No one could miss the headline screaming "Whitacre wants more sales—NOW!" on the top of the front page in that week's Automotive News. *And as the story attempted to flesh out Big Ed's growing impatience with the whole "sluggish sales" quandary that continued to vex GM—and the reassignment and in some cases jettisoning of sales and marketing executives—and after observing the day-to-day chaos that seemed to define GM of late, I was getting the distinct impression that Whitacre still didn't have a clue as to what he was dealing with here in the auto biz. So I thought I'd give Big Ed a few pointed reminders.*

DEAR ED:

I'm sure you've figured this out about now, but just in case you haven't, this business isn't about consolidating "Baby Bells," or fixin' to make deals, or playing phone and cable customers off against each other. And it's not about packaging cable, phone, and Internet service into tidy little bundles that people can deal with by the month, at the expense of a competitor you want to bury.

No, Ed, this business has been distilled down to the fundamental reality of trying to get people to forget twenty-five years of rampant mediocrity, when the Detroit automakers—and *especially* GM—squandered their rich, historical legacy of putting this nation on wheels, forging the Arsenal of Democracy, and becoming the shining beacon of American industrial might by unleashing a series of crappy vehicles that—except for a very few noteworthy instances—were not only stunning in their lack of imagination, originality, and vision, but were equally stunning for their horrifying lack of quality.

It was during this time, Ed, that the American consumer became painfully aware that, for the most part, the Detroit automakers really didn't give a shit about them, and when they went looking elsewhere—at the Toyotas, Hondas, BMWs, Nissans, et al of the world—in many cases they found excellent vehicles that were screwed together properly and offered good value. And for most of them that was more than enough and they never looked back.

As a matter of fact, they put the Detroit automakers entirely off of their radar screens for a generation and a half, only encountering domestic-made cars at the car-rental lots at airports or in taxicabs in big cities. It's so bad, Ed, that there are households all across the land that have *never* had a domestic-sourced vehicle in their driveway. Ever.

And given the realities of this situation, all you can bring to the table is your impatience? I know being an "outsider" can be terribly difficult, Ed. I've seen countless executives from other industries who got here before you, who not long after were either forced to leave or who left of their own volition, muttering under their breath as their planes lifted off the tarmac at Metro Airport, never to return.

Much to most outsiders' chagrin, this is the most complicated, relentlessly unforgiving, perilously difficult business on the face of the Earth. I'm sure you like to point to other industries that you consider equally difficult, but I would beg to differ. No business combines the depth and breadth of challenges that the auto business does. Why do you think so many outsiders flat-out fail and turn tail?

Not that I'm condemning all outsiders to this industry to a pile of hopeless irrelevance—after all, Alan Mulally gets it, but, then again, we know now that he's a once-in-a-lifetime executive who will go down in the one-hundred-plus-year history of this business as truly one of the all-time greats.

But saying that, where does this leave you?

I'm afraid that leaves you in the corner of the "finger snap" experts, Ed, the ones whom I have found to be *the* most loathsome over the years. The ones who show up with an attitude that suggests that this business can't possibly be all *that* complicated, right? The ones who believe that if they were stars in their chosen avocations, then why not here and why not now? The ones who actually believe—at least for a fleeting moment in time—that all of this mess can be fixed with a finger snap. Just. Like. That.

For your information, Ed, two shining examples who bristled with that attitude almost ran GM right into the ground a decade earlier. And after John Smale and Ron Zarrella—and their handpicked acolytes—got through unleashing their brand of P&G mumbo-jumbo on GM, the company was almost left for dead, a lifeless carcass festering by the side of the road.

Not that I'm equating you with those two, Ed, but you must admit the tone and tempo are eerily similar. The impression that you know better than anyone what needs to be done, discounting everyone who came before you and every painfully hard lesson learned. Believing that if you rearrange the deck chairs just so it will all come good overnight as if by magic. Or believing that the good times are just around the corner, just you wait and see.

And what if that doesn't happen, Ed? Are you just going to stomp your feet until the sales trajectory starts pointing in an upward direction? In other words, you're going to *will* it to happen? Is that it?

Well, I can safely say at this point that it doesn't work that way, Ed, and I'm getting the distinct impression that you clearly don't have a clue at to what you're talking about, no matter how many "Aw, shucks, I'm just a nice guy trying to help y'all out" platitudes you spread around.

At this point—and in case you don't realize it, we're talking desperation time here, Ed—this business is about recapturing the hearts and minds of hundreds of thousands American consumers who got let down by the "bad old days" when Detroit was at its worst.

And you're not going to do that overnight.

It's going to take people being drawn into your showrooms by the pure excellence of your vehicles, a level of excellence that can no longer be ignored by your critics, the media, or consumers on the street.

And then once you lure these consumers into your showrooms, they need to be pleasantly surprised by switched-on dealers who get it and who understand what this whole "putting the customer first" thing is all about.

And then should you be so fortunate as to have some of these consumers actually choose to drive out with an Equinox, an SRX Turbo, a Malibu, a LaCrosse, or an Enclave, etc. And over the entire time they own that vehicle absolutely nothing can go wrong with it. Not even a misaligned cupholder. Not even anything.

And during that time, if when asked by their friends and neighbors, they say nothing but good things about their vehicles, that's when the word-of-mouth "buzz" begins—still the most powerful form of advertising there is—and then you will begin to gain real traction in the market, the kind that has eluded GM for so long.

And finally, when that consumer has to consider getting a new vehicle three or four years down the road—and he or she comes back to get *another* GM vehicle—then you'll really know, Ed. Then you can safely say that GM is reaching the customer again and that the ugly past is fading away.

Again, that's not going to happen overnight, Ed. No, in fact it's going to be a l-o-n-g drawn-out slog fraught with myriad opportunities for things to go horribly wrong.

So you can throw your tantrums and snap your fingers and demand results, but I hate to break it to you, it's not going to make one damn bit of difference.

GM needs to *exceed* the competition in all respects to even get a place at the consideration table. Not just *gain* market share, mind you, Ed. There's a huge difference between the two. I hope you can see that by now.

That means it will come down to the people who know the business and understand what it takes to succeed. And that means people like Mark Reuss, Ed Welburn, and Tom Stephens leading their troops into battle with a laser focus and unwavering purpose. And that means that the "new" GM must deliver extraordinarily compelling designs, boldly remarkable engineering, surgically precise manufacturing, top levels of quality (not *among* the best, but *top*), and a flawlessly seamless dealer experience, and do so consistently day in, day out without hiccups, missteps, interruptions, or horror stories.

Anything less, Ed, and it's game over for you *and* GM.

In closing, I have a suggestion: Seeing as I don't believe you're bringing anything of value to the table other than the occasional exhortation of the troops for the "I'm large and in charge" window-dressing effect, I suggest you settle into a more suitable role as official company "greeter." You know, the guy that GM PR can trot out to functions and photo opportunities, and who can throw out the "Aw, shucks" platitudes about the "new" GM with vigor.

It's not a bad assignment when you think about it, especially with your financial package keeping you comfy and cozy, hard by the RenCen. (I mean, we know it's just play money and all to you, but it's nice to know you're covered at least.)

Because the harsh reality of the situation, Ed, is that you clearly got nothin' else to offer.

And being clueless in the Motor City has never been a good look.

Chapter 56

The One Thing I didn't want to write about this week

The auto industry had been on an endless cycle of intense Sturm und Drang for going on three tumultuous years. Churning through financial upheaval, bankruptcies, mergers, acquisitions, boneheaded maneuvers, brilliant plays, technical excellence, wild-eyed hubris, unfettered greed, and an exuberant design renaissance, I can safely say that the entire 125-plus-year roller-coaster history of the automobile business had been encapsulated and exposed for all to see in the previous thirty-six months. During that time we had seen giants fall (GM and Toyota), giants rebound (Ford), giants on hold (Chrysler-Fiat), emerging giants (Hyundai and Kia), giant new markets (China and India), and, yes, a giant bowl of Not Good for assorted movers, shakers, and players who heretofore seemed incapable of screwing things up but somehow did, and in spectacular fashion too.

SINCE OUR ISSUE DATE didn't fall on April 1 last week (much to a few readers' chagrin, I might add), I was going to do this week's column—as a stealth April Fool's "Rant"—on, well, let's see, my world-class collection of PEZ dispensers. Or how about the debut of our new website, lawnornamentextremist.com, on June 1. Or my upcoming new book: *In Praise of the Porsche Cayenne—Brilliance in a Box*.

Ah well. Maybe next year

No, just when I think I'm free of the shackles of writing about the recurring themes that have dominated this business of late, *they pull me back in.* Thus, the One Thing I didn't want to write about this week. . . ..

The hand-wringing was subsiding, the nightly hits on the national news were fading from view, the Internet frenzy had begun to wane, and the sales had not only rebounded (albeit because of its scorched-earth incentive programs), but caught fire, and BOOM, here comes the Supreme Waffler (a.k.a. Transportation Secretary Ray LaHood), telling the public yesterday that, "We now have proof that Toyota failed to live up to its legal obligations. Worse yet, they knowingly hid a dangerous defect for months from U.S. officials and did not take action to protect millions of drivers and their families." And not only that, but the feds were seeking a $16.4 million fine— the maximum—for Toyota's transgressions. Ouch, Baby. No, not for the fine—because let's face it, with a $35 billion–plus war chest, that amounts to a rounding error for Toyota—but for the "knowingly hid a dangerous defect for months from U.S. officials and did not take action to protect millions of drivers and their families" part. If nothing else, this will give the ambulance-chasing, ball-busting, sleazebags (a.k.a. the marauding trial attorneys) looking for their next score and lining up for their cut from this debacle all the ammunition they need to extract huge settlements from sympathetic juries.

But that's not all, because the touchy-feely minions (a.k.a. the typical Toyota customers who think the company can do no wrong) now have yet another sliver of doubt sticking in their craws, as in, "They didn't really know, did they? I mean, they wouldn't really do that, would they?"

And the answers to those queries are—at least according to the piranha attorneys—"Yeah, kinda" and "Uh-huh, absolutely."

(Do I think cosmic rays may have caused intermittent electronic interference sending Toyotas careening out of control? It's possible, but then again it's possible I could be named Ed Whitacre's replacement, too. No, I firmly come down on the side of gross driver error being the cause of these incidents, especially given this nation's overall level of incompetence behind the wheel.)

What have we learned about Toyota after all of this? That it's a Japanese company that started out being in love with building cars and trucks with exceptional levels of consistent quality—and little else— that grew into an emerging global industrial juggernaut. But along with that unbridled success came a virulent strain of hubris that infected legions of new-wave executives who didn't much care for the Toyoda legacy, but instead cared more about making their personal marks on the company and the business itself. And with that new breed of executive fueling its global ambitions to be the biggest, baddest car company in the world, Toyota became careless and supremely arrogant. And the mistakes cascaded from there.

"The Toyota Way" was jettisoned in favor of "Toyota Right Now," and the Japanese government—Japan, Inc.—willingly went along by giving Toyota everything they needed in terms of jiggering their currency to extract the maximum profits from the markets they competed in, especially here in the U.S.

And the rest, as they say, is history. Except that in this case history is going to be played out for Toyota in courtrooms all across America for many, *many* years to come. Oh, and that hefty war chest? Let's just say that Toyota will need a big chunk of it to weather the upcoming storms headed its way.

As I said weeks ago (echoed by "Maximum Bob" Lutz in New York last week), Toyota is no longer on its own pedestal, safely ensconced above the mere mortal car companies that have to fight and claw and scramble for every scrap of business they can cling to.

No, Toyota is now the one thing it never wanted to be—*just another car company*, lost in the swirling maelstrom of chaos that has come to define the automobile business here in North America.

Chapter 57

It's time to take the "alternative" out of our energy development

The pictures from the Gulf of Mexico were relentlessly depressing and beyond sad—for lack of a better word—and they'd continue to get even grimmer as each day passed. And as the disaster in the gulf unfolded, I feared it would not only send our southern coastal states directly affected by it into a lingering, decade-long, depression-like tailspin, I argued that it would fundamentally alter this country's perception of our dependence on oil forever. This column wasn't about laying blame at the doorstep of those responsible for what had happened in the gulf, because there was plenty of that going around as it was. No, it was about hammering home what should have been the final realization for this country, its citizenry, and its leaders, and that realization was that our dependence on oil—foreign and otherwise—needed to be dramatically reduced, if not outright eradicated, and much sooner rather than later.

THIS NATION NEEDS to get serious about alternative fuels and alternative sources of energy, and in a hurry. It does absolutely no good to be outraged about what's happening in the gulf if we—as a country—are unwilling to do something about it.

And what does "doing something about it" entail, exactly? There are companies and individuals striving to make a difference all over this country, feverishly hard at work at turning waste of all types into fuel.

253

From farmers turning cow manure into a dependable, accessible source of fuel to support power grids, all the way to the legions of talented and inventive people—the best and brightest this country has to offer—working on real-world, workable solutions that will turn waste of all kinds into cellulosic ethanol that can be created, transported, and delivered to our existing fueling stations at a competitive price.

There is alternative-fuel research and technology of all kinds out there that is being exploited and explored as you read this, and we just may be on the verge of a breakthrough, *if we're willing to devote this country's considerable resources to it.*

None of these solutions, of course, will come cheap or easy, and I have no doubt that the transition will be painful in a lot of ways and for a lot of people. But this country needs to wake up, and I believe that this looming disaster in the Gulf of Mexico just may be the final kick in our collective asses to get us off of our seats so that we can demand a fundamental shift in the way we power our nation's fleet.

Everywhere I go these days I'm hearing things like "I'm disgusted" or "It's just outrageous," and the sense of helplessness and hopelessness is growing about what's going on in the gulf. But you can be sure it doesn't come close to the outrage and despair hovering over the people of Louisiana and the other affected coastal areas.

If you've never been there then you have no idea what this horrific disaster means. It's one thing to read the paper or the Internet, or watch the television newscasts, but it's quite a different story if you live down there, or in an instant find out your livelihood is at stake. And remember, we're not just talking about a momentary hardship of a lost summer fishing season, either. We're talking about a fundamental, life-altering event that will destroy a way of life down there for a better part of a *decade* or longer.

None of us in this country should be saying "It's sad, but it doesn't affect me," either. This unmitigated disaster will affect all of us, and in ways we can't even imagine yet. And needless to say, none of them will be good by any stretch of the imagination.

As far as I'm concerned, the Gulf of Mexico disaster should be the final straw. No, check that. It should be the final sledgehammer in our collective foreheads, the one that we've needed for a long, *long* time.

There are better solutions out there and I believe this nation is talented enough and creative enough to find them and make them work. Because depending on hostile regimes and woefully precarious drilling operations for our future energy needs—as we've come to find out—is a recipe for disaster.

Thanks to this devastating crisis in the gulf, I believe we've finally reached a turning point.

We have finally come to the realization that alternative energy can't be "alternative" anymore.

Chapter 58

Still clueless after all these years

Even though we'd had a spate of spectacular warm weather of late, I offered as to how our readers should just be glad they weren't around here this week. Why? Because we had to endure something called the "Constitutional Convention" of the United Auto Workers that took place down at the Cobo Center. And that meant we'd been subjected to all of the hot air generated by the attendees and their so-called "leadership," with our local media dutifully reporting every nonsensical utterance. Not that our local media had much of a choice. After all, this is the one state in the country that had been subjected to—no, make that held hostage by—the union movement to the detriment of everything else, so if our local media mavens decided to let the UAW twist in the wind—as befitting the most ineffectual and out-of-touch entity of its kind in the world—then the long knives would come out and the emboldened hordes of the UAW would unleash their considerable bombastic fury on the local journalistic establishment for all to witness.

DETROIT, OF COURSE, is unfortunately the perfect environment for something called the UAW "Constitutional Convention," because, after all, this is the epicenter of the union movement in America, the one place in the country where the unions have been allowed to flourish unfettered and virtually unimpeded for decades.

Ever since long-ago Mayor Coleman A. Young planted his jaundiced flag in the heart of the city's government and slowly and systematically removed the last shred of common sense when it came to rational governance and replaced it with a virulently insidious strain of entitlement compounded by a level of self-righteous "What's in it for me?" that still knows no bounds within the city limits, no matter how hard the current Mayor Dave Bing tries to rectify it. And ever since, the city of Detroit has been stumbling about in a perpetual state of mediocrity, paralyzed by its own willful intransigence and slowly but surely grinding itself into smithereens.

So we've had to put up with every sound bite—each one sounding more outrageous and ridiculous than the one before—and wade through countless headlines and the endless streams of misplaced rhetoric, just so Ron Gettelfinger—the outgoing president of the UAW—can hand over the reins of power to UAW vice-president Bob King, yet another in a long line of overhyped and overblown "statesmen" to come out of the UAW whose sole contribution to societal discourse has been to consistently and relentlessly redefine the term "intractable."

The gist of the convention—just so I can spare you the more outrageously infuriating details—is that the UAW is out to reclaim all of the concessions it was forced to make in order to keep the domestic automobile industry from totally imploding, so that they can get back to the way things used to be, like none of the *Sturm und Drang* of the last twenty-four months ever happened.

Really?

With Chrysler still very much in limbo, Ford finally just now righting itself after years of teetering on the brink, and GM still reaching for every positive development it can latch onto while it continues to claw its way out of the most humiliating corporate bankruptcy in American industrial history, the UAW is now ready—make that *expecting*—to have everything returned back to "the way it used to be" so that they can go back to getting "theirs"?

Yes, *really*.

How appalling has this display been down at Cobo? They even enlisted the president of the AFL-CIO, a guy by the name of Richard

Trumka, to come on down and add his two cents to the proceedings, which he willingly obliged by spouting, "The three major U.S. companies are making profits again. We salute their success and we demand that they do right by the workers who have done right by them. Just as there has been shared sacrifice in periods of pain, there must be shared prosperity in periods of gain."

Huh? Not that I'd expect any union leader to be encumbered with the facts by any means, but in case anybody bothered to look beyond the somewhat rosy headlines dealing with the state of the domestic automobile industry of late, they'd find that none of these car companies—*including* Ford—are anywhere near being out of the woods yet. Not even close, in fact.

The bottom line is that the domestic automobile industry is still on the brink. Yes, there are real signs of optimism if you can learn to decipher the tea leaves properly, but make no mistake, the "recovery"—no matter which way, shape, or form it takes—is going to be excruciatingly s-l-o-w. There will be no finger snaps resulting in "happy days are here again" profitability, and there is never going to be a domestic automobile industry that even *approaches* what it once was at its peak. It's just notgonnahappen.com.

So into this somber reality marches the lame-brained leadership—old and new—of the UAW. In his farewell speech to the conference, Ron Gettelfinger exhorted his minions in the rank and file to light the fires again. Here's an excerpt:

> *Employers have always known that a union is the only instrument that gives working men and women any form of equity and justice in the workplace. Most employers have consistently and vigorously opposed unions with every means at their disposal. During and since the auto crisis they focused their smear tactics on the UAW like never before.*
>
> *Their rhetoric has become a drumbeat of anti-union chatter. It has no merit but it continues to shape and form opinions against unions. These pro-employer, anti-worker,*

anti-union forces continually attack unions and workers who want to form a union. Those they represent belong to organizations that help them to gain clout in the employer community but they prefer to have the ability to trample on workers' rights individual by individual. These anti-union forces are simply motivated by greed.

We are driven by equity and justice in the workplace, and, brothers and sisters, in the end, we will prevail.

Gettelfinger went on to say that, "Today, more than ever, we need to feel the passion of the labor movement."

Really, Ron? Passion? How about that's the very *last* thing the "movement" needs.

Instead, it would have been much better if you had performed a public service for the UAW members in attendance—and the rest of the nation for that matter—by injecting a large dose of reality into your "Constitutional Convention."

By that I mean being straight-up with what's left of your constituency by urging them to get their collective heads out of the sand and then telling them to turn off the white noise emanating from their so-called enlightened leadership—especially Bob King—because it will count for absolutely nothing going forward.

It's hard to believe that at this juncture, with everything that has transpired in the global economy and with the near-death experience of the domestic automobile industry still raw in everyone's mind, the UAW leadership is *still* clinging to hoary notions of entitlement and squawking about getting their "fair" share.

And even more outrageous to contemplate that the UAW actually believes that they—and their "cause"—still have relevance in this age of brutal global competition, where leaders of newly invigorated countries manipulate everything in their path to extract an economic advantage over the rest of the world, while at the same time doing everything in their power to court automakers and convince them to do business there.

The bottom line in all of this is that time ran out on the UAW a long time ago.

Enabled by a domestic auto industry that kept acquiescing to escalating union demands out of fear of what would happen if they didn't, the UAW and "Detroit" wandered down the primrose path to oblivion together, smugly ensconced in their pathetic self-righteousness and maniacal short-term thinking while staunchly convinced that The End would never come and that the good times would last forever.

Well guess what? The End *did* come and with a ferociousness and finality that even the most jaded among us couldn't have predicted.

Everything that worked, everything that used to be accepted as standard operating procedure in this industry, is now gone, never to return. This industry has undergone a fundamental transformation requiring a scope of change only witnessed once before, and that was during World War II.

It's just too bad that no one over at the "Solidarity House" got the memo.

Out of touch, out of time, and totally irrelevant, the UAW is an entity whose time has most assuredly passed.

Chapter 59

Caution: You're entering the Notgonnahappen.com Zone

*Little did I know that one of the most creative television shows from the late '50s and early '60s—*The Twilight Zone, *created by Rod Serling—would seem so eerily appropriate in those dog days of summer 2010. But there was certainly enough craziness and weirdness—and cessation of rational thinking—to go around back then to make even the most seasoned observers in this business stop and ask,* WTF?

*"You're traveling through another dimension, a dimension not only of sight and sound but of mind; a journey into a wondrous land whose boundaries are that of imagination. That's the signpost up ahead—your next stop, the Twilight Zone." —*Rod Serling

LET'S START WITH the whole Tesla Motors charade. As in are you kidding me? Really? The *frenzy* going on out there right now for the Tesla IPO is simply stupefying. Are people really that gullible, naïve, flat-out stupid, etc., etc. enough to talk themselves into going all-in on a glorified kit-car company that has managed to cobble together 1,000 wildly overpriced $100,000 sports cars for sale *in the entire history of the company?* And that has managed to lose $246 million over the last three years while doing it? And now they want to raise money in an IPO to *allegedly*—and I mean that in the strongest possible terms—build a new "Model S" that will *supposedly* be "affordable" at $50,000 and will instantly transform the auto industry overnight?

261

Remember the old adage that there's a sucker born every minute? Memo to all of you out there screwing yourselves into the pavement while chomping at the bit to get a piece of the action: Welcome to The Club.

A club, by the way, that was unfortunately endorsed by the rumbling, bumbling, stumbling idiots in our federal government at the Department of Energy who ponied up a staggering $465 million loan to Tesla so they could build a Shiny, Happy Green factory that would build Shiny, Happy Green Smiley Cars someday that will more likely than not never see the light of day, at least not in the volumes that anyone is dreaming about anyway.

As a matter of fact I will predict right now that this will be the current administration's equivalent to the Northern Ireland/John Z. DeLorean fiasco that ended so badly. Don't think so? Tell me what's different. A bright, egomaniacal P. T. Barnum–like character with a vision and a plan—oh, let's call it for what it really is: an idea that's wrapped in a frickin' wing and a prayer—but with not enough cash to see it all the way through and who manages to talk a government entity into partially bankrolling it. Sound familiar?

What? The IPO makes it different? How so? That just means more investors will be hurting when it blows up real good. And what about the fact that Toyota "invested" $50 million in Tesla Motors? Well, let's see, Toyota destroyed most if not all of the goodwill they had accumulated in California when they closed the NUMMI facility and threw their employees under the bus. So they throw $50 million at Tesla, let them exist in a tiny corner of the largely unoccupied NUMMI facility, tell them to hire back some of their workers, and call it good. That's not a ringing endorsement by any stretch of the imagination. That's just Toyota distributing some guilt money around and trying to look like upstanding corporate citizens for doing it.

(Oh, I almost forgot, Daimler partnered with Tesla to develop an electric version of the Smart Car, too, but this development is so insignificant as to barely even warrant a mention, by the way.)

The Bottom Line in all of this?

People want to believe in the electrification of the automobile as the savior of all mankind to the extent that they're making stupid calls—and investments—on a business that they don't have even the first clue about. Will the electrification of our transportation system be a factor going forward globally? Absolutely. But the electrification "revolution" will be confined to massive urban centers where these kinds of cars can and will—in certain applications—make sense. People have to remember that electrification will be just *one part* of a bigger picture of energy resources involving every possible combination of fuel on the horizon now, and some we haven't even imagined yet.

Tesla? This company hasn't made any sense since Elon Musk started popping up on the daytime business TV shows, selling himself as some sort of modern-day reincarnation of Billy Durant, and the gullible minions started getting in line to kiss his aura. Remember that at the time this guy was riding the wave of the Chrysler and GM bankruptcies, exploiting Detroit's "failures" for all they were worth, and insisting every step of the way that he would not only show Detroit how it's done but that Silicon Valley would be the new center of the automotive universe. And some pretty smart people who should have known better suspended all rational thinking long enough to get sucked in. And witnessing the stunning success of the IPO today, they're still getting hooked by the minute.

Well, guess what? Elon Musk is broke by his own admission, and to make matters worse he's in the midst of an ugly divorce that will be sure—one way or the other—to remove the whole enterprise from under his control.

And then who will be left holding the bag? Yup, you guessed it, our esteemed braniacs in the Department of Energy who threw money at Tesla on the come—which means the collective "us" out in the real world outside Washington, D.C., get stuck with the bill—and countless financial institutions and individual investors out there who were all looking for the next silver bullet and that 100 percent sure thing that would have surely put them over the hump and on easy street.

Oh, and one more thing: Let's not forget the *other* giant electric pipe dream that is lurching toward trouble as you read this. It seems that Henrik Fisker (speaking of P. T. Barnum) is having some major financial problems getting his much-vaunted $88,000 Fisker Karma plug-in luxury GT car off the ground. Production was supposed to start this year but now it has been pushed back until next year at the earliest. Wait a minute—didn't Fisker get over a half–billion-dollar loan from the government too? Yup, he sure did.

The automobile business looks so easy to the countless "experts" out there who just *know* if given the opportunity they'd do it better than an industry that has been up and running for going on 125 years.

Well, folks, it just doesn't work that way, especially with new technology that requires massive research and development, and massive amounts of investment cash on top of that.

I'm all for the kind of creativity, innovation, vision, and the pioneering entrepreneurial spirit that forged this industry from its beginnings. We will need all of that and more to solve this nation's—and the world's—energy needs going forward. But the history of the transportation business is littered with people who had a good idea and nothing else, whose runaway egos drove them—and their investors—to financial ruin.

I submit Exhibit A—Tesla Motors—and Exhibit B—Fisker Automotive—as the latest examples of entities with too much ego-infused hype, too much runaway hubris, and too much blind faith in their abilities—and in OPM (other people's money)—to let a nagging little thing like reality creep into the equation.

So to paraphrase the brilliant Mr. Serling. . .

> *There is a fifth dimension, beyond that which is known only to electric automotive dreamers. It is a dimension as vast as space and as timeless as infinity. It is the middle ground between light and shadow, between science and superstition, between common sense and abject stupidity, and it lies between*

the pit of man's fears and the summit of his knowledge—albeit limited—of the auto business. This is the dimension filled with rampant delusion. It is an area that we call The Notgonnahappen Zone.

Chapter 60

A midsummer's daydream: Five things

After my last column generated enough buzz and controversy to get a whole bunch of people's panties in a bunch, I thought it might be a fine time to assess some Things in the business at the midpoint of the year. You know, the kinds of Things that weren't what they seemed, or the kinds of Things that needed to be exposed for what they were—without the spin—or the kinds of Things that just were, for no apparent reason other than the "we've always done it this way" ingrained inertia.

THE GREEN HORDE.

The suspension of all rational thought in defense of a Green Nirvana that is simply notgonnahappen.com is just plain ludicrous and further proof that their pap finger-snap solutions for this nation's energy future are not only misinformed and flat-out pathetic, but if we allow our energy future to be hijacked by their woefully misguided ideas and ideals we'll be living in a third-world country in no time. If the Green Horde's dogmatic attempts at subjecting the greater population of this country to a mantra of "learning to live without"—while we sit back and watch as our sacrifices make not one damn bit of difference in the Big Picture of things, especially given China's insatiable desire for an elevated standard of living that will consume every last resource known to man at the rate they're going—are successful, we will soon realize that the headlong rush to force questionable choices upon us when it comes to this nation's transportation fleet will result in exorbitant vehicle prices, an overtaxed electrical grid, and an unsustainable driving future. I keep waiting for someone—*anyone*—speaking on behalf of the Green Intelligentsia to step forward and admit that this "all-in" stance on electric cars will only result in fulfilling a small *part* of our vehicle needs going forward—specifically in the urban arena—and to suggest otherwise is simply lunacy.

The blind embracing of Tesla—again, that glorified kit-car company that hasn't produced even a whiff of profit or even demonstrated even the remotest suggestion of being able to bring a mainstream electric sedan to market—is Egregious Example No. 1 and proof-positive that the Green Horde will suspend all vestiges of reality in order to shove their view of a transportation future down the rest of this nation's throat, even if the infrastructure doesn't exist to support it now, not to mention that the funds to even begin paying for it are nowhere to be found on the horizon.

Blind faith in the "new" or the "next" is one thing—I can embrace and encourage blue-sky thinking and innovation as much as the next person—but abject stupidity in the face of a burgeoning reality borders on the criminal.

Our sustainable driving future will be based on a kaleidoscope of options going forward, including hybrid, electric, natural gas, diesel, cellulosic ethanol, and, yes, believe it or not, gasoline. And make no mistake, that last item—and the internal combustion engine that goes with it—will be the dominant motivating factor in our nation's fleet for at least another two decades, not that you could get anyone from Planet Green to admit it.

That's Thing No. 1.

SERGIO, SERGIO, WHEREFORE ART THOU, SERGIO?

After trying to get through the beyond-tedious "interview"/schmooze-fest conducted by the *Wall Street Journal*'s Paul Ingrassia over the weekend, I'm really trying to figure out this "thing" that some of the media have for Fiat-Chrysler's Sergio "I'm Smarter Than You'll Ever Nnow" Marchionne. Is it the fact that he turned around

Fiat against all odds going on several years ago now? That seems to be a lot of it, although Fiat isn't doing so hot at the moment and hasn't been for quite some time, so what makes people think that this time around will be automatic for Sergio and Fiat-Chrysler? I simply don't get it because the facts are stacked against success for Chrysler, and there's nothing, and I mean n-o-t-h-i-n-g, automatic about it. Throughout all of Marchionne's grandstanding pronouncements it has always been the jaw-dropping volume numbers being bandied about that strike me as disingenuous to say the least. Take the new Grand Cherokee, for example. Make no mistake, it is a fine piece of work, but the assumption that consumers in this market—one that's losing traction by the minute—will disregard all of the excellent choices out there and jump on board the Grand Cherokee bandwagon as if it were a *fait accompli* is simply laughable.

Remember, this is a company that has long been off of the consumer radar screens and is just now cranking up advertising and marketing initiatives to get its mojo back. But it's not that easy and whenever Sergio suggests matter-of-factly that Fiat-Chrysler will meet all targets—no matter how fanciful they might be—his credibility takes another hit. The bottom line at this point is that the new Grand Cherokee will not only have to be a hit, it will have to be a *runaway bestseller* on top of it to make a dent in moving Sergio's "Plan" forward. And that's asking *a lot*.

But again, everything Sergio says asks for a lot. A lot of suspension of belief and rational thinking from where I sit, to be exact. But that's just "Sergio's Way," and we're all supposed to go along with it. Well, I'm not buying it. Sergio's plan has more than enough holes that you could easily question just about everything in it. It's all based on one market number *over here* and that assumptive chunk of the market number assigned to Fiat-Chrysler *over there*, and it's all supposed to come out in the wash and come good, because, after all, "I've done it before," as he likes to say.

Well, guess what? The market isn't cooking like everyone thought it was going to be and the so-called "recovery" is going s-l-o-w. So slow, in fact, that Sergio's master plan could soon end up in jeopardy, and then what?

Well "then" is what I've been saying all along: Sergio's *real* plan was aimed at establishing Fiat North America in this market on the bones of Chrysler, with minimal investment and cash outlay on Fiat's part. It wasn't a Chrysler or media-friendly idea at the time he was trying to get everyone's buy-in on the idea of Fiat's takeover, but I don't doubt for a moment that's what his true plan was all along. And now that his grandiose plans for Chrysler are so intricately dependent on everything falling into place "just so"—from the economy to the successful execution of the products *and* <>marketing—it's going to be damn near impossible for Sergio to hit his targets. I've been in and around this business for going on too many years to count, and I will tell you that *nothing* ever comes together "just so" in this business. Ever.

And that's Thing No. 2.

Toyota credibility? The Oxymoron of the Year.

The fact that I'm still writing about Toyota's problems at this point is simply shocking to me. How this company could fall so far, so fast will fill B-school case studies for decades to come. It's simply the most stunning corporate implosion in recent memory—well, except for the BP debacle, that is, which by the time the disaster in the gulf plays out will go down as the biggest corporate collapse in recorded history, but I digress. With the latest recall of 138,000 Lexus models—and really, we're *still* talking about Toyota product recalls after everything that has transpired?—Toyota can no longer hide the fact that there is, or at least *was* a fundamental corporate culture at work in its hallways based on deliberate obfuscation, a pattern of stonewalling, and a steadfast refusal to admit guilt for *anything*. It's as if the powers that be at Toyota started to believe that they were, in fact, infallible and that nothing of any consequence would happen to derail their inexorable march to the top of the mountain in the auto business. And that they couldn't possibly be dropping the ball on quality—no, *not* possible. Well, it did, and now they're toast. Will they still sell boatloads of cars and trucks? Absolutely. But will Toyota ever enjoy the stature that it once did? In a word, no. It's *just another car company* competing for the proverbial "jump ball" in the marketplace that plays out every single business day.

Not Good and Not Pretty by any stretch of the imagination.

And that's Thing No. 3.

OH, FOR THE HONDA OF OLD.

There was once was a pretty damn impressive little car company called Honda. Energized by its total gearhead founder, and reveling in the fact that its official corporate name was the Honda *Motor* Company, Honda was the car company that marched to a different drummer, fueled by imagination and creativity, and powered by a willingness to take chances and push the outer limits of thought when it came to building cars. And build cars they did. *Great* cars that bristled with innovation and creative thinking while executed to a high standard. Yes, Honda was the one Asian automobile manufacturer that proudly waved its freak flag high, comfortable in the knowledge that what they were putting on the street at that very moment was the very best they could possibly do. Different from everyone else certainly, but usually wonderfully enticing nonetheless.

But alas, things got weird.

Honda got sidetracked chasing segments they didn't belong in, while losing sight of its founder's vision. In short, they started playing it safe, pulling back on the throttle when in the past they would have pushed down harder. Soon, creativity gave way to a sober predictability—both in their designs and in their thinking—and everything Honda became known for was systematically watered down or neutered to the point that the company and its products were barely recognizable. Today, Honda is flailing about while clearly lacking focus and direction. Its products are woefully predictable—the new CR-Z is a massive disappointment with its blatantly "safe" execution, like they pulled up halfway through and called it good—and a car that would have never seen the light of day at the "old" Honda.

Honda, the company that once regularly stood this industry on its ear with its rampant creativity and innovational prowess, has been running on autopilot for too long now. A creeping conservatism has swept through its ranks and now the company is filled with upper-management types who could easily blend in at any other car company, but who wouldn't have passed muster at the old Honda not all that long ago.

Something has got to give. We need and want the old Honda back. This *industry* desperately needs the old Honda back to show how it's done and to demonstrate what's possible when you allow creative thinking to run unfettered and free.

And that's Thing No. 4.

GM: A Giant in training or the two-steps-forward-five-back mobile frustration app of yesteryear?

I get that everything that GM is doing right now has a cadence and purpose. Big Ed is allowing his top lieutenants to do their thing and GM might just have the best team in place that it has had in years, maybe even decades, because in the recent past, when GM would have its financial shit together something else would be weak. Or if it had its engineering and design functions firing on all cylinders, its marketing would be pathetically out of touch. It was always something in the GM of yesteryear, whether it was the wrong people, the paralyzing structural bureaucracy, or the mind-numbing processes, GM managed to bring any shred of momentum to a screeching halt before it even got out of the gate simply by the sheer force of its own ineptitude.

But everything has changed. And now, GM not only isn't making excuses, it's focusing on making the best cars and trucks possible, with everyone seemingly—remarkably enough—on the same page. I won't bother throwing around the names of the people who deserve the credit right now (they know who they are) because there's no need for anyone down at the RenCen to stop for anything. They need to have the attitude ingrained that nothing has been "fixed" and nothing has been "won" and if they stick to that they'll be just fine.

But two things concern the hell out of me about this company. One is the Chevrolet Volt. The Volt will *not* be an automatic homerun by any stretch of the imagination. Once the Green Swells in California and D.C. get their fill of it, then what? We're talking about a car that has been dissected and displayed for going on two years now in its present, finished form. Once the novelty wears off I believe the Volt could be the toughest marketing job of this or any other year. It's a giant "we'll see" at the very least.

Secondly, as good as the Chevrolet Cruze is—and it best be better than they say it is—there's no question that its conservative design language will play against it, no matter *how* good it is. The odd thing about the Cruze is that for all its built-in goodness it doesn't have "new" written all over it. Instead it reeks of "familiar GM," which is about the last thing that car needs.

It's going to be interesting to say the least because those two vehicles are not only the future of Chevrolet—they're the future of GM to boot.

And that's Thing No. 5.

Halfway through 2010 and we're just getting warmed up. Fasten your seatbelts, ladies and gentlemen—it's going to be a wild ride.

Chapter 61

The Shit Disturber cometh

Many months ago, long before Ron Gettelfinger retired as the president of the United Auto Workers union, I predicted that Bob King—the clear heir apparent—had the potential to set back all of the conciliatory, somewhat progressive, and decidedly more realistic discussions and agreements that had marked the union movement at the end of Gettelfinger's reign. I also suggested that King, in about fifteen minutes or so, would go out of his way to blow up any of this "enlightened" thinking—and of course the reduced union contracts— the ones that fundamentally pressed the reset button for the Detroit automakers and allowed them to survive the economic crisis relatively intact while armed with a new competitiveness. And then, true to form, King cranked up the hoary union rhetoric and reminded everyone that things weren't all that different.

UNFORTUNATELY FOR ALL OF US who are in this business and in this industry—and particularly in this town, state, and region—it looks like Bob King's fifteen minutes are at hand. And make no mistake, this is the most unfortunate scenario that could unfold and the biggest bowl of Not Good headed this industry's way since this nation's financial crisis itself.

While being subjected to King's hairball pronouncements and his belligerent demeanor right out of the gate—the tone of which is clearly punctuated by his blind ambition and his uncanny ability to studiously avoid the realities of the modern-day global economy at every turn—it's clear that this guy is a throwback to an uglier, much more confrontational era. An era that saw the domestic auto industry acquiesce to a constantly escalating series of demands by the UAW while effectively being held at gunpoint, knowing that if they didn't cave, the gravy train of profitability would be over, even though with each corrosive agreement the table was being set for the bankruptcies that unfolded by the end of 2008.

Forty years of UAW belligerence—compounded by the domestic automakers' steadfast unwillingness to put the brakes on the insanity—led this industry down the primrose path to the Abyss, and it damn near meant the destruction of one of the key pillars of this nation's manufacturing base.

Yes, the domestic automakers were more than culpable, what with their refusal to believe that: 1. Anyone else in the world could build a decent car, and 2. Even if they did manage to build something decent, American consumers wouldn't want anything to do with them.

And we all know how that turned out.

Not only did American consumers embrace the imports in droves, an entire generation walked away from the Detroit Three's run of slipshod or nonexistent-quality vehicles, never to return.

But the UAW didn't do themselves any favors by making it their mission to consistently ignore the big picture. When it was suggested that the import manufacturers build plants here to help "level the playing field," that's exactly what they did, and except for a few glaring instances—NUMMI in California to be exact—the imports avoided the myriad negatives associated with the UAW by ignoring the issue altogether, running nonunion plants and making no bones about it. And as the Detroit Three struggled mightily to make money—while being hamstrung with crippling UAW labor agreements—the import manufacturers made even more strides with American consumers, and slowly but surely the domestic automakers saw their share of the market plummet in a continuous downward spiral for the last twenty-five years.

Then again we know all of this. And I get the fact that King is trying to mark his territory by dusting off the hoary rhetoric from yesteryear in order to get his constituency juiced for the long fight ahead, blah, blah, blah.

But what's going on this time is different.

Bob King isn't just dusting off the old rhetoric to generate sound bites for the content-starved hordes in the media; he actually *believes* the time is right to bomb this industry back to the Stone Age, effectively bringing back the notorious UAW "entitlement" mentality of less work/more pay + benefits with a resounding chorus of "What's in it for us?" thrown in for old time's sake.

King's first offensive aimed at getting back to the bad old days is to start "informational" picketing at Toyota dealerships—specifically in California, but watch for it to spread quickly to other media-visible states—in order to strong-arm Toyota into allowing the unionization of its U.S. plants and to protest Toyota's decision to close its NUMMI plant in Fremont, California, which was closed when GM—Toyota's partner in the manufacturing facility—went bankrupt.

Not long after Toyota closed NUMMI, it resumed finishing construction of a new facility in Blue Springs, Mississippi, about two hundred miles northeast of Jackson—which had been put on hold when the economy slowed—where it will build Corollas, *without* union labor, of course. This seems to have rankled Mr. King to no end and he just can't seem to fathom why Toyota would do such a thing.

But given all of the negative evidence accrued over the years pointing to the inherent drawbacks of UAW involvement, why would Toyota consider doing it any other way? So now King is now even more hell-bent on "converting" Toyota's facilities in the U.S. to become UAW plants.

Memo to Bob King: It's notgonnahappen.com. Not in this lifetime, or any other lifetime either. That the ship has sailed on the union movement in this country is apparently news only to the old hands clinging to the past at the UAW. Yes, the union movement once served a purpose in the development of industrial America, but that was so long ago that no one currently involved with the UAW can separate the historical facts of that era from the modern-day distortions stemming from the union's warped reality that has been going on for four decades now.

The "entitlement" mantra gleefully idolized by the anointed, hand-holding minions in the UAW became obsolete the moment Toyota and Honda first established their assembly plants in this country. And the fate for the UAW—and for the soon-to-be woefully out-of-touch domestic automakers—was sealed from that moment on too.

But that Bob King is tone deaf to the nuances of the global—and national—reality shouldn't be a surprise to anyone. After all, this guy's roots are deeply embedded in the UAW's past. A past fueled by grandstanding histrionics and a maliciously calculated and confrontational intransigence. So it's no wonder that he's come out with guns blazing, sounding for all the world like a guy lost in a permanent fog of irrelevance.

What could Bob King do to become even *more* irrelevant, if that's possible?

As hard as it is to believe, King is now throwing in his lot with—speaking of grandstanding histrionics—one Reverend Jesse Jackson. You know Jackson as the guy who seems to show up—Zelig-like—whenever there's a whiff of controversy in need of his "talents." What you probably don't know is that this guy has made a career out of shaking down corporate America in the guise of "justice" and "equality"—with the unspoken threat of playing the race card to the media if he isn't able to extract the amount of the "donation" he wants.

These two blowhards are taking their respective organizations—the UAW and the Rainbow PUSH Coalition—and forming a coalition along with other various unions and organizations to fight for urban revitalization, fair trade, and jobs. They're even organizing a march in Detroit on August 28 to kick off the campaign for "jobs, justice, and peace."

Perfect, isn't it?

In the midst of crawling out of the rubble of two bankruptcies—and trying to make Detroit's products desirable again—while dealing with the perpetual din of negativity in national media stories about this industry and this city, here comes Bob King doing a pitch-perfect impression of a UAW leader from 1970, with Jesse Jackson trundling along for the ride in case there's need for hysteria and custom-delivered, agitating sound bites.

How is this helpful? How—after all that has transpired in this industry over the last twenty-four months—can projecting to the rest of the country that this miserable excuse for a "union" is *still* involved in the Detroit Three's fortunes going to get people to view Detroit—and its cars and trucks—in a different light?

I'll answer that one for you: It won't.

Chapter 62

The Autoextremist Interview: Reddy Kilowatt— The man, the myth, and the mystery

As the din from the Green Horde continued unabated and frenzy over the electrification of the automobile reached fever pitch, it was time for a bit of perspective, which I chose to provide in the form of an "interview" with that famous twentieth-century icon, Reddy Kilowatt.

CONCEIVED AND CREATED BY Ashton B. Collins, Sr. for the Alabama Power Company, Reddy Kilowatt made his debut on March 11, 1926, as an ambassador for the use of electric power. Reddy was so popular that he was eventually licensed by over three hundred electrical companies across the United States. He starred in local ads, a comic book, and even a movie at one point. But then, things got weird, as we like to say.

Much to Reddy's (and his creator's) chagrin, some rural electric cooperatives and public-utility districts created a competing character named Willie Wiredhand. Willie had electric plugs for his legs and feet, a lamp socket for his head, and strange hand coverings rendered to look like farming gloves. This did not go over well with Reddy or Mr. Collins, so Collins sued Willie's corporate handlers—the National Rural Electric Cooperative Association—for trademark infringement in 1957 and promptly lost. The court found that the two characters were distinctly different.

Bitter and disillusioned, Reddy soldiered on knowing there was a rip-off artist out there nipping at his heels in rural America, and even though his popularity continued, deep down, Reddy could smell a change in the air, and it wasn't just the Iowa cornfields or the pot smoke hovering over the '60s. As the use of electrical power in this nation shifted from a growth strategy to an energy-conservation platform, Reddy's visibility gradually waned. And it wasn't too long before he was relegated to the scrap heap altogether, discarded like, *ahem*, an old, burned-out lightbulb.

The rights to Reddy were bought by the Northern States Power Company back in 1998, and that company set about to manage Reddy's affairs, creating a subsidiary focused solely on Mr. Kilowatt. But he was rendered irrelevant again when that company created a character named Reddy Flame, who was tasked to promote natural gas. Despondent, Reddy went into seclusion, never to be heard from again. Until now. We tracked Reddy to an undisclosed location in rural Wisconsin and after harassing him relentlessly over several months, he agreed to meet me last weekend in Elkhart Lake, Wisconsin, to talk on the record, for the first time in eighty-five years.

I met Reddy in the parking lot of the famed Siebken's bar in downtown Elkhart Lake. He was taller than you might think, and his lightning bolts much redder than I expected—his DayGlo yellow shoes were shockingly vibrant too—and his fixed grin was more than a little off-putting, to be honest. And the sound he made was eerie, kind of like a combination bug zapper and microwave. Weird. But he seemed eager to get on with it, so without further ado, the one and only Reddy Kilowatt, in all of his cantankerous, high-wattage feistiness.

PMD: Reddy . . . can I call you Reddy, by the way? You've been in seclusion for years, is that by choice?

RK: Yes, I had been ripped off, humiliated, and marginalized to the extent that it didn't matter anymore, I just couldn't take it and I just couldn't go on. And Reddy is fine. It's better than Mr. Watt, which some jackass called me back in '36. I mean, really, do I look like a "Mr. Watt" to you?

PMD: WELL, FRANKLY, NO. BUT I DID NOTICE YOU'RE REMARK-ABLY WELL PRESERVED. AND NICE SHOES, BY THE WAY.

RK: Thanks, I think, and of course I'm well preserved. I have current running through me constantly, like 5,000 volts at any one time. I get a jolt every morning, if you know what I mean. [*Reddy has a big, stupid grin on his face that eerily never changes.*] Get it? Jolt? Volts? God, I crack myself up sometimes. [*He also has this odd cackle when he amuses himself, and his lightbulb nose flashes like a strobe when he laughs. Weird.*]

PMD: UH, YEAH. SO, REDDY. WHY TALK NOW, AND WHY ME?

RK: Well, you're a persistent S.O.B., I'll give you that. And Andrea-Marie thought it would be a good idea to talk to someone after all these years. That it might make me less cranky.

PMD: I HESITATE TO ASK, BUT WHO THE HELL IS ANDREA-MARIE?

RK: Andrea-Marie Ampere. She's a descendant of the famed Andre-Marie Ampere, the French math whiz and physicist. He was a *very* big deal, like the godfather of electrodynamics, among other things. I met Andrea-Marie in Paris back in 1958. After we lost that bullshit trial, I went to Paris for a couple of months in the hopes of getting my juice back, and needless to say, "Amp" or "Ampie" or "Miss Amp," as I like to call her, definitely got my juices flowin' again, if you know what I mean. We've been inseparable ever since.

PMD: THAT'S FUNNY—THERE'S NEVER BEEN ANY MENTION OF YOU HAVING A LIFE OUTSIDE OF YOUR POWER COMPANY DUTIES. YOU WOULDN'T BE BULLSHITTING ME NOW, WOULD YOU?

RK: Yeah, well they never mentioned Willie Wiredhand was a fraud and a degenerate gambler either, so now you know.

PMD: WHY DO I FEEL LIKE I'M GETTING THE INSIDE STORY OF THE PEOPLE WHO PLAYED THE MUNCHKINS IN *THE WIZARD OF OZ?*

RK: Hey, pal, you got me here, so I might as well get it all off my chest in one sitting. And I'm going to let it fly.

PMD: I ACTUALLY DON'T KNOW HOW ANYTHING STAYS ON YOUR CHEST, UH, SEEING AS YOU'RE BASICALLY A LIGHTNING BOLT. AND BY

THE WAY, WHY DIDN'T "AMP" COME WITH YOU THIS MORNING?

RK: She wanted it to be my show, one-on-one. She's been push-ing me for years to say what I needed to say, and besides, she's not big on mornings so, trust me, it's much better she's not here. Besides, we were up late last night partying and watching the latest *Terminator* movie—great electrical special effects, by the way—and after we put our charges together—repeatedly and enthusiastically, I might add—I let her sleep in.

PMD: OH MY, I THINK WE'VE JUST CROSSED THE THRESHOLD INTO TMI TERRITORY.

RK: What, you don't think I can have a sex life? Or should I say "WATT"? [*There's that strobe-enhanced cackling again.*]

PMD: LET'S MOVE ON, SHALL WE, AS THE THOUGHT OF YOU AND MISS AMP GETTING IT ON IS A BIT DISCONCERTING TO SAY THE LEAST, ALTHOUGH I'M SURE IT'S . . . *ELECTRIC?* SO REDDY, WHAT DO YOU MAKE OF ALL OF THIS "ELECTRIFICATION OF THE AUTOMOBILE" TALK? WHERE DO YOU THINK THIS IS GOING, AND IS IT REALISTIC FOR THE CURRENT ADMINISTRATION TO EXPECT ELECTRIFICATION TO BE THE BE-ALL AND END-ALL?

RK: First of all, the words "reality" and "realistic" don't apply to this administration, but thanks for using the word "current," it always gives me a little charge. [*His damn strobe nose starts going off again as he cackles to himself.*] But if we're speaking of reality here, as much as I'm an obvious booster of electric power, there is no way in hell that this mass electrification of the automobile is going to happen.

PMD: THAT'S A STRONG STATEMENT, NEEDLESS TO SAY, ESPE-CIALLY COMING FROM YOU. WHY DO YOU SAY THAT?

RK: We tried it as a nation back at the beginning of the last century, and guess what? It didn't work. This is a big damn country in case you hadn't noticed. And we can't expect these little electric shit boxes to move our goods, take us on vacations to Glacier National Park—I highly recommend that trip, by the way—or power us to a getaway weekend in the Smokies, for instance. It's just notgonnahappen.com, as you like to say.

PMD: But Reddy, you don't believe in energy conservation? I know the Green movement basically ended your career so it's understandable you'd be bitter, but don't you think we need to conserve our resources and reduce our carbon emissions into the atmosphere?

RK: Yes, of course I do, what do you take me for, a moron?

PMD: Well, no, of course not.

RK: Look, yes we need to watch what the hell we're doing as a nation. But while some in this country are threatening to banish us back to the Stone Age while pushing Liposuction Fat–powered lamps and Flintstone-mobiles, China and India are going to keep right on consuming their way to oblivion. Didn't I just read where China has now exceeded America's daily energy usage?

PMD: Yes, that just came out this week.

RK: Uh, well, just off the top of my cute little head socket, that can't be good, right?

PMD: Uh, no. It's definitely a giant heaping, steaming bowl of Not Good, to be exact.

RK: Right. So if there's no push to get those countries to adopt mass conservation, we're all toast. And by the way, China's headlong rush into electric power and electrification is all fine and dandy except for the fact that they have the highest polluting, dirtiest coal-fired plants in the world. How is that going to work? I mean, yeah, I'm an electric ambassador and all that entails—blah, blah, blah—but electrification for electrification's sake is never a good idea, because something has to generate that electricity, and the way we're going about it is crazy at this point.

PMD: What do you suggest?

RK: First of all, this administration has to get real. Shoving touchy-feely "green" electric cars down everyone's throat—when we don't have the infrastructure to support it—is pure insanity. Who's going to pay for all of these electric car subsidies so that they're actually affordable in the real world? Who's going to spring for all of these on-street charging meters and all of the associated cost that goes with that? That's right, you and me, the taxpayers. And last time I checked, we're pretty much tapped out at this point. And besides, other than a few HugVilles in California and a three-block area in Manhattan designated by Mayor Bloomberg as a "Shiny Happy Smiley Green Zone" we can't get there from here.

Secondly, everyone has to get real about the scope of the electric car movement in this country and around the world. Yes, in a few megacities we'll see electric vehicles make inroads, but it's never going to be this idyllic, Shiny, Happy world that's portrayed by this current administration. Electric vehicles for short hops in urban centers make sense, *somewhat*. But they're never going to meet our inveterate need to roam, to experience, and to explore. Instead, we'll need to develop alternative fuels—I'm really digging the idea of cellulosic fuel from waste, by the way, and that new OPOC engine—and we're going to have to learn how to use the energy from the sun more efficiently too. Do I like the fact that we're dependent on petroleum? No, but to pretend that it's not going to be around for another forty to fifty years is just plain silly.

PMD: Reddy, what about the advancements in battery technology? Doesn't that excite you?

RK: Excite me? Uh, no. Amp *excites* me; advanced battery development just pleases me. But again, electric vehicles and electrification are not the salvation for the human condition. I've been around for a long time, and I'm confident that there's a whole bunch of technological developments and inventions coming that we can't even imagine. As much as it pains me to say it, electricity is just one component of a wide variety of energy solutions going forward, but *just* one. And as much as I'm proud of my contributions to the cause, I'm a realist. Electricity—and electrification—has very defined limits, even though the people who have a ton invested in selling us on the Electrification Future want us to believe otherwise.

PMD: Interesting—and controversial—coming from someone whom I consider to be the preeminent electrification ambassador of the last century.

RK: Well, thank you, but you know, the only thing I've gained after all this time is perspective. One minute you're hotter than hot and the next minute you're yesterday's news, forgotten and ignored. I'm aware of my contributions and I was always aware of my role. When we were trying to build up the concept of electric power to a nation weaning itself off of oil lamps, I served a very important purpose, and I'm very proud of that. But this extreme—I would say *blind*—rush into electrification for electrification's sake is going to bite us all in the ass, and hard. It will be more costly, I can guarantee you that. *Much* more. The Dirty Little Secret? Electricity costs are high. And this whole rebuilding-the-infrastructure thing will be just the tip of the iceberg of those costs too.

People need to get real—although politicians in California and Washington don't count, they wouldn't know real unless it served them a subpoena—and people need to understand that the promise of a Bright Shiny New Day just around the corner because of the electrification of the automobile is unmitigated bullshit. And that's the High Wattage Truth.

PMD: Funny.

RK: I knew you'd like that.

PMD: Well, Reddy, it has been a distinct honor and pleasure talking to you and we here at Autoextremist wish you and Miss Amp the very best in the future.

RK: Well, thank you, and I have to admit it wasn't painful at all. Oh, and one more thing? There's no such thing as "free" or "cheap" electricity. It simply doesn't exist. Use wisely, my friends.

Chapter 63

High-voltage hysteria

You knew that when such automotive "experts" as Rush Limbaugh started weighing in on the Chevrolet Volt— complete with his misinformed and wildly off-base knee-jerk- isms in full bloom—the electric car hysteria in this country had reached critical mass. That Limbaugh had no idea as to what the Volt represented or the first clue as to how it operated was not a surprise, but it was clear that he wasn't alone, and that GM marketers had their work cut out for them. The Volt would prove to be everything promised and more once the media got a hold of it, and GM's big image gamble appeared to have worked. There was nothing in the market like the Volt, and for one brief shining moment, GM would have the attention— and mostly positive too—of the nation's media.

IT'S IMPORTANT TO REMEMBER that both sides of the political spectrum have clear-cut agendas when talking about the Volt. On the conservative Right, it's the anti-bailout, anti-"subsidized" GM (and Detroit), and anti-*anything* Obama fervor that encapsulates the frenzy. To this faction the Volt is nothing short of e-v-i-l and represents everything wrong and bad about the current administration and the direction of the country itself.

While on the Left, we have that mind-numbing "we know what's best for you and you will like it" smugness that envisions the sheer joy that will result after American consumers are forced to embrace mass electrification overnight, even though for more than 85 percent of the country it makes zero sense. And yet this group will be delirious over the fact that after an entire nation is brought to its knees by woefully misguided policies based upon theoretical "best case" scenarios rather than functional, real-world realities, a Shiny, Happy Green Nirvana will result overnight and it will be Good.

Given the noise generated by both of these factions, it will be a miracle if the American consumer public can ferret through the cacophony and discover what the Volt is—and what it *could* mean and how it *could* perform—for their day-to-day driving regimen.

Clearly the whole "range anxiety" factor will loom large in the consideration process. That most consumers view the Volt as just another one of those electric golf carts that are all the buzz of late shouldn't be a surprise. GM has pounded out the fact that the Volt goes forty miles without a charge and to *most* consumers that doesn't sound like much, even though if they actually analyzed their daily driving they'd discover that in an urban setting that figure would suit them just fine.

But while hammering the "forty miles per charge" figure into consumers' heads, GM has failed to make a big enough deal about the fact that that the Volt is an *extended-range* electric vehicle, and that the onboard engine will allow you to maintain enough of a battery charge to go a very long way.

It's easy to see why marketing the Volt will be such a monumental challenge. First of all, the political hand grenades lobbed in from the sides and the relentless posturing will never go away, and GM marketers would be best served by steering far clear of that noise. If they think they can spin the spin-meisters, they're sadly mistaken, so instead they better go after the consumer intenders intrigued by the concept, the people who will have the power to make or break the Volt, because without the warm embrace of these early adopter/zealots the Volt will never get out of the gate.

And secondly, GM has to avoid—as much as possible—the whole "electrification of our driving future" angle, because in reality the electrification of the American automobile—the concept that has the left-leaning pundits in such a frothing frenzy—remains a distant pipe dream and one conducive to urban areas only. And this will be true for a long, long time to come, as much as the "finger-snap" experts out there suggest otherwise.

No, the Chevrolet Volt—at least for the time being—will be the ultimate niche vehicle of this young century. It will have limited appeal to a limited number of consumers in limited parts of the country, and it will all work out just fine if GM marketers remember that, even though the natural tendency will be to shout from the rooftops that the Volt is nothing short of the reinvention of the automobile.

And just for the record, for some consumers the Volt *will* be the greatest thing since sliced bread, and *that's fine, man*, as The Dude would say, but it doesn't mean that feeling will automatically translate beyond the first-on-the-block frenzy.

The bottom line?

Somewhere in this kaleidoscope of hysteria GM has to figure out how to market an extended-range electric vehicle called the Chevrolet Volt. And somehow—as GM marketing chief Joel Ewanick has rightly suggested—GM has to convince a skeptical American consumer public that it's a real car, and not a marketing gimmick or a toy.

Sounds simple, doesn't it?

Chapter 64

Sergio's "chaos theory" coming to a Chrysler showroom near you

I continued to be amazed at some of the genuflecting minions in the media who were still buying into Sergio Marchionne's "vision" for the new Chrysler, er, Fiat-Chrysler, er, let's just call it for what it is: Fiat North America, *circa 2013. These lesser computer keyboard–stained wretches among us—who seemed to have suspended all rational thought for the temporary comfort provided by Marchionne's soothing "wisdom"—were falling all over themselves trying to pretend that the new Fiat-Chrysler product plan was not only pure whimsy—or abject lunacy, take your pick—but a burgeoning showroom train wreck of immense proportions.*

LET'S REVIEW, SHALL WE? Marchionne's plan calls for at least twenty-three new models in Chrysler showrooms by 2013. (In case you're wondering, Chrysler's walking-wounded dealer body has seventeen to contend with right now, and for comparison's sake, Ford has twenty-one models currently, sans Mercury.)

And just what, pray tell, are Chrysler's dealers going to do with all of these vaunted new products? Let's not forget that the great shrunken car company formerly known as Chrysler has stripped out its dealer body to the point that it's damn near approaching skeleton crew status. And, not to state the obvious—although some out there in media land are choosing to ignore it—Chrysler's latest financial numbers are skewed heavily toward fleet sales, while the retail side of its business continues to struggle.

According to Sergio, however, the new Jeep Grand Cherokee will fix any infirmities on the retail side of the equation and set the table for surefire future product success overnight. Make no mistake, the new big Jeep is a fine piece of work—as I've stated previously—but there's no fixing what ails Chrysler overnight, I don't care how great one single product is.

No, Sergio is setting up his dealers for failure, as sure as I'm writing this and here's why. Sergio's chaos theory of automotive marketing suggests that his marketing corps will be able to differentiate the four brands—Chrysler, Dodge, Ram Truck, and Jeep—in the remaining Chrysler showrooms with a flip of a switch, creating a distinctive, unimpeachable persona for each.

This sounds all well and good but given the overall quality of the remaining Chrysler dealers—and hold your emails because, yes, there are plenty of good ones left, just not nearly as many as Chrysler would have you believe—*and* the propensity for the general public to avoid Chrysler showrooms at all costs, how is this all going to work, exactly?

And to actually get up there and suggest to the media—and I mean you, Sergio—that all of this working out is just a mere formality and that once it gets rolling it will all come good overnight is bordering on sheer lunacy.

A depleted, semi-demoralized dealer body unused to having visitors in its showrooms—let alone buyers—is all of a sudden going to be able to not only understand the myriad brands and models that are suddenly overrunning its showrooms, but is going to be able to explain the differences and nuances between them to its customers, even though these new products—particularly the compact and midsize offerings—are going to be stepping all over each other on the showroom floor in terms of size and price?

Uh, Not. So. Much.

Some Chrysler dealers have already gone on record as saying the more products the merrier—that the long national nightmare brought on by the bankruptcy is over and happy times are just around the corner again—but the smarter ones know better and are understandably leery of what's to come. The more rational among the Chrysler dealers are fearful of a looming mini train wreck in their showrooms, with too many models crashing into each other with a redundant thud, and with little rhyme or reason given to any of it.

And there's no amount of marketing money that will solve any of it either, certainly not within the timeframe Sergio's banking on.

And what about that whole marketing thing? Let's not forget one other very important point that Marchionne has conveniently managed to gloss over in the midst of telling us all how great it's going to be, and that is the fact that achieving a targeted, cohesive awareness of your product out there in the big, bad, real world of competing messaging that exists today—automotive and otherwise—is extremely difficult and consumes billions of dollars. Not millions, but *billions*.

It's one thing to play fast and loose with the financials, because apparently you can spin just about anything these days and someone out there will buy it. Just look at the latest round of Chrysler financial numbers that everyone went gaga over—even though the retail sales component was woefully lacking—and you can see what I mean. I guess if Sergio says it's okay to not put too much emphasis on the retail component and focus instead on the Big Picture, then it's okay. Or, maybe not.

But when it comes to marketing—and shoving the equivalent of fifty pounds of new product into the equivalent of a twenty-five-pound bag—and trying to sort it all out on the fly, with a weakened dealer body *and* a consumer public that will need more than a few good reasons to show up on your dealers' doorsteps, it gets more than a little complicated.

And it takes time, too. Not Sergio "finger snap" time, but a plodding, grind-it-out, move-the-ball forward kind of slog that takes years to come to fruition. Not months, but *years*. And there are no shortcuts, at least none that will achieve the kind of consistent, sustainable, let alone instantaneous results that Marchionne so desperately needs.

And yet here's Marchionne insisting that with his brilliant guidance—as translated through his marketing acolytes—four distinct brand personas will emerge unscathed from the wreckage of past Chrysler train wrecks, an infusion of new models will be integrated seamlessly into the American consumer consciousness with nary a hiccup or even a whiff of confusion, and the depleted Chrysler dealers will sort it all out and be wildly successful.

All by 2013.

I'm all for some glass-half-full optimism now and then, but this is flat-out ridiculous.

Memo to the wildly optimistic Chrysler dealers out there: I say good luck, but don't be surprised if the Marchionne "vision" leaves a lot to be desired in three years' time. And maybe it's best that you learn to live with disappointment now, so the shock won't be as bad.

And to the smart, more skeptical Chrysler dealers out there who are making a cottage industry out of hedging their bets, I say be smarter and even *more* skeptical, and you won't be disappointed in the least.

Chapter 65

Akerson's to-do list revolves around two key points, plus one

In the hand-wringing frenzy of media coverage surrounding "Big Ed" Whitacre stepping away from the GM Corporation CEO job in favor of sixty-one-year-old Daniel Akerson, there were many in the media expressing surprise about the move, at least those in the media who hadn't been paying attention, that is. But it shouldn't have been a surprise at all because Big Ed made no bones about the fact that he wasn't going to be around forever (and his home was in Texas and he wasn't moving here, thank you very much). And since the entire raison d'être for GM now was to get out from under the "Government Motors" tag, the company's focus was clearly on appeasing Wall Street and making sure the IPO that was imminent went off successfully and without a hitch. Big Ed's "interim" leanings weren't a positive part of the plan.

WALL STREET NOT ONLY doesn't like surprises, they want to know that a company's management team that's in place on the eve of an IPO is going to be the management team that will be there to see it through. *All* the way through. And that's why the change was made. Akerson gets the CEO title on September 1 and the chairman title when Big Ed steps completely away at the end of the year.

GM absolutely needs this IPO to go well because the entire future of the company rests on it. Until GM can get out from under the tainted "Government Motors" moniker there's no amount of smart marketing—they have several crucial launches coming up, Chevy Volt and Cruze, to name just two—from Joel Ewanick's troops that will be able to overcome that ball and chain. That's how crucial all of this is.

The moment the "Government Motors" tag is buried, GM has a shot. Until then its future is cloudy, at best, no matter how good their hot new products are.

Much has been made of Akerson's ball-busting tendencies, his use of "colorful" language, and that his take-no-prisoners style is exactly what GM needs right now, blah, blah, blah. But to put a finer point on things, Akerson's day-to-day managing will revolve around two things: Speed and Accountability.

Speed in that GM has finally—finally—begun to leave its sedentary ways to the dusty old history books and is acting like a car company that gets it, one that realizes that months of meetings and territorial posturing is not a way to bring a vehicle to market in this *right now* global automotive economy we live in today. And that agile decision-making and the ability to marshal the company's resources are what will allow GM to compete both here in this market and around the world. Akerson has to emphasize this speeded-up decision-making and product action every day. If GM's newfound tempo slides just a little or they ease up on the gas in the least, it's not going to go well for them. And from all accounts Akerson understands this and lives by it. I certainly hope so anyway.

As for Accountability, the fact that I'm even mentioning it means that I am not firmly convinced that GM is out of the woods just yet. Far from it, in fact. Oh, the right people are engaged in all the right management positions now, but that doesn't mean the entire organization gets it. Akerson would do himself—and the "new" GM—a huge favor by rooting out the last vestiges of the complacency and lack of accountability that have plagued GM's vast bureaucratic middle for over forty years now, because it's exactly this cancerous, odorous quagmire of "not invented here" myopia, combined with a stunning lack of decision-making responsibility, that contributed mightily to this once great company's downfall into bankruptcy.

And Akerson must be absolutely ruthless in eliminating it if GM is going to thrive after the IPO.

And the plus one?

Akerson needs to make sure that Mark Reuss and Ed Welburn and their respective product teams have all of the tools and resources necessary to do their jobs. And then he needs to step away *and stay out of the way* so that they can execute the various product plans commensurate with their considerable capabilities. The fact that Akerson isn't a "product guy" ultimately won't matter, as long as he keeps out of the way of the people who are.

If Akerson can do all of that—without allowing his considerable ego to get in the way—this company has a shot to be great again.

If not, well, let's just say that Akerson and the rest of GM will be hearing from me about it.

Chapter 66

By the people, for the people . . . oh, never mind

As we stumbled into the final weeks of the summer around here, the hot and steamy weather had begun to resemble the economy, as in slow-to-stagnating. To make matters worse, people in this business clinging to a glimmer of hope that the good times were just around the next bend were now having to deal with the fact that this so-called auto industry recovery was going to be excruciatingly painful and drawn out, with nothing resembling instant gratification on the horizon, or even close for that matter. But it wasn't just the weather or the economy causing the lingering late-summer headaches for this business, it was the stark realization that the U.S. government was hell-bent on becoming a direct, hands-on player in this industry—well beyond the existing bailout/overseer role it already occupied—and it was a role no one in this business wanted to see expanded. And, High-Octane Truth be told, it shouldn't have sat well with consumers out there in the real world either.

LET ME START BY ASKING a couple of key questions: Are there people out there who actually believe in their hearts that they know what's best for the rest of us? Or do they just get off on telling us not only what to do, but how it's going to be when we're doing what we're told, too?

How does all of the above sound?

The latest sign that The End is near as far as the automobile—or at least the freedom associated with the automobile—is concerned? The government wants to change the now ubiquitous EPA mileage stickers on our cars and trucks so that they'll be even more nanny/nag-like, assigning an actual letter grade to our cars and trucks that will rate fuel economy and emissions performance.

In other words, if your vehicle isn't a Shiny, Happy Prius or one of the zippy new electrically enhanced modes of transportation, your vehicle will be assigned an average to poor grade. In other words, our government regulators plan on shaming us into buying a better grade of transportation—at least in their minds anyway—than we'd normally opt for.

Because we are, after all, too stupid to figure it out for ourselves.

This, in case anyone wants to delve into it any deeper, makes perfect sense in the minds of regulators in Washington. After all, as Gina McCarthy, the EPA's assistant administrator for air and radiation—nice title, by the way—told the *Wall Street Journal*, the rules are designed to reflect major advances in car technology: "We think a new label is absolutely needed to help consumers make the right decision for their wallets and the environment."

Really?

I see it a little bit differently. I see it as an example of the classic—albeit tragically typical—bureaucratic regulator mindset that seems to thrive in places like Washington and in The Free Republic of Sacramento. The same mindset brought to bear on our behalf each and every day, unfortunately, that automatically frets about the fact that we—the general citizenry "out there" in the hinterlands—are barely capable of negotiating our typical day without the guidance and suckle of the all-knowing and all-seeing regulators who are charged—at least in their minds—with saving us from ourselves.

And that if it wasn't for these aforementioned regulators and well-meaning benevolent bureaucrats we'd all be wandering around in a daze, careening though life unfettered, unruly and incoherent, generally causing societal chaos by our abject refusal to follow the rules. Or to be even blunter, generally screwing things up because we don't acquiesce to the whims and wishes of the bureaucratic regulators who, after all, *know what's best for us.*

The undertone in all of this nonsense is that this ugly bureaucratic mindset operates under the assumption that, collectively, we—meaning you and me—don't have the faintest of clues about anything to do with our cars and trucks, and that given our feeble state we can't possibly understand even the most rudimentary issues when it comes to the environment or anything to do with our transportation choices.

But even worse than all of this? Now the table is being set to have these same regulators, with that same *we know what's best for you* bureaucratic mentality in full flower, veering from giving us emissions/economy ratings on our vehicles—that we all presumably can understand, now that they've been distilled down to elementary-school levels of comprehension—to actually ladling out *opinions* on which vehicles are worthy of our consideration.

Just off the top of my head, this is a Cowboys Stadium–sized bowl of Not Good.

Next thing you know, they'll be requiring the manufacturers to actually add the grade as a decal on the vehicle somewhere, which will be followed by decal grades on our garage doors—like scarlet letters for all the world to see.

Between now and then, however, I predict yet another giant disconnect between the bureaucratic regulators and the rest of the American driving public, as the Shiny, Happy "A"-graded vehicles are left collecting dust in showrooms all across the country as the "C," "D," and "F" vehicles fly off of the lots.

As the Wicked Witch of the West once famously said, "Oh what a world! What a world!"

Chapter 67

Pinheads, WallSqueaks, and Bad Lieutenants: The High-Octane Truth at full throttle

This was me being done. With the "instant" auto experts who were keeping this business from rising to greatness again. It was also about my frustration with this era of rampant national naïveté and crushing lack of awareness as to what this global competition thing really means for this nation going forward, and how our national epidemic of self-absorption and vacuity can no longer be viewed as an excuse, but only as a humiliatingly annoying embarrassment.

THAT THIS BUSINESS CONTINUES to be a seething cauldron of brilliance punctuated by flat-out incompetence is undeniable. With a portion of the players actually reveling in a focused commitment to greatness and the rest engaged in a two-steps-forward-five-back dance of mediocrity, it's no wonder that on this Wednesday in late September I find myself asking: Is this the best we can do?

I mean, really, folks. Steven Rattner? Are you frickin' kidding me? Give me one example—just one—in his much-touted *Overhaul* book that actually counts as a revelation about General Motors. Seriously. What, that it was FUBAR and had been for years? This counts for news? *Really?* That its vaunted accounting troops were borderline incompetent and the bureaucratic fiefdoms in the "vast middle" were more powerful at times than any chief executive? Wow. And this is why some lesser lights in our esteemed media are falling all over themselves canonizing the little WallSqueak as some sort of Beacon of Light as he conveys his knowledge about one of the most pathetic chapters in American corporate history? I'm sorry, but I think it's time you all replay the scene from *The Untouchables* when Robert DeNiro (as Al Capone) gives his team a little pep talk about teamwork around the dinner table. With a baseball bat. Because right about now it's clear that it's going to take a baseball bat rattling across some foreheads to knock some sense into some of you out there.

The GM story—the story of the pre-implosion company at any rate—is in the past. The "old" GM achieved astounding greatness for decades, but by the end of the '70s it started its long, slow march toward oblivion. When I started documenting the decline of GM—and the U.S. auto industry—from both an insider's *and* a historical perspective back in June of '99, I was viewed as one who was writing incendiary, axe-to-grind attacks at best, and a flat-out malcontent who needed to be taken out at worst, *especially* to those whose cages I was rattling.

And that was understandable, in hindsight. After all, even though others had danced around the isolated bureaucratic mindset of Detroit in the past in various books and screeds, nobody had done it after growing up personally in the midst of Detroit's heyday and then having spent over two decades in and around the trenches and the battles and the swirling maelstrom that have come to define the "car biz." That was different and that *was* cause for worry.

Because I *knew* what the Detroit mindset—in all its sedentary, myopic, the-empire-will-live-forever-and-a-day-and-the-good times-were-just-around-the-corner-again—felt like, and I *knew* what that "first order of business is to cover your ass" mentality smelled like because I had to live with it and witnessed it up close and personal in all of its ugly permutations. And I *knew* that to attack that piece of this town—the core of its very existence, by the way—was sheer heresy.

But I saw too many good and talented people get their careers blown up because they weren't practicing the go-along-to-get-along shuffle that accounted for standard operating procedure in this town and in this business. The kinds of people who could have made a real difference if they had just been allowed to be heard.

And conversely I saw too many pinheads, incompetent fools, and unconscionable ball-busting bad lieutenants get promoted and get rich after wreaking havoc wrapped in rampant mediocrity everywhere they went, destroying product programs, killing great ad campaigns, and generally wrecking everything they came within fifty feet of. *These* were the bastards who had to be exposed, this was the behavior that had to be called out in no uncertain terms, and this was the "Detroit mindset" that clearly was sending this business—at least as practiced in this town—on the road to ruin.

And I was hell-bent on doing it.

Even though I was viewed as being treasonous by some of the very executives who knew me and had worked with me over the years—especially given my family background—there were others both in the trenches and in the hallowed halls of executive management, however, who knew that I was speaking The High-Octane Truth. And the fact that my writing resonated like a bulldozer in an herb garden could not be ignored, or its impact ultimately contained.

And eleven and a half years later this business, this *thing* we call the Motor City—a.k.a. Detroit, "The Hard Life"—has been praised at times for putting America on wheels, for providing the Arsenal of Democracy, and for being one of the steadfast pillars of this country's manufacturing base. It has also been vilified for countless sins both real and imagined, for squandering its legacy in a choking haze of incompetence, for being a monument to mediocrity and not-invented-here malignance, and for a virulent complacency that's awe-inspiring in scope and deflating in its impact.

And all of it is true.

That Detroit has changed fundamentally and forever is true, too, and as I've said repeatedly, the selling of the "new" Detroit—and its ultracompetitive new vehicles—is the toughest marketing job of this or any other era. And with the ever-boiling global market we live in now—which is a cacophony of fractional discord, blatantly malicious governments in the business of business, and brutal, take-no-prisoners competition—Detroit's success is not only essential to this town and this region, it's essential to the nation.

Not a popular assessment in this era of rampant national naïveté and crushing lack of awareness as to what this global competition thing really means for this nation going forward, to be sure, but our national epidemic of self-absorption and vacuity can't be viewed as an excuse, only as a humiliatingly annoying embarrassment at this juncture.

Instant auto "experts" like our "esteemed" politicians in Washington, Sacramento, Michigan, et al, and the Steven Rattners of the world who parachute in, do their thing, and then go off to manufacture horrifically bad legislation or write books stating the painfully obvious—while basically being financed at the taxpayer's expense—should not be applauded. Instead, they should be called out for what they really are: Two-bit carpetbagging hacks who couldn't find a clue if you spotted them the "cl" and the "e"— who dine on the American taxpayers' trough with impunity and without one single shred of remorse.

For the record? That should *really* piss you off.

Chapter 68

Tweet this: The current state of the auto biz in 140-character bursts or less

The Twitter phenomenon had escalated to the point of annoyance, with the whole universe insisting that their 140-character communiqués were worth contemplating, no matter what the topic. Understanding that, and understanding that people like me who insist on writing long-form missives with real thought behind them were becoming part of a dying art, I decided to give the people— as in the ADD generation—what they wanted: the auto industry summed up in 140-character bursts.

Now THAT THE short-attention-span generation has taken over the world and the Internet has distilled our daily lives down to a series of talking-cat videos, vacuous celebutards emoting for the cameras, and maniacal conspiracy theorists, we are reduced to a day-in, day-out slog made of blips, burps, bites, and an occasional cogent thought every, oh, couple hours or so. And for some, that's plenty. They usually can't be pried away from their video games for any more time than that.

The rest of us? We'll just have to suck it up and keep fumbling through our oh-so-*outré* printed newspapers and magazines, and digesting long-form TV news programs and online journals in a futile attempt at sifting through the rapidly deteriorating concept of what used to pass for rational public discourse, trying to make sense of it all. Or as Jerry McGuire once famously said, "I am out here for you. You don't know what it's like to be *me* out here for *you*. It is an up-at-dawn, pride-swallowing siege that I will never fully tell you about, okay?"

So here's to the minions, the gamers, the coddled and the entitled, the I-don't-give-a-shit-just-ask-me hordes who want the world broken up in 140-character bits because anything more is just too tedious to contemplate. This column—the current state of the auto biz in digestible 140-character morsels—is for you.

Enjoy it. Or just count to one-one thousand and it won't matter anyway.

GM Marketing: Joel Ewanick gets the band back together. Improved, intelligent—with a dollop of tenacity—but still a long, *long* way to go.

GM Marketing, Part II: Ad agencies Goodby (Chevy) and Fallon (Cadillac) grade "C" and "C," respectively. Better, but not nearly good enough.

Chrysler: Perpetual Marchionne-driven "just you wait and see" state. We're still waiting, they're still dreaming. And the "new" 200? Oh. My.

Honda: Lost in the bland-tastic wilderness still searching for its mojo. When the Odyssey is their best product you know they're in trouble.

Toyota: Arrogance still intact they've now allegedly rediscovered their Hot Rod Hearts. Jalapeño sauce on white bread doesn't = credibility.

Mitsubishi: Missing in action for so long it just doesn't matter anymore. Irrelevant, invisible, and in need of a quick one-way ticket home.

BMW: Being all things to all people just wasn't enough. Now the Niche Market Kings are hot for a lineup of FWD cars based on the Mini. Ugh.

Corvette: Achieved global respectability but long overdue for a makeover. The C7 can't come soon enough but it's unlikely to go far enough.

Ford: Mulally-led upward trajectory still going according to Plan. "A" management + "A" products + "A" marketing = continued market success.

Porsche: In spite of 4-door sedans and a burgeoning truck line-up, still enough sports car juice to stay cool with the hardcore faithful.

Mercedes-Benz: They still believe they're the only automaker worth mentioning. The reality? It's just another car company chasing a niche.

Audi: Confident, strong, and sure of every move they make, these automotive Masters of the Universe show no signs of fatigue—or letting up.

VW Group: On a Dr. Piech–led, double-timed death march toward total world domination—or oblivion—depending on which way you look at it.

VW of America: Germanic automotive sweetness to soulless robot cars by 2018. Worst case of Toyota envy we've ever seen and a crying shame.

Mazda: When good, *very* good, excellent even, but a lack of consistent messaging beyond Zoom-Zoom has killed them. A new ad agency will help.

Acura: A rudderless mass of confusion with the most horrific design language in "the biz." A car company with no *raison d'être* whatsoever.

Infiniti: In a desperate race to reinvent itself yet again, this brand needs a transformational idea. By the looks of it, they got nothin'.

Lexus: The Pursuit of Perfect vanilla has its limitations. A foray into performance can't change the fact that it's rolling White Bread.

Subaru: Shiny, Happy followers, continues its inexorable climb. How far? No one really knows. The link-up with Toyota? The jury's still out.

Nissan: Two steps forward, five back and an endless struggle for respect. New marketing direction is innovation. Really? That's all you got?

Rolls-Royce: Until further notice, the very definition of "f***-you money" and the answer to the question that some people are still asking.

KIA: Straining to be something other than Hyundai's little brother and now carving out a growing piece of the pie for itself. One to watch.

RANGE ROVER: As long as people have money to burn on stuff they don't really need, there will always be an overwrought vehicle for them.

VOLVO: Backed with plenty of Chinese money and gaudy visions of grandeur, a brand still in search of an identity, naughty or otherwise.

ELECTRIC CARS: A niche wrapped in an enigma in search of decent batteries and a sustainable infrastructure. Other than that, it's all good.

ELECTRIC CAR ZEALOTS: A movement based upon a pipe dream and fueled by a fundamental refusal to accept reality, even when the truth hurts.

JAGUAR: Some signs of life, although the new XJ looks like a parade float, btw. Let's face it—the C-X75 is the only Jag worth talking about.

HYUNDAI: Aggressive and irrepressible. Pure unbridled automotive ambition, Korean style. Caution, however, there *will* be bumps in the road.

ASTON MARTIN: What's not to like? But just how many variations on the same theme can they regurgitate? And no, the Cygnet doesn't count.

BENTLEY: Part of Piech's luxury stable, Bentley has exceeded all expectations. The refined Continental GT is simply gorgeous. More please.

LAMBORGHINI: Another shining star in Piech's luxury stable, but no matter how hard Lambo tries, it's the perennial No. 2 Italian sports car.

FERRARI: High-Octane Truth & Beauty. When this red-hot Italian sports car maker is "on"—as in the 458 Italia—it's Dead. Solid. Perfect.

So there you have it, kids. The current state of the auto biz in 140-character bursts, if you're into the whole brevity thing, that is.

Chapter 69

It's all about respect, Mr. Akerson

*As the real Dan Akerson—GM's newly minted CEO—
emerged, I had the sickening feeling that we were about to see
a bad movie all over again. Here was an opportunist with a
heavily-laden financial background who had the top job at
GM thrust upon him for no apparent reason other than that he
was in the right place at the right time. And to make matters
worse, he was making noises that he had instantly become an
auto expert capable of making product decisions—without any
accrued credibility in the business whatsoever—and he was
doing it with a prickly management style that left a lot to be
desired. GM's past history was littered with bad times when
financial suits who were diametrically opposed to the product
people—the True Believers who actually got things done—
still saw fit to weigh in on major product decisions anyway,
much to the detriment of company fortunes. This was one rerun
I could do without.*

As THE GHOST OF PONTIAC passed over the weekend—with the
last of the existing dealer agreements expiring on October 31—the
"new" GM was looking ahead. *Way* ahead. As the company's financial
boffins were preparing the much-anticipated road show (a.k.a. "The
WallSqueak Circus") to sell the company's IPO—in the quest to get
out from under the "Government Motors" moniker and see their way
clear to financial and decision-making freedom—I doubt anyone down
at the RenCen could be bothered with the thought of the demise of

Pontiac. After all, that was the "old" GM and it had nothing to do with the "new" GM and where it needed to go, right?

Not so fast.

As I have said repeatedly, Pontiac will always hold a special place in my heart, and the lessons learned from its triumphantly exhilarating heyday to its criminal mishandling and neglect at the hands of ham-fisted GM marketers and corporate bean counters—through to its eventual and ultimate demise—are still fresh and applicable to today's GM. And judging by developments of late, the Pontiac perspective couldn't be timelier.

Example No. 1? I have no idea what possessed freshly minted CEO Dan Akerson to boast to anyone who would listen last week that the new Cadillac ATS models coming in 2012 and slotted below the CTS—in order to take dead aim at the BMW 3 Series and Mercedes-Benz C-Class—would basically kick the competition's ass and take names, but that's exactly what Akerson did. And it said more about what Akerson *doesn't* know about this business than anything I could have written.

Even though there once was a time-honored tradition among Detroit car executives of making grandiose pronouncements about how great things were going to be—who could ever forget Lido Iacocca saying in so many words that the U.S. automakers would "drive the Japanese imports back to the ocean"?—Akerson's comments were irresponsible and indefensible.

I mean come on, really? The new Cadillac ATS is going to displace the perennial "best all-around sports sedan"—the BMW 3 Series—and a pretty nice piece of work in its own right—the C-Class—right out of the box? Ridiculous. And no, it's not because the men and women involved in this new GM product program can't deliver the goods, because I will state emphatically that they absolutely can. They're more than capable, as a matter of fact.

But part of the rationale behind the campaign by Detroit automakers to distance themselves from the hoary image of the "old" Detroit is to not do things that the "old" Detroit *used* to do.

And running your mouth off about how good it's *going to be* instead of shutting up and delivering outstanding products that speak for themselves is symptomatic of the same old Detroit bullshit, as far as I'm concerned.

I'm sure the product-development teams working on the new Cadillac ATS would have preferred that Akerson had kept his mouth shut, that they'd much rather earn good comments about these new cars, having those favorable comments bubble up from the ride and drives, the reviews, and the word-of-mouth chatter. That's how it's done when a majority of the consumer car–buying public out there is pathologically skeptical about anything and everything to do with the American car companies and the products they build. That's how it's done when you're picking yourself off of the mat after a knockout punch called bankruptcy and the taint of "loser car company" that comes with it.

Instead they have a Wall Street money guy—who, by the way, was handed the reins of the company for no apparent reason other than the fact that he was in the right place at the right time at the right board meeting and he was the next man on deck who knew how to hang with and speak the language of the WallSqueaks—running his mouth off to the media about a car not many have seen, no one has driven, and no one wants to automatically attach greatness to just for showing up.

I have heard enough about Akerson's so-called management style—complete with the in-your-face fear and intimidation tactics—to know that the blunderbuss approach isn't going to work down at The Silver Silos. It may work in the murky world of investment banking Akerson came from (the land he parked himself in after steering one company into the ground)—where the size of the *ahem* "nut" you're managing is directly proportional to how big of an asshole you can be—but in a business in which Akerson has no credibility whatsoever?

Not so much.

I'm sure the whole blunderbuss thing has a lot to do with a wayward mentor in Akerson's background, but it's certainly no excuse for making stupid pronouncements. It not only says that Akerson doesn't have the first inkling as to what this business is all about, it says that he doesn't have even a shred of respect for the people who actually *do*.

I brought up Pontiac for a reason. What Bunkie Knudsen did when he took over Pontiac in 1956 could provide just as valuable a playbook for GM going forward, because the same fundamental issues were all present and accounted for even back then. Even more so, in fact. Faced with a moribund industry nameplate that was getting lost in GM's corporate shuffle, Knudsen assembled the best and brightest car people he could find—Pete Estes and John DeLorean just to name two—gave them marching orders to juice up the looks and the performance of the Pontiac lineup, and then stood back and let them do their thing while giving them the financial wherewithal and support they needed every step of the way. And for the better part of thirty-five years after that—minus a few missteps here and there—Pontiac thrived as the maverick car company that marched to a different drummer and lit up the industry by delivering hit product after hit product, as well as huge profits to GM (at least in the glory days of the '60s through the mid-'70s).

That GM lost touch with Pontiac—and the fundamental High-Octane Automotive Truths that powered it to greatness during its glorious heyday—was no surprise, given the fact that in recent history there were far too many people at GM who didn't have the first inkling as to what the car business was all about and who had no clue as to how to go about fixing what needed to be fixed, either. Toward its humiliating end, Pontiac was something completely beyond GM's level of understanding, unfortunately, which was a complete travesty.

To a degree, what GM has managed to accomplish with today's Cadillac mirrors the Pontiac story of long ago. Cadillac was so far lost in its Landau roof, Vogue tire haze more than a decade ago that it was clear that things could not continue if the iconic American luxury nameplate was to survive. And in order to save it, a team of dedicated car people came together and chartered a new course for the brand while totally revamping its design and engineering focus. And now, eleven years later, the fruit of their vision and dedication is manifested in brilliant cars like the Cadillac CTS-V and CTS-V Coupe, cars that need no "pretty good for an American car" apologies or disclaimers to be considered among the best in the world.

The key point here is that in order to succeed in the automotive business of today, the focus must first and foremost always be on the product, just as it was fifty-five years ago. That means designing, engineering, and building exceptional machines that bristle with quality, deliver a level of performance *with* overall efficiency that's consistent with today's market-driven environment, and most important, machines that register on an emotional level with customers and connect with people in a way that make them too compelling to be ignored.

And as a car company, you can't do that without having a fundamental respect for the product and the people who are able to deliver those products. From the designer who pushes the design envelope that much further to the suspension development engineer who keeps searching for that perfect combination of nuanced ride and handling, all the way to the assembly technician on the factory floor who comes up with a way to do it more precisely and consistently—make no mistake, success in this business is all about respect.

I find it beyond puzzling that Mr. Akerson was handed the reins of the "new" GM just because of his familiarity with Wall Street. That might be politically expedient during this IPO process that's looming large over the company over the next few weeks—after all, Wall Street types are more comfortable dealing with their own kind—but after that, then what?

I'll tell you what.

I fear for a "new" GM that's shaping up to be way too much like the GM of the bad old days. *That* GM was dominated by financial "experts" unleashed during the Jack Smith era who were woefully out of touch with the realities of the business and who were wildly out of sync with the people—make that the True Believers—who were battling in the trenches to make the products the best that they could possibly be (and against all odds, I might add, too).

Back then there was a fundamental lack of respect for the product and the people who could make the products great—if given the resources to do so—and that giant disconnect was the beginning of the end as GM's long, slow slide to oblivion picked up speed.

Dan Akerson has a role in the "new" GM whether I happen to like it, or not, so I will be happy to give him a few pieces of advice:

1. GM's success is not dependent on you and your financial minions; rather, it's totally dependent on the True Believers battling away every day in the trenches to make the products great. Make sure they have the resources to do their job and then step out of the way. And stay there.

2. Avoid commenting on *anything* to do with product. You're simply out of your league and you have zero credibility in that arena. You have two gentlemen in particular—Mark Reuss and Ed Welburn—who are more than capable of addressing any and all issues concerning product. Stow your blunderbuss attitude and listen, and then again, make sure they have every resource you can muster in order to help them do their jobs.

3. When it comes to marketing, see points 1 and 2. You have the right team in place, so let them do their jobs, and yes, make sure they have the resources to get it done.

4. If all else fails, shut up, listen, and learn. Just because you're the designated CEO of the moment doesn't mean that you're qualified to fulfill that role. Unfortunately for everyone hard at work in the trenches at the "new" GM, your actions aren't exactly engendering boatloads of confidence at this very moment. Why? Because it's painfully obvious that you don't get it and your ramp-up time is going to be a rollercoaster ride of bad decisions, bluster, and poor judgment. You've already put your foot in your mouth once—and that's just in public—and from what I'm hearing—and believe me it's not pretty—that's just the tip of the iceberg.

It's all about respect, Mr. Akerson. In order to get it you're going to have to earn it, and trust me on this, thrusting yourself into situations and areas of expertise that you have no business weighing in on is no way to go about getting it.

And remember one very crucial thing: After the dust settles from the IPO, the real work begins. Right now—with all things on the table and the future of the "new" GM at stake—I'm finding it difficult to envision a role for you once that happens.

Chapter 70

GM's image will be a work in progress long after the IPO frenzy

What a rollercoaster ride it had been. Two years earlier GM represented everything wrong with corporate America, and the public flogging by politicians and in the media was relentless, with GM held accountable for myriad sins both real and imagined. Now, we had an entirely different type of frenzy going on as Wall Streeters fell all over themselves to get in on the IPO action for the "new" General Motors Corp., the slim-downed, unencumbered, back-from-the-brink car company that all of a sudden was looking strong and righteously invigorated. Did the government-directed taxpayer money save GM? Unequivocally, yes. It also saved an entire industry—not just any industry, but a pillar of the American industrial fabric—from going down for the count, inexorably altering this country's ability to compete and its economic future in one fell swoop. Was it popular? Oh, hell no. There were still vast swaths of the country that didn't care to go near a GM vehicle again because "they took the money." Was GM out of the woods? Not yet, and not by a long shot either. But it was upright and profitable, its new products were ultracompetitive, and management was bound and determined that GM would never allow itself to be put in that position again. It was still a giant "we'll see" for a lot of politicians and industry pundits, but there was no question that GM—and the U.S. auto industry—was back from the brink and prepared to compete over the long haul.

313

AFTER WITNESSING THE U.S. auto industry bashing over the last two years I must admit it's a little bit stunning to see the frenzy over GM's IPO. The run-up of Ford's shares I can understand, as this is a company that has been focused and on an upswing almost from the moment Bill Ford, Jr. brought in Alan Mulally and asked him to "fix it." But GM?

Two years ago GM represented everything wrong with corporate America. The public flogging in the media was relentless, with GM held accountable for myriad sins both real and imagined—everything from being equated to terrorists by the resident blowhard of the *New York Times*, Thomas Friedman, a.k.a. the patron saint of the green-tinged intelligentsia—and pilloried by members of Congress for being blatantly and maliciously incompetent, which, given the notorious stumblebum political players involved, would have been laughable if it weren't so relentlessly tedious and insulting.

In the height of the pre-bankruptcy frenzy Friedman even went so far at one point as to suggest that GM and the rest of the U.S. automobile industry should be put to sleep and out of its misery in favor of Toyota becoming America's only car company, because the Pious, er, I mean the Prius, was just so much better than anything Detroit could muster that the most logical thing—at least through Friedman's emerald-tinted glasses—would be to shut down the U.S. auto industry and put hundreds of thousands of people out of work. Remarkably prescient—*not.*

Now we have an entirely different type of frenzy going on as Wall Streeters fall all over themselves to get in on the IPO action for the slim-downed, unencumbered, back-from-the-brink car company that all of a sudden is looking strong and righteously invigorated.

The unencumbered part is what really has the financial wizards frothing at the mouth. Stripped of debt and costs by way of the bankruptcy and drawing a "pass" on a $45 billion tax obligation because of the way the government-orchestrated deal was constructed—maybe the sweetheart of all sweetheart deals in the annals of corporate America, by the way—GM is a refueled corporate rocket poised to launch itself into the golden profit stratosphere, a stratum where the sun never sets, the bonuses are huge, and the payoff is damn near unlimited.

Sounds deliciously simple, no?

As Lee Corso likes to say, *Not so fast my friends.*

As frenzies go, I admit that GM's is worth more than a little excitement because, when you look at the financials, GM has not only been handed a new life via bankruptcy, it has been gifted a formidable new competitiveness, something that rankles its competitors to no end, I can assure you. But then again, all this "unencumbered" excitement going on doesn't mask the fact that as a company and as an industry player, GM still has a long, *long* way to go.

It's one thing to be the darlings of Wall Street; it's quite another to be the darlings of Main Street. And to be blunt, GM isn't there with the Rest of America yet. Not by a long shot. Everything associated with GM is a work in progress, especially when it comes to its image—or lack thereof—with the American consumer public.

For every single person touched by a favorable review of the Chevrolet Volt, Buick LaCrosse, or Cadillac CTS-V, and every smile brought on by Chevy's "Dogs in Pickups" commercial, there are just as many consumers out there who are not only still furious that GM took *their* taxpayer money, they're even *more* pissed off as the full ramifications and scope of the cozy tax break "deal" that GM was handed becomes understood.

That to me suggests that there's still a giant disconnect between the glitzy and glamorous GM IPO—and all of the Wall Street swells who will benefit from it—and the true reality of GM's image in this market, which to millions of consumers shopping in the retail trenches—the ones who will have to give GM another chance if the company expects to thrive, let alone survive—leaves a lot to be desired.

Ironically enough, the product is the one area I'm not as concerned about when it comes to the "new" GM. This business is, was and *always* will be about the product first and foremost, and GM is definitely firing on all cylinders in that department. As a matter of fact, GM is on a new-product roll, and each new vehicle execution they deliver to the streets and byways of America seems to be dramatically better than what came before, and not by just a little bit.

But after stating that fact I'll paraphrase the great Vince Lombardi's famous quote about winning as translated for the freshly minted, IPO-flush GM: Image isn't everything, it's the *only* thing. And GM's image is definitely a work in progress, at best.

Before any high-fiving can go on down in the hallways of the RenCen, GM must figure out a way to reinvent its image. Removing itself from the taint of bankruptcy by paying off most of the money—yes, that would go a long way toward improving GM's image balance sheet. But it's going to take more than that, and it's going to take more than multiple variations on the Volt theme too.

GM has to figure out a way to connect with the hearts and minds of the American consumer, and it's going to take image-wrangling of the highest order—and over many years to come—in order to get it done.

Chapter 71

The looming train wreck at General Motors

The 2011 Detroit Auto Show (we have permanently banned the use of NAIAS around here) by all accounts was a smashing success, with a distinct note of optimism hanging over the proceedings like a big puffy cloud of happiness, with fleeting moments of giddiness thrown in for good measure. It wasn't all sweetness and light of course, but nonetheless compared to the two previous dismal years, Detroit 2011 was pretty decent and intermittently impressive even. But now that the smoke has cleared from the shock waves of media coverage of the show, it's time to assess what really happened beyond the chrome and glitz and hot air wafting through Cobo Hall. Beyond all the positive vibes and in some cases, flat-out euphoria from the show, the fact remains that the overall industry is facing daunting challenges, formidable obstacles and recurring questions on the way to having a more-than-decent 2011. And none of that changed just because there was a feel-good auto show in the Motor City. The most dramatic development to come out of the show is the major image push from GM surrounding their new CEO Dan Akerson. As the industry's newly-minted "instant" expert, "Lt. Dan" is now large and in charge of the Silver Silo dwellers and it's not going so well. He talks too much, he's already making dubiously questionable predictions as to the scope of the company's future product success, and worse, he's starting to walk the walk and talk the talk like he's been there for the bad times and he can now take credit for stuff that he hasn't done or been involved with during the good times. Not Good doesn't even begin to cover it. So is GM PR serious about their barrage of positive spin, or are they being forced into it? Do I really have to ask this question? Given a choice do you really think the pros on the GM PR staff would willingly generate the embarrassing image-shaping barrage they've been orchestrating for "Lt. Dan" on their own? Of course not. But it's tres *embarrassing nonetheless. Listen, folks, don't kid yourselves for one minute, Akerson is a bull that has been unleashed in the U.S. auto industry china shop and this situation is going to get a lot worse before it gets better. Powered by a hard-headed, remarkably arrogant mindset, a general operating principle that he's never wrong—okay maybe once back in '72 but you get the drift—and the growing certainty that oozes out of him more each day revolving around the fact that he's mastered this business in a matter of months making him the King of the "instant" experts hands down, and worse, that he's hell-bent on leaving his mark on it, and you have a recipe for disaster that no PR offensive on earth can sugar coat. And before the lights from the Detroit Auto Show were even dimmed, Akerson began his personal mission to reshape GM, cloaked in "consumer-focused" doublespeak, and the looming train wreck that was sure to follow began to take shape. Needless to say it was the very* last *thing that GM needed at this moment in time.*

AFTER UPENDING GM's product development function by punting former Chief Tom Stephens up and out of the way to the new title of Chief Technical Officer and promoting Mary Barra as the new head of GM's product development function, it's clear to me that GM CEO Dan Akerson is hell-bent on "reimagining" GM in his own image, even though that image has disaster written all over it. Marching to the dulcet tones of a soundtrack based on his own unimpeachable convictions—even though they are unencumbered with any real depth of knowledge or understanding of what this business of making cars is really all about—"Lt. Dan" Akerson has launched an offensive to put his stamp on the company, no matter what the cost. And I predict those costs will be cataclysmic for GM and may just cripple the company down the road, just when it needs to be firing on all cylinders.

If this is a business about product cadence—which it most definitely is—then the "new" General Motors is on a runaway train to Hell. After all, this is a guy who has proudly admitted "I'm not a car guy" from the get-go, underlining that statement by making some plainly horrific comments to the *Wall Street Journal* in a revealing interview conducted right before the Detroit Auto Show.

Do you want to know just how dangerous this guy is to the future stability of GM? In that interview Akerson insisted that GM has too many engines globally, and he's going to "fix" that. Uh, and he's basing that on what, exactly? Secondly, Akerson is quite certain that GM is spending too much time and money differentiating sheet metal between the divisional nameplates, when a little creative marketing would suffice.

Oh really?

The last guy who believed that at GM was John Smale and we all know how that turned out, don't we? The Smale "Reign of Terror" (executed by his Chief Acolyte, Ron Zarrella) was so mind-numbingly wrong-headed that it ended up unleashing a string of products bristling with all of the P&G-infused, marketing-driven mumbo jumbo that the Smale/Zarrella brain trust could muster—revolving around the fundamental premise of *it doesn't matter how good the product is, because brilliant marketing can overcome anything*—and resulting in the most woefully uncompetitive and out-of-touch products in the market. Not only was it a complete disaster, it ultimately helped set the table for the most humiliating corporate bankruptcy in American history.

How is the Smale/Zarrella "Reign of Terror" any different from "Lt. Dan's" vision for the future of GM? Let's review, shall we?

Let's see, carpetbagging interloper plucked from corporate obscurity by a flat-out incompetent board of directors and then handed the keys to the candy store just for showing up that day? Check.

Instant "expert" who has studied the business for oh, about ten minutes, and who now boasts about how he will set the industry straight and show everyone how it should be done? Check.

Talking "customer-focused" decision making while putting product development on a cost-cutting binge that takes precedence over everything else, because after all, we'll fix it in marketing, right? Check.

Guess what? I've seen this movie before and it doesn't end well. The only difference between GM then and GM now is that this is a company that has only recently emerged from the Abyss of bankruptcy, one that can ill-afford a single misstep brought upon by misguided leadership, even though it has the most competitive lineup it has had in decades. And make no mistake: Dan Akerson's "leadership" is at the very least misguided.

How misguided? The provocative statements Akerson has made to the press—implying that he has ordered the product development troops to cut $10,000 worth of cost out of the Volt, for instance—don't even come close to the bone-headed orders he regularly fires off behind closed doors.

And the personnel changes GM has announced this week? They're emblematic of the intense turmoil going on within the company stemming from the fact that Akerson is wreaking havoc on product development, something he doesn't have a feel for or the qualifications to do, to put it charitably.

The True Believers in GM Product Development have chafed under the barrage of nonsensical orders and pronouncements emanating from Akerson by the minute, and they have pushed back, hard. And one thing you don't do to "Lt. Dan" is push back, because if you do, you're either moved or exited from the company.

And after reading all of the gushing media coverage this week giving Akerson credit for being an "enlightened" leader as if he's some altruistic Big Daddy for promoting a woman to a top position in this business—and there *are* thousands upon thousands of superbly talented women in this business who are often overlooked, a reality that remains a glaring and historically documented failure of this industry—I'm going to have to throw an ice cold pitcher of water on the proceedings.

By all accounts Mary Barra is an exceedingly bright woman who is an excellent manager but make no mistake, Ms. Barra didn't get her new assignment because she's the most qualified individual for the position. No, Mary Barra got her job because "Lt. Dan" needed someone in that position who would do his bidding, and who will bow to his wishes and execute his "plan," as convoluted, misguided, reactionary, and wrong-headed as it may be.

Because the True Believers in Product Development weren't buying what he was selling. And they weren't buying his unmitigated bullshit calls or his inability to grasp even a shred of the reality needed when it comes to the business of designing, engineering, and building automobiles. In other words, true product people can smell an instant automotive "expert" when they see one.

And Akerson isn't just setting a new standard for instant "experts" in this business—a rogue's gallery chock-full of executives who left a trail of tears and destruction at various times throughout this industry's history, by the way—he's writing an entire new chapter right before our eyes.

The most glaring thing that Akerson fails to understand about this business? He thinks that the product development function is a process that is solely controlled by cost, when in fact product development is an ever-changing kaleidoscope of technology utilization, engineering philosophy, product vision, cadence, *and* cost, with a large measure of gut feeling and passion thrown into the mix. And that last part, the "gut feeling and passion" part? That is quite simply the Black Art of this business, the very essence of which—if orchestrated properly—separates the outstanding product executions from the merely good or mediocre ones.

But when you're Dan Akerson and you don't have even a rudimentary understanding of what this business is all about, and you have difficulty grasping the "gut feeling and passion" part, then putting in a manager to speed the product development "process" along makes perfect sense.

Add to all of this the fact that Akerson conducts himself as if he's on a search-and-destroy mission, with his bull-in-the-china-shop management "style" routinely lacking even a whiff of subtlety and nuance, and you have a recipe for disaster.

Now, I know some of my esteemed colleagues in the media and the blogosphere have bought the spin generated by GM's PR troops on Akerson's moves hook, line, and sinker, regurgitating such pre-packaged pap as, "Visionary moves by GM's CEO," "Akerson puts his stamp on a new, tech-savvy, customer-focused GM," and "Akerson promotes diversity in the new GM," etc., but the real story has none of that sheen or carefully orchestrated gloss.

No, the real story is that "Lt. Dan" is an egomaniacal corporate opportunist with an overwrought sense of himself, one who will shake the neck of GM until it falls limp in his hands so that he can then rebuild it in his image. And believe me that image is not pretty. It's not one of a customer-focused, enlightened, tech-savvy automotive company of the future, by any means. Instead, it will be a company stripped to the bone in the interest of delivering short-term eyeball-popping profits for the next couple of years, which will then be left a woefully uncompetitive hollowed out husk of a company by 2016 because of a product development "process" decimated by functionaries imbued with the Akerson gospel of speed and cost cutting—product relevancy and integrity be damned.

So please spare me the hyperbole associated with Dan Akerson and how he is the latest in the long line of saviors for General Motors. "Lt. Dan" is a corporate blunderbuss masquerading as a "switched-on" visionary auto executive, except there's nothing visionary about the shallow reservoir of knowledge that this guy brings to the table every day. Instead, it just falls under the time-honored dictum of a little bit of knowledge is a very dangerous thing.

The Bottom Line?

Dan Akerson is the wrong guy, at the wrong time, at the wrong car company.

And as long as he's at the wheel, GM's long-term future is at risk.

Afterword

IT HAS BEEN A LONG and at times excruciatingly painful road for the U.S. auto industry over the last decade, and it's about to get even tougher.

We are now witnesses as the center of the automotive universe undergoes a seismic, fundamental shift to the Far East, where the biggest automobile market in the world for the next fifty years at least will be centered in Shanghai.

We've also seen the anti-car movement in this country gain steam with each and every passing year over the last decade. Led by the abhorrent histrionics of High Priest Tom Friedman and his smugly self-righteous acolytes, pockets of the American population have not only turned their backs on Detroit and dismissed America's eroding industrial base as a nonissue, they now equate the automobile as being the No. 1 societal pariah, something that must be expunged from our cities, streets, and byways before we are all consumed by its exponentially multiplying negatives.

That some of these same people are now reeling in horror as the true cost of the implosion of the U.S. auto industry hits home all across America—even in places where the "it won't affect me" zealots blissfully reside—would be humorous if it weren't so devastatingly heart-wrenching for the people directly consumed by it.

Hard on the heels of the anti-car zealots is the emergence of the green-at-all-costs devotees, the armchair environmental fanatics (insert your favorite celebrity du jour here) who not only think that the radical transformation of the American industrial fabric can happen overnight, but that it can happen with the minimal effort akin to a finger snap too.

That the anti-car intelligentsia and these green fanatics are coalescing into a movement that's unfettered by such quaint notions as cost, technical feasibility, or reality is not surprising. That whole factions of the media and hordes of our elected representatives in Washington have willingly bought into the movement hook, line, and sinker—while abandoning such irksome little details as the inconvenient facts along the way—is not surprising either.

How all of this will shake out and what effect it will have on America's manufacturing base remains to be seen, but initial signs aren't good. We are losing manufacturing in this country at an alarming rate, and there just aren't enough Shiny, Happy Green startups to make up for the lost plants and the lost jobs. Not even close, as a matter of fact. And even worse, it seems to be impossible to get people to care about it.

There are even some in this country who believe that the continued erosion of the U.S. manufacturing base is no big deal, that we can exist swimmingly fine as a Starbucks Nation of consumer zombies who devour everything in sight but who don't actually make anything of value. But if we as a country lose the ability to manufacture things and lose the ability to successfully compete globally with our heavy industries, the end result will be that we will become a second-tier nation, which would be the quintessential definition of Not Good.

Suffice to say, a lot has happened in this business, in this country, and around the world since 1999. But one of the most fundamental changes—if not *the* most when it comes to this country at least—is that the domestic automobile industry that's embodied in the one-word moniker "Detroit" will never be the same again.

The anti-car zealots seem to be trying to force this country into a future fraught with restrictions and reduced expectations, while the auto industry races to transform itself to meet a new level of environmental responsibility and fuel-economy regulations. One side demanding total capitulation and annihilation, the other side embedded in reality, trying to respond to a challenge that will actually benefit the country. One hundred eighty degrees apart doesn't even begin to cover it.

It's easy to question the automobile's future role in this mania-cally whipsawed environment. A lot of the "anti-" people are insisting that the automobile will never have the same impact, will never enjoy the mass acceptance of large swaths of the American population, and will never hold sway over the American consumer consciousness like decades past.

But I vehemently disagree.

Exhibit No. 1 is the new Chevrolet Volt from General Motors. At the end of the day this dazzling new machine is a technological tour of force for this or any other century and a glittering reaffirmation that there *is* such a thing as American ingenuity, that we haven't completely devolved into a parasitic consumer society that can't build anything of consequence anymore, and that we *can* and *will* fight our way out of this morass of mediocrity that has plagued this industry—and this country, I might add—for far too long.

Personal mobility is a powerful concept and the freedom it brings to people cannot be overstated. And it will remain that way too. Yes, in our urban city centers compromises must and will be reached. But this is a vast country, and people will still want to roam to the far reaches of it. And the automobile—newly reinvigorated and environmentally cleansed—will still play an integral role in America's every day life for a long, *long* time to come.

In closing, I think it's important to point out that in the face of a business that grows more rigid, regulated, and risk-averse by the day, there are still lessons to be learned and new heights to achieve.

If anything, we *must* remember what really matters in this business above all else, and that is to never forget the *essence* of the machine and what makes it a living, breathing mechanical conduit of our hopes and dreams.

And that in the course of designing, engineering, and building these machines, everyone needs to aim higher and push harder with a relentless, unwavering passion and love for the automobile that is so powerful and unyielding that it can't be beaten down by committee-think or buried in bureaucratic mediocrity.

And one more thing.

This nation is facing a clear choice. With the halcyon "Morning in America" days long faded, we—as a people—have to decide whether we're staring into the abyss of a life of reduced expectations and the collective and unfamiliar drudgery of a nation that suddenly finds itself mired with a second-tier status, or whether we're on the precipice of greatness, fueled by a renewed passion, boundless creative energy, unbridled ingenuity, and a relentless, unwavering conviction.

I, for one, am choosing the latter.

CPSIA information can be obtained at www.ICGtesting.com
Printed in the USA
LVOW07*2250071015

457358LV00005B/16/P

9 780982 173374